DISCARD

THE YEARS OF OPPORTUNITY:

The League of Nations, 1920–1926

THE YEARS OF OPPORTUNITY:

The League of Nations, 1920–1926

by Byron Dexter

The Viking Press, New York

Copyright © *1967* by Byron Dexter
All rights reserved
First published in *1967* by The Viking Press, Inc.
625 Madison Avenue, New York, N.Y. *10022*
Published simultaneously in Canada by
The Macmillan Company of Canada Limited
Library of Congress catalog card number: 67-20299
Printed in U.S.A. by H. Wolff Book Mfg. Co.

65844

ACKNOWLEDGMENTS

I would like to give thanks here to the publishers of the two great histories, both basic books of reference for events of the early years of the League of Nations, upon which I have drawn: Oxford University Press for *A History of the League of Nations* by F. P. Walters, and Harvard Univeristy Press for *A History of the Weimar Republic* by Erich Eyck, translated by Harlan P. Hanson and Robert G. L. Waite. I would also like to give special thanks to the editors of *Foreign Affairs* for permission to quote freely from articles published in that quarterly and to adapt in this book articles of my own that have been printed there.

Payment of debt is a pleasure when the coin is friendship. My personal debts are large: to Hamilton Fish Armstrong, stimulating friend and colleague for many years; to Donald Wasson, director of the indispensable Foreign Relations Library of New York; and to the Baker Library of Dartmouth College for its limitless hospitality; to Helena Stalson of the Council on Foreign Relations, for one of her characteristic miracles harmonizing kindness and statistical expertise; to my neighbor Philip K. Crowe, for good cheer and good sense; and my neighbor John H. McDill, who to my immense advantage read the entire manuscript with perceptive critical care; also to Denver Lindley and Henry Volkening for professional assistance beyond the line of duty; and to Lorraine LeHuray Dexter, for preparing the index and preserving the life of the author during the time it took to write the book.

—B. D.

Contents

MAPS

Introduction

This book is intended to suggest how interesting, how fresh, how heartening even, in one great particular, is the story of the early years of the League of Nations. They were the years of opportunity, when the League enjoyed the chance of effectiveness in its political task that the United Nations has never had.

The League of Nations was designed to solve the problem that Sir Edward Grey could not master in the years before the First World War: the construction and maintenance of a defensive coalition to meet and discourage the threat of war by a great expansion-minded power. The founders of the League hoped to reach the solution by placing the problem of peace and war in the largest possible framework—a world-wide organization of states under principles and procedures for common action in the event of armed attack upon one of them by a member or nonmember state. But the League gave a dusty answer to the question of the possibility of such "collective security." It became an accessory to aggression and died in disgrace.

The long library shelves with the books and documents of the League years ranged upon them now tend to be dusty too. And why, it may be asked, should the old papers be disturbed when the causes of the failure are so well known? The statesmen at Ver-

sailles devised a worthless settlement. The League was made responsible for the maintenance of the boundary lines of the peace
treaty—the notorious *status quo* of the League's ten thousand dis-
gusted critics. And, anyway, the United States refused to join. The
League never had a chance.

This book reasons that, on the contrary, the Versailles Treaty
was, in the main, a fair and moderate settlement, certainly worth
upholding; and that the League had its chance because, for some
years, there was peace in Europe. The peace was maintained by the
power of France and Britain—sufficient for the purpose so long as
those nations came together at times of crisis. The League was
their intelligent instrument, and sometimes guide. The work of the
judicial agency of the League system—the Permanent Court of
International Justice—witnessed the actuality of peace, though neither the United States nor the Soviet Union subscribed to its statutes and almost all the disputes brought before it originated in European or Mediterranean lands. The cases included none of the
major disputes of the "interwar" years, but the body of law that the
Court interpreted and began to develop was respected. Every judgment and advisory opinion—more than sixty in all—was obeyed.
Given peace, and such homogeneity in membership as was enjoyed
by the League, the great dream of nations under law seemed, for a
time, not impractical. But the work of the Court came to an end
when Hitler achieved domination over League and Europe.

The book does not speculate as to whether the League would
have succeeded in its political objective had the United States been
a member. Certainly the story would have been different—but
different in what way? Such major interventions as the United
States made in Europe during the interwar years appear to have
been more harmful than helpful to the stability of Europe. Had
Americans been fully engaged in the affairs of the Continent from
1920 on, would those interventions have shown more understanding of European problems? Or might the American influence have
been more constantly disruptive? Speculation of the kind is point-
less. Similarly, the narrative does not attempt to guess whether

Japan would have embarked on its Far Eastern adventure had it not been evident even before the Great Depression of the 1930s that another German war was impending, or whether and to what degree membership in the League would have altered the American response to the Japanese challenge.

It is argued in the following chapters that the decisive turning point for the League and Europe, from peace to war, came several years before Hitler gained power in Germany. In a deliberate choice in 1925, Great Britain turned to a policy of disengagement on the Continent and assumed the role of mediator between France and Germany; and Weimar Germany was granted admittance to the League on terms that undermined the Treaty of Versailles and opened Eastern Europe to German adventure. Then Hitler was the beneficiary of an illusory peace, and the League of Nations encouraged the aggressions it was organized to suppress.

The League was essentially a European system. Its story is of interest for what it tells about the effort to amend and apply the procedures of collective security, as outlined in the Covenant, to the practical problem with which the League was faced: the maintenance of stability on the Continent. Both the Council and Assembly of the League benefited from the leadership of responsible, experienced, resourceful statesmen; their failures, their successes, and, most of all perhaps, the times they nearly succeeded offer many things for us to reflect upon today.

In an essay such as this, historical but not a history of the League of Nations and written for the general reader, useful "lessons" are likely to occur by the way. As the writer selects what seems to him significant in present perspective, for the story he has to tell, so the reader composes his picture of the past in relation to the questions that are in his mind today. Answers will be different; only those that the reader finds for himself can be valid for him. Narrative and analysis in the book focus upon the League; the United Nations is mentioned only occasionally, in passing. I hope the book will be read primarily for the stimulation of sharing a re-creation of the League's experience. At the end, however, I have offered a generalized conclusion applicable not only to this story but to the incomplete story of the United Nations also.

Despite the ignominious ending of the first effort toward world organization, its restricted scope made certain that the outcome would be considered inconclusive and that the experiment would be repeated on a larger scale. Again the President of the United States was the prime mover, but this time with strong support at home. It is hardly correct to say that the United States fought without political objective in the Second World War. From the time of the 1943 Four-Power Declaration on General Security at Moscow, the perpetuation of the wartime "alliance" in a new league was the explicit American purpose.

The Charter of the United Nations followed the outline of the Covenant in general principles and in many of the arrangements—though in more and cloudier words. It is significant that two of the major departures—the provisions for a Great Power Military Staff and the heightened power of veto for permanent members of the Security Council (including a veto over new memberships)—were intended to help ensure the maintenance of the wartime collaboration. Stalin made an important concession in withdrawing his demand for a veto over the mere consideration by the Security Council of intergovernmental disputes, and all the powers agreed upon an ambiguous grant of independent initiative to the Secretary-General—a sign of great expectations, good intentions, or indifference. The Western nations hedged their bet on postwar collaboration between parliamentary and Communist governments by provisions in the Charter authorizing regional defense organizations; Stalin hedged his bet by military occupation of all Eastern Europe up to the Elbe.

Each of the two superpowers was perhaps, however, as surprised as the other by the developments of the two years after the signing and ratification of the Charter—the United States by the evidence of intended Soviet expansion into Iran, Turkey, Greece, and the central Mediterranean and the USSR by the American decision to contest it. When the Security Council made an issue of the failure of the Soviet Union to withdraw its troops from Iran, as pledged, the United Nations became the arena of another war, of a new kind. Instead of harmonizing the purposes of the Communist dictatorship and the Western powers (as the United States expected) or insulating them from one another (as the Russians may have assumed) the principles and procedures of the world-wide United Nations brought the conflict between Communist and non-Communist countries to a head. The Soviet riposte to defeats in Iran and Greece and to the Truman Doctrine and Marshall Plan was the seizure of government in Czechoslovakia and the attempt to starve isolated West Berlin into submission. The blockade was thwarted by American airpower and the courage of the Berliners, and the Russian offensive brought the formation of an organized core of power in the West by a dozen North Atlantic members of the United Nations.

Stalin's reply to that was an undeclared war in the Far East—in Korea—an area in which the United Nations had asserted its authority under American leadership. Of the members of the NATO alliance, only the United States had direct interests in this area. The Soviet attack by means of the North Korean cat's-paw was carefully prepared and mounted; preparations included the signing of an offensive-defensive alliance between Russia and Communist China and the successful beginning of the production of atomic weapons by the USSR. Stalin apparently expected a "League" response from the United Nations—a "resolution of protest" (as Philip E. Mosely put it in a perceptive analysis)[1]*—but no effort toward enforcement. He had withdrawn the Soviet representative on the Security Council and withheld him from the meeting called by the United Nations Secretary-General, Trygve Lie, to consider the overt armed attack. Stalin's purpose, presumably, was to avoid the necessity of showing his hand by an explicit defense of the North Korean invasion and by too conspicuous a veto of the ex-

* Reference notes begin on page 215.

pected vote of condemnation. But President Harry S. Truman followed the Security Council's words of protest with immediate action. Stalin was denied his quick conquest and a Communist outpost dominating Japan on the Tsushima Strait.

In the fighting that ensued the North Korean army was routed, and it seemed for a moment as though the United States intended to press a counterattack on the peninsula in an advance to the north validated by the United Nations General Assembly. But the Soviet ally, China, raised the bet. The Assembly declared the Chinese People's Republic an aggressor, but Chinese troops inflicted a defeat on unwary United States forces in northern Korea, and the United States hastily abandoned the counteroffensive and sought negotiations. So suddenly the wind veered: fifteen United Nations members gave help of some kind to Americans and South Koreans in the more than two years of warfare that accompanied the protracted negotiations, but all pressure was on the United States to end the fighting, with the Chinese People's Republic the intoxicated victor on the field. That was the end of collective security.

The ratio of atomic bombs in the possession of the two sides was, we may guess, enormously in the Americans' favor. Did the pressure—especially effective from two leading NATO countries, Great Britain and Canada—turn against the United States and the South Korean victim of the attack for fear that the terrible new weapons would be used, or from fear that they would not deter Stalin from resorting to the familiar tactic of a strike in the west to make good the setback in the east? However that may have been, there was no need for Stalin to show his hand further. The United Nations Command—in practice, the United States—remained agonizingly on the defensive.

President Eisenhower is reported to have threatened to resort to atomic weapons if the Communists did not abandon their delaying maneuvers at the Panmunjom conference table, but the paradoxical aspect of this first war in which such weapons were in existence from the beginning was that the stronger side fought the war under conditions imposed upon it by the weaker—a very unusual state of affairs indeed, particularly in "limited war" as that had hitherto been understood. (Bismarck's politically limited wars were not military stalemates!) But the truth or falsity of the paradox cannot be estimated, for the war is unfinished. There is only an armistice. The Communist claim to South Korea is constantly advanced. There is sporadic fighting on the tense and closely guarded border where the armistice was signed, and the questions left unsettled at Panmunjom have been reopened in combat on another strategic outpost of the coast of Asia—Vietnam. The immediate question is whether a Soviet ally or client can be defeated in a "war of liberation" which it chooses to begin; the long-range issue is the balance of power in the Pacific.

So much remains the same—and so much has changed. Before Stalin died, he indicated, in a theoretical formulation, the conclusion he had drawn from the Korean experience. Between the conventional groupings of "socialist" and "imperialist" camps in Soviet doctrine, he inserted another grouping—the "peace camp." This was to be composed of the uncommitted, the underdeveloped, and the anticolonialist nations and peoples of the world—the vulnerable flank of the West. Long-range competition for the allegiance of this camp would determine the outcome of the contest between the other two. In sum: no more tries at quick conquest. The preparations had not been careful enough; resistance had been made too easy for the enemy and for its instrument, the United Nations. Henceforth a war of the new kind, "peaceful" ("cold"), would be pressed on a vast new front, where the allies of the United States would have everything to lose and the USSR nothing. Guerrilla "wars of liberation" would be permitted, indeed encouraged, as always in Communist doctrine; but they had to be prudently masked.

The new formulation was a master stroke, turning Soviet miscalculation in the Korean adventure to Soviet profit. It accurately estimated the effect that the American acceptance of stalemate would have upon neutrals, and it provided the breathing space necessary if the USSR were to catch up in the development of the new weapons.

Moreover, it not only made identification of disputes "likely to endanger international peace and security" infinitely complicated for the diverse group of countries that constituted the United Nations but also made "peace" an instrument of conquest.

"A conqueror is always a lover of peace," Karl von Clausewitz, one of the great students of war, remarked in an acid passage in his early-nineteenth-century treatise. "He would like to enter our country unopposed." Clausewitz was thinking of Napoleon, who was sincerely indignant when coalitions resisted his projects. Lenin had copied the witticism in his notebook and underscored it, and Stalin borrowed the joke in his interview with H. G. Wells in 1934. "Communists do not in the least idealize methods of violence. They would be very pleased to drop violent methods if the ruling class agreed to give way to the working class." Khrushchev made it one of his favorites. The formulation was adopted by the Nineteenth Party Congress in 1952 and reaffirmed by Stalin's successors after his death.

The result of the competition for the allegiance of the third camp was a rush to decolonization. One of the cloudy passages of the Charter (Paragraph 2 of Article 1) included the "self-determination of peoples" among the principles and purposes of the organization but employed the phrase without qualification, in a breathless sentence that seemed to assume that "peoples" and "nations" were synonymous and that the more nations there were the friendlier would be the relations among them.

The Western powers accepted the absurd premise with reluctance at first, then in a panic of accommodation—urged on by the United States, which was motivated seemingly by an unanalyzable combination of good will, desire for justice and votes in the Assembly, self-righteousness, and domestic self-interest. After the package deal of 1955 for the accession of new members to the United Nations in blocs of Communist and non-Communist countries (in contravention of an advisory opinion by the World Court as to the legality of that procedure under the Charter) the world organization itself engaged in an orgy of "nation-building," without "standards, common sense or clear objective," as a respected authority in international law, Clyde Eagleton, had foreseen in a timely but disregarded warning. "There is no gain to anyone in pressing every possible cleavage in the community of nations," Professor Eagleton wrote, "nor in reducing the strength of the free world by breaking it into helplessly weak units. The fears and desires of small states deserve consideration, and valid needs should be met; but the community of nations to which the apostles of fragmentation appeal also has rights and needs." [2]

The result was the United Nations as we now have it at the Plaza on the East River: a conglomeration of nations, non-nations, and fluid groups of individuals, all denominated sovereign, independent, and equal states—one hundred and twenty-two of them at the moment with some twenty or thirty to come. Many are bankrupt and in chaos, but all possess the exciting power of voting resolutions (called laws) in the democratic Assembly, on the democratic principle of one nation one vote: doctrine run wild.

"Peaceful competition," interspersed with wars and threats of wars, is an approach designed to keep the enemy always off balance, economically and politically. At times the ebullient Khrushchev (having acquired his nuclear missiles) seemed to depart from the long-range policy in search for quick successes—notably, in Berlin in 1959, in the Congo in 1960, and in the Cuban adventure in 1962. The first two episodes ended in embarrassing rebuffs; yet each time the dictatorship seems to have retreated the better to advance.

When hot war threatened over Soviet demands for "normalization" in Berlin, President Eisenhower said in a news conference (March 11, 1959), "We will do what is necessary to protect ourselves, but we are never going to back up on our rights and responsibilities." There could be no mistaking what he meant, and the Soviet challenge faded.

Three years later, however, came the Berlin wall, uncontested by the West, and the fifty-eight-megaton nuclear explosion: and in due course, "disarmament," with the partial nuclear-test-ban treaty the first step to making disarmament "general and complete." This first step, was, at very short range, a blessing; an intermediate political effect seems to have been the disruption of NATO, the partial test-ban treaty having been aimed (on the American side) particularly at France. For the long-range effect of these hurried American commitments we must, naturally, wait.

Khrushchev's effort to rush arms to a standard-bearer whom he had chosen in the turmoil in Leopoldville—one Lumumba—would be recalled as a comedy had it not had so tragic an ending for Dag Hammarskjöld. With the death of this truly neutral Secretary-General of the United Nations—accepted by both sides in the cold war to replace Trygve Lie, who had been forced from office by a Soviet boycott—the hope of any effort of peace-keeping by the world organization that might restrain a Soviet client disappeared. Only the Secretariat now held the riven world organization together, and if the non-Communist members wished it to continue in existence, their only choice was to accept as Secretary-General the candidate desired by the Soviet Union.

In the Cuban episode the United States reminded the Russian dictatorship that Americans would, indeed, fight in cases of plain aggression—with nuclear weapons if necessary. And the confrontation cast light upon the full significance of the change that had taken place in the United Nations since the Korean War. Now the Secretary-General spoke forthrightly for the peace camp which he represented, not from rancor at the object of the aggression, but from principle—the principle that peace itself must be the overriding objective. He at once brought his influence down on the side of the power threatening war. He proposed that the hitherto secret Russian nuclear missiles remain in place during a cooling off period while talks began. He asked the Soviet dictatorship to pledge that nuclear reinforcements loaded on Russian ships then approaching Cuba would not be used to build up the installations, and he asked the United States to refrain from heightening the crisis by putting into effect a plan for the blockade of the approaching freighters.

That is to say, he asked that no action be taken by *either side,* aggressor or defender. For practical purposes, it was a duplication of the response of the League of Nations after Hitler's occupation of the Rhineland in 1936. Following a quite different route, the United Nations had come out at the point reached by the League shortly before its career ended.

As it happened this time, however, the young President and the country for which he spoke were resolute. The United Nations proposal was brushed aside. The blockade was pressed. The Soviet ships veered off; after direct negotiations between President Kennedy and the Soviet dictator (aspects of which remain unknown) the missiles were withdrawn from Cuba. It is interesting that the American Ambassador to the United Nations, angered at Communist Russian duplicity, used the powerful sounding board of a Security Council debate to win a propaganda victory in the cold war. By these American responses, the ultimate in hot war was averted. There was a truce in the Atlantic after the American victory, indeed, an era of good feeling—the interval used for disarmament. The riposte was to come in the Pacific, as President Kennedy discovered to his sorrow in later personal conversations with the Soviet dictator.

Once in this fifteen-year stretch of peaceful competition, there was a serious setback for the socialist camp. The Chinese ally of Russia, head in the clouds after the triumph in Korea, which it so fatuously assumed was the product of its own armed strength, sought a quick success in a thrust across the Gulf of Quemoy in 1958. It was humiliatingly repulsed by a well-prepared counteroffensive. Parliamentary democracies can learn from experience too, and President Eisenhower and his Secretary of State, John Foster Dulles, showed that they had. There was none of the political confusion that accompanied the brief and unhappy effort of counterattack in Korea. Political aims were clearly limited. The defender—the American ally, the Nationalist Chinese on strategic Taiwan—was trained and ready, and one new superior weapon—

the "sidewinder"—took the trick. Communist China's great partner refused to come to its assistance, and the open split between them appeared.

Whether the Politburo advised against the adventure from the beginning we do not know. The split may now be irrevocable, though it is relevant to keep in mind the fact that China was organized after the Second World War not by Japan but by Russia, and that the chess players in the Kremlin look several moves ahead. But who can know when, or even whether, the Chinese People's Republic will recover from its madness and become capable of rational thought?

We do know, however, that Russian military support has been essential for the continued prosecution of the Communist war of conquest in South Vietnam. And when the inevitable retaliation for the determined resistance of the United States and its Pacific allies to that war of liberation came in the West—in the Mediterranean in June 1967—we learned once again that in Soviet theory and practice "peace" is a Communist weapon for the waging of world war. We learned also, once again, that the riven world organization whose headquarters are on the East River in New York is helpless before that system of waging war and, perforce, an instrument of it.

We can only guess whether the timing of a people's war upon Israel by the United Arab Republic was approved by the Kremlin. It may be that the USSR intended only a credible threat of overt war —date left open—in this troubled and sensitive region to spread fear and discord in the West through the arming of Egypt and Syria and the encouragement of their belligerency. But when President Nasser ordered his Russian tanks to go forward and the United Nations peacekeeping forces to get out of their way, he certainly expected a victory—peaceful or forcible, as one may choose to call it —and so, evidently, did the USSR. The Russians rejected out of hand the French proposal—accepted by the United States—for a four-power meeting to formulate terms of a Middle East settlement before the guns were fired. The Russian representative at a hastily summoned meeting of the Security Council also refused to join the

Western powers in calling for a cease-fire until it was evident that Egyptian and Russian estimates of relative Arab-Israeli military strengths had been mistaken.

The Egyptian-Syrian declaration of war was, of course, made by the two heads of government in the modern manner—via the air waves, not in any state document. But it used words that were blows, and Israel responded to the informal announcement of its prospective annihilation and to the ring of armor that closed around it with blows that in six days left the Russian planes and tanks shattered in the desert, the Russian missiles emplaced in Syria in Israeli hands, and Israeli forces in advanced positions within enemy territory.

Significantly, it was the Soviet Union that took the issue of peace terms in the Mediterranean from the hands of the Security Council after a week of inflammatory wrangling and put it before a special session of the one-hundred-and-twenty-two-member General Assembly. The Soviet Union failed to get a two-thirds majority for a resolution that would have authorized Russian intervention in the Middle East—"Communists in blue helmets"—under the United Nations flag, but the week of unrestrained political warfare in the Assembly postponed to a distant day any possibility of actual peace between Arabs and Jews, which requires major concessions from both. The "safety valve" blew the roof off. Meanwhile, the Russians poured fresh arms into the Middle East.

The interesting aspects of the Russian statements in these late June and early July days were the depth of hostility disclosed toward the United States, the frank insistence on the Communist terms for a settlement in Vietnam—unconditional cessation of bombing followed by "complete withdrawal" of United States forces—and the distance the Soviet spokesmen went out of their way to charge West Germany with responsibility for Israeli resistance, along with the United States and Britain. Ironically, moreover, while demanding unconditional withdrawal of Israeli forces from positions they had occupied, the Soviet Premier took the opportunity to explain that the USSR based its peace policy on "respect for the boundaries established after the war [the Second World War], including those between the two sovereign German states." The USSR, he said in further elucidation of the peace policy, would continue to support all wars of liberation in colonial areas.

Mere propaganda, to make friends and influence people? Propaganda, surely enough, but statements of Soviet doctrine are not "mere words," and these were coldly doctrinal statements. To rivet the message, the Communist Party of the Soviet Union issued an extended formal statement in Moscow on June 25 (the day the Soviet Premier returned after his meeting with President Johnson at Glassboro, New Jersey) reaffirming the principles of the Stalinist declaration of 1952 on Soviet peaceful competition and people's wars. The formal statement, distributed in excerpt by the Associated Press on June 26, was identified as a formulation of policy preliminary to the observance of the fiftieth anniversary of the Bolshevik Revolution in November 1967.

What will the next step be? Berlin again? If it should by any chance be so, there is, of course, the NATO collectivity to provide help in an emergency.

Is it there, in reality? In one of the supreme ironies of our time, France has condemned the United States for assuming the responsibility for two-front resistance to an expansion-minded Central Power that France itself assumed almost single-handed in comparable—though more restricted—circumstances in the 1920s. France is no longer a world power, but France is a great European power and deserves to be treated as such. Should we not remember, moreover, that the United States failed to comprehend the realities of the French predicament and the French strategy last time? And must we not, indeed, admit to some lack of comprehension in recent years of the role that France and the Federal German Republic—now the two powers of Europe with the closest common interest in the unity and freedom of the Continent—have sought to play together in an effort of unification in Western and Central Europe?

If the NATO collectivity proved to be all veto, or were thought to be so in advance of a test, could it be possible that John Foster Dulles—now so fashionably despised—keeping his mind on the problem and learning from mistakes, found in the Pacific an answer for Europe? The SEATO arrangement that has so well met the test in the Pacific has the appearance of a collectivity, but in actuality is a group of bilateral pacts between the United States and each member. All members of the alliance are welcome to take part in resistance to aggression in the area if they consider that to their interests; but none has a veto over the decision of any other.

Such a modest form of international organization—provisional and practical—is a long way removed from the ideal with which the search for a secure and peaceful world began half a century ago. An age of war and revolution has proven unkind to grand designs. To move forward "one step at a time, close to the ground" in such a storm calls upon all resources of mind and will. Indeed, it is said, often angrily, that the very effort to construct a kind of grouping of nations that anticipates and hence discourages the challenges of the warlike will intensify the danger it seeks to avert. That was Sir Edward Grey's problem sixty years ago, with which the story of the League of Nations begins.

—BYRON DEXTER

South Woodstock, Vermont
July 8, 1967

THE YEARS OF OPPORTUNITY:

The League of Nations, 1920–1926

I. THE LOGIC OF
THE LEAGUE

1. Sir Edward Grey's Problem

The logic of a system of world-wide collective security—foreshadowed by the Covenant of the League of Nations, though not achieved in practice—is most readily understood by an effort to see the problem of war and peace in the years before the First World War through the eyes of Sir Edward Grey, the British Secretary of State for Foreign Affairs from 1905 to 1916. There was no one more fair-minded.

It was Grey who had determined the form of the loose French-Russian-British Entente, constructed to counterbalance the Triple Alliance of Germany, Austria-Hungary, and Italy, and it was Grey who was held responsible when the arrangements he had made failed to restrain Germany and Austria-Hungary in 1914. Italy had held aloof at the August crisis and then changed sides.

Grey was criticized in abusive terms for opposite reasons—for failure to assert British neutrality and for failure to make plain that England would fight. "An incompetent Machiavelli," George Bernard Shaw called him in a gibe that set the fashion for the postwar generation of debunkers in England and America. Later evidence of what German domination of the Continent would have meant and first-hand experience with the thorny task of maintaining defensive alliances disposed of the abuse on both shores of the Atlantic. The essence of Grey's policy toward Germany was to play for time. He lost, therefore his estimate must have been wrong; but men's imaginations have never been able to rest with the verdict.

Grey's problem was uniquely difficult: more nearly than any statesman of his time he saw the problem whole. Though this quality indicated fineness of character, perhaps, in the cruel circumstances of international politics, it was also a defect. Not "a great man" but "a great example," Lord Vansittart said of his former chief in the Foreign Office at the end of his own disappointing career. Vansittart disagreed with the policy of Grey the statesman, but he revered the man.

Grey disliked a system of competing alliances, but he had respect for the procedures of traditional diplomacy. Until the lights went out in the summer of 1914, he never lost the hope that the successive crises between the great powers and their allies and clients could be successfully dealt with in the manner of the old diplomacy. That procedure ruled out efforts at grand settlements of complicated conflicts. It sought to isolate issues and adjust them in as prosaic a way as possible, so that there would be no spectacular failure or success for either side. Such an approach was admittedly artificial. Everyone concerned knew that small and large issues interlocked. Everyone also knew that upon adjournment of any conference some nation or group would be disappointed, at best, and probably angry and determined that things should go differently next time. But it was generally assumed that the concert—the community—in fact existed and that no contestant could gain by destroying it. Underlying all was the assumption that the political objectives of the powers were limited.

How these procedures and assumptions worked is illustrated in the last episode of the prewar era in which the old diplomacy actually worked. The London Conference of 1912-1913 averted an immediate threat of European war over territorial quarrels arising from the Balkan Wars and brought a temporary lessening of the mounting hostility between England and Germany.

The Balkan melee was both cause and product of the disintegration of a colonial empire—Turkey's in Europe. The territorial dispute at issue was whether Serbia—which, in alliance with Greece and Bulgaria, had emerged from a six-week campaign against the Turks with "her reputation greatly increased, her territories enlarged, her aspirations inflamed" [1]—would annex the former Turkish province of Albania. Austria was prepared to go to war to prevent it.

Sir Edward Grey was the moving spirit in assembling the representatives of the six great powers for this last meeting of the concert. There was no pressure exerted in public for a conference; he ascertained that the others would be willing to come together and left it to them to choose the place of meeting. London was chosen, though Grey preferred Paris. His reasons were characteristic: he wished to play down his own and Britain's role in bringing about any settlement, and he would have been pleased to be spared the extra work and the tedium of presiding at the prolonged sessions. Had the conference met elsewhere than at London, the British ambassador at the particular capital would have taken his place.

As it was, the ambassadors to St. James's from Germany, France, Italy, Russia, and Austria met, under his chairmanship, afternoons from four to about seven—with an interval for tea—over a period of about seven months—with intervals of suspension. The ambassadors were friends. All wanted the conference to succeed but all were under instructions from their governments. Personal friendships would have had no bearing on the outcome had not the governments also felt it to their interest to avert war on this occasion. That being the case, interminable but subdued arguments among these diplomatists droned along. The conference never formally adjourned; its particular mission accomplished, it simply stopped meeting, to everyone's relief.

Such, at any rate, is the tone in which Sir Edward Grey tells the tale. In his heart-searching memoir, *Twenty-Five Years,* he permits himself only one lively passage in regard to this last exemplification of the old European order.

At one point in the proceedings Serbia, he explains, claimed "a village called Djakova," but Austria, through Count Albert von Mensdorff, her ambassador, insisted that it be included within the boundary of Albania. Count Alexander Benckendorff, speaking for Russia, said that it should go to Serbia. There was a deadlock. The conference was forced to suspend its sessions and there was an ominous feeling of rising pressure.

"Probably I saw Mensdorff and Benckendorff separately, and perhaps Lichnowsky [Prince Karl Max Lichnowsky, the German ambassador] too, to explore the possibilities of concession," Grey says, "but of this I have no certain recollection." Suddenly, however, Count Mensdorff sent a messenger to ask him for an appointment, speaking with urgency, and Grey invited him to come at once to his house. He describes the climax in the following words:

> In a few minutes Mensdorff arrived. The room in the house that I occupied then was small; on a table in the middle stood daffodils and other spring flowers sent to me from Fallodon and placed in tall glasses of water. Mensdorff entered briskly, even a little breathless with haste, delighted with the good news he brought and exclaiming, "We give up Djakova!" As he bustled quickly into the room, his full-skirted frock-coat, swaying as it passed the flower-table, brushed the heads of some daffodils; the resentful daffodils tilted their glass and emptied the water down the skirts of Mensdorff's coat. Some perturbation ensued; I fetched a towel and swathed the coat as best I could. Then we fraternized over Djakova. Mensdorff was genuinely pleased to bring the news.

In return for the concession, Austria stipulated that Serbia should evacuate certain other areas in favor of Albania. Grey "strongly urged" that this condition be accepted in St. Petersburg, and it was accepted. "The incident was over; the Great Powers were in agreement. More trouble remained about other things, but by these methods, and in this spirit, we got through." [2]

In sum, Serbs were told that they would not occupy Albania, which was made an independent kingdom under a German prince chosen by the powers, but Serbia was given an outlet to the sea. Boundary lines between Serbia and Albania were drawn with rough justice and the settlement was imposed, with the aid of some monetary compensation for Montenegro.

Though no other Foreign Secretary in the world would think of making the spring flowers from his country house the principal actors in the tableau that symbolized the postponement of a world war, this north-country Englishman was aware of the crucial aspect of the situation that he was omitting when he thus described the episode. The counterpart of his representations to Britain's associate, Czarist Russia, urging moderation had been similar counsel from Germany to its ally, Austria. That saved the peace in 1912-1913.

Grey's problem was to maintain a defensive coalition against Germany in a situation which he believed had not yet crystallized. In other words, his policy was geared to holding Germany within the concert, not to amassing a preponderance of force against it.

The construction and maintenance of a defensive alliance to meet the threat of war from a great power is diplomacy's hardest task. From its inception such an alliance confronts a potential aggressor with a check to his plans, and thus it challenges him to adopt the one measure most likely to separate any allies—to inflict upon one of them a defeat, military or political, which the others are unable or unwilling to prevent. And since the formation of such an alliance implies the shift from a passive to an active policy by the threatened nations, it puts into the hands of their antagonist a conqueror's most powerful political weapon—the opportunity to make the victim appear the aggressor.

In a conqueror's eyes, the victim of his aggression starts the fighting by the act of resistance, and therefore is responsible for the bloodshed. Similarly, an "arms race" begins because the weaker state looks to its defenses. Only the aggressor can offer every antagonist a sure method of avoiding war—surrender. In the diplomatic conflicts of alliances, the high cards are in the hands of the most warlike power.

An incident that took place not long before Grey entered office suggests the complexity that had been added to this problem of a defensive alliance by the development of modern parliamentary government. In 1889 Count Paul Hatzfeld, the German Ambassador in London, told the British Prime Minister, Lord Salisbury, on Bismarck's instructions, that peace could best be secured by an Anglo-German defensive alliance against France. Salisbury, professing gratification at the proposal, replied, "We unfortunately no longer live in Pitt's time, when the aristocracy ruled and we could conduct an active policy. . . . Now the democracy rules, and with it come personal and party government, which has made every English Government absolutely dependent on the *aura popularis*. This generation can only be taught by events." [3]

The reply was somewhat disingenuous, for though Britain and France were angry at each other over colonial matters at the time, we may guess that Salisbury was none too sure where the threat to Britain actually lay. But it indicates well enough the dilemma an alliance presents to the leader of a parliamentary government. To wait until the outbreak of war makes plain the need of a commitment to fight is to lose any hope that the alliance will forestall the war; but to make the commitment before public opinion is convinced of its necessity is to risk starting the war and losing both alliance and war. In short, the formation of the alliance brings matters to a head and invites an attack at the vulnerable point of the union—the area in which the immediate interests of the allies are most uneven.

Grey awaited events before accepting the obligations of a binding alliance with France or with Russia—indeed, he awaited the ultimate event, German violation of Belgian neutrality. The British people went to war united, but the war that Grey sought to avert had begun before Britain made up its mind.

In his effort to understand the nature of the Germany, and of the German government, of the time, Grey deliberately did not look extensively into the writings of the Pan-German expansionists. He wished to keep as free as possible from emotional judgments. England, too, had her jingoes. He tried to damp down the acrimony of press exchanges. A speech to the Delegates of the Dominions in London in 1911 is a fair sample of the position he took.

There is no "appreciable danger of our being involved in any considerable trouble in Europe," he said to the delegates, "unless there is some Power or group of Powers which has the ambition of achieving what I call the Napoleonic policy. That would be a policy on the part of the strongest Power in Europe, or of the strongest group of Powers in Europe, of first of all separating the other Powers outside their own group from each other, taking them in detail, crushing them if need be, and forcing each into the orbit of the strongest Power. . . ." [4]

This, of course, was a warning of danger. The Dominion delegates knew which was the strongest power in Europe; all knew that Grey meant Germany. Yet he did not name Germany. To do so was the precondition of an effort to transform the loose French-Russian-British Entente—to which Grey had carefully promised "diplomatic" but not military support—into a firm alliance for waging a possible war against a recognized enemy.

Dangerous to Europe Germany had certainly become. It was looking for something: "a place in the sun"—an expression of a general restlessness. The German diplomatic method in earlier major crises had been that of ransom—to spring to an exaggerated position and then negotiate a partial withdrawal. The rational objective of the German fleet-building program, in so far as it had one, was to force England to be neutral if Germany engaged in war with France; moreover, with such a man as Wilhelm II—erratic, vain, childish, though sometimes brilliant—in command of the strongest army in the world, no one could tell what might happen. The dangerous results of Bismarck's successful bullying of the German people and their neighbors were real.

Yet this was but half the picture. The fact was that Germany was a deeply respected nation. The world's scholars turned to her for guidance. There was no Iron Curtain about the Reich to provide a plain yardstick for measuring aggressive intent. In the 1900s German citizens went freely abroad, sought and welcomed for the gifts they brought with them.

Bernhard von Bülow, Foreign Minister and then Chancellor, Bismarck's heir (or so he called himself), was cultivated, witty, cosmopolitan. Though a former Hussar, he was a career diplomat. He thought he could safely build the navy that Admiral Alfred von Tirpitz and Wilhelm II wanted if he talked about it soothingly. He thought he could divide Britain and France if he rattled the sword. He was an accomplished courtier and spent prodigious amounts of energy and time in court feuds. It was impossible to tell where he stood with regard to Russia, since he did not perceive the relevance to Russia of a German attachment to the fortunes of the dissolving Austro-Hungarian Empire. He wanted no war with England. He was apparently not averse to a war with France if he could separate France and England. He left for posthumous publication an incredibly petty, vindictive, and naïve autobiography that revealed him as a mountebank. "The only man who ever succeeded in committing suicide after his death," the Kaiser is said to have remarked.

Grey's policy was intended to cope with a government of which von Bülow was typical—that is to say, to deal with it by firmness but not by threats. His policy recognized that the German Empire was off balance, but it assumed that there was hope that time—and the experience of self-government which time might bring to the German people—would restore them to balance without a terrible bloodletting.

Moreover, there was Russia. The unity of French and British interests, though perceived only after the turn of the century, was established. To maintain it was Grey's unswerving purpose. But a binding alliance to amass preponderant force against Germany also had to make binding commitments to the Czarist empire, which he called a despotism without discipline.

Grey had had experience of Russia. He had supervised the settlement with Russia which divided Persia (Iran) into British and

Russian spheres of influence, thus effecting a truce in Russian-British conflicts in southwest Asia and making possible the loose arrangements of the Entente. But open conflict was ever on the point of boiling up again: the simple sequel to the Persian settlement had been a Russian military occupation of its sphere.

Grey was also well aware of Russian intrigues in the Balkans. And always vivid in his memory was that odd episode in the North Sea in 1904 when the Russian fleet, setting out for the Far East to meet the Japanese, had come upon a group of British fishing boats and blazed away with all their guns. No one ever found out how the guns happened to go off.

So Grey played for time. There were two sides even to the Russian coin. The British Prime Minister, Sir Henry Campbell-Bannerman, had read everyone's thoughts in his calculated indiscretion of 1905, when the Czar had shut down the Duma while a delegation of its members was on the way to London for ceremonies with British parliamentarians. *"La Duma est mort! Vive la Duma!"* Campbell-Bannerman said in his toast to the Russian visitors. It was an expression of faith in the forces of liberalism in Russia. The Russia intelligentsia was highly trained and one of the most talented in the world. It shared, and sometimes led, in every civilized experience save one—the experience of political liberty. Was not that on the way? During the subsequent period of land reforms under the Czarist minister Peter Stolypin, Lenin, indeed, despaired of revolution in his lifetime. Five years, Bismarck believed, are the furthest any statesman can hope to read the future. Suppose Grey had had five years more?

The possibility, however slight, that war could again have been averted, as it had been in 1913, had there been some standing machinery for consultation when the Archduke of Austria, Ferdinand, was assassinated at Sarajevo a year later was one of the factors that helped form the idea and machinery of the League of Nations. In 1914 the gigantic armaments of the powers seemed self-activating; the rush to destruction seemed so insensate that such words as "blunder," "stumble," "drift" were—and still are—employed to explain, if only to those who use them, how the catastrophe occurred.

But, except among complete savages, war is an act of policy, and these statesmen and generals of Europe were cultivated men. Grey tried to assemble a conference in 1914, but now Germany refused. In this instance, when Serbia replied in conciliatory tone to an Austrian ultimatum, Berlin did not advise moderation in Vienna but the contrary.

In July 1914 von Bülow was out of office and Montz von Bethmann-Hollweg and Gottlieb von Jagow were respectively Chancellor and Foreign Minister in the German government. They were serious men. Grey confessed to a feeling of anger at them, rare for him, when they proved unresponsive to his plea for moderation. But that feeling vanished. The fact was, he believed, and probably correctly, that in communicating with them he was not communicating with the governing power in the German state. Power lay elsewhere, and decisions were being made by others. Military counsels had superseded political.

That being the case, the restraint of superior power was needed to keep the peace. Where could it have been obtained? England had the strongest fleet in the world, and also a well-trained expeditionary force of seven divisions prepared by Lord Haldane, Grey's closest friend. There was no system of conscription. Could one have been instituted at any time after 1904 without precipitating a showdown among Englishmen of different views, and between England and Germany, that might quickly have brought war? England would then have been considered the aggressor.

There was one further aspect, evident only in retrospect. In 1910 Sir Arthur Nicolson, British Ambassador to Russia, recommending to his chief the reconstruction of the Entente as a binding alliance, assured him that Great Britain, France, and Russia would be more than equal to the Central Powers. But they were not. The German General Staff had estimated correctly that they were not. Even after they had strained every nerve to develop their resources they were barely equal in strength to the combination against them; and after the Russian Revolution their strength became inferior.

In the course of a discerning analysis of Grey's conduct of office, Algernon Cecil has speculated on some of the "ifs" of the situation —if Grey had made an early flat statement that Britain would fight for Belgian independence, if Italy had placed her troops in support of the French right flank, if Theodore Roosevelt had been the American President—if, that is to say, all the other powers had acted together. The one hope of restraint powerful enough to avoid the final break between Alliance and Entente lay in lifting the whole issue into a large framework. *That was the logic of the League of Nations.* Grey became President of the League of Nations Union in Britain after his retirement as Foreign Secretary and devoted the remainder of his life to that cause.

2. The French View of an Alliance

For most British—and American—proponents of the League of Nations, the Continental system of alliances, with the fears it engendered and the sensitiveness with which it registered shades of national prestige, was itself the source of war. "Alliances, made with war in mind, lead to war." But to a diplomatist such as Paul Cambon, French Ambassador in London, such generalizations were a superficial reading of the circumstances of the prewar years. In his view, and in that of most Frenchmen, the question was not whether the formation of a binding alliance might fail to deter a German attack but whether France would again have to withstand a German attack alone.

Partly because of Napoleon III's blunders, but primarily because Bismarck and General Helmuth von Moltke wanted a war and deliberately made one, France had fought in 1870 and been crushed in a brief campaign. Because it had recovered with unexpected quickness from the punishment—including the indemnities—of that defeat, Bismarck had not scrupled to threaten war again in the 1880s. His policy included no such moderation toward France as he had shown toward conquered Austria in 1866. German soldiers had taken pains in advance to checkmate him if he intended to seek reconciliation with France. He had no such intention. The seizure of Alsace-Lorraine was the symbol of the enmity Bismarck intended to perpetuate.

The French Minister of Foreign Affairs, Théophile Delcassé, tells the story of an episode of 1903 which registered the end of the British period of splendid isolation and the sense of relief with which France greeted it. He had gone to London to talk to Lord Lansdowne, then the British Foreign Secretary, in furtherance of the convention which brought an end to the friction between Britain and France in Egypt and established their entente. Suddenly and casually, Lord Lansdowne said, "You ought to open the way for some rapprochement between ourselves and Russia."

"I felt that my head was about to burst," Delcassé related. "But I did not show anything of the feeling these words had stirred in me. I was content to remark that I should avail myself of every opportunity to praise in the presence of Russian statesmen the satisfactory working of the Entente Cordiale." [5]

Before the British settlement with Russia could be consummated, von Bülow tested the French accord with Britain. The leverage was a warlike demonstration by Wilhelm II at Tangier, Morocco, in 1905, accompanied by a veiled demand for the dismissal of Delcassé and the holding of a conference. France, frightened, acquiesced in both demands and also appropriated two hundred thousand francs to improve its frontier defenses. At the conference, held at Algeciras the following year, Sir Edward Grey gave France firm backing, and a formula—proposed, surprisingly, by President Theodore Roosevelt—was found to satisfy international claims in woefully misgoverned Morocco. There was no further humiliation for France.

In the terminology of international politics, Delcassé's dismissal was a blow to French "prestige." For France it was a direct challenge to her national independence. In the circumstances the words "freedom" and "prestige" were synonymous, as they are whenever a foreign country asserts a veto on the choice of foreign minister—

and hence of foreign policy—of another. Once armed force had been used against France, the threat of force sufficed: the word was the blow.

Even in the conference of 1912-1913, when France had no direct interest in the disputed Balkan territory and a strong concern in damping down the threatened warfare between Serbia and Austria, Cambon, with utmost politeness, conveyed to Sir Edward Grey the impression that Britain was making the unguarded assumption that all the powers shared common aims. He thought that Grey was being too detached—too neutral. Cambon feared a political defeat for France's ally, Russia, such as Russia had suffered at the hands of the Central Powers in 1908 when Austria annexed the former Turkish provinces of Bosnia and Herzegovina contrary to the treaty to which Russia was a party. In Cambon's view, the interest of his pledged ally was his own.

By 1912, the German population was a third greater than that of France. Germany's economic resources were much greater. Moreover, the major French industrial plant stood on the border of the open northeastern gateway. The German government was an absolute monarchy; France was at the mercy of arbitrary decisions by the German Emperor and his soldiers—and soldiers and state were revered by a well-drilled people. Literally and figuratively, Germany was the Central Power of Europe. Because a great, expansion-minded central power can be restrained only by opposing power on two fronts, an alliance with Russia was, for France, not a step toward war but a defensive action that offered at least a possibility of maintaining national independence.

The role of mediator in international conflicts is a delicate one, and the party which comes forward as conciliator is often enough, Cambon knew, a country which is in process of changing sides. Its weight, if merely removed from one side and held suspended, swings the balance in favor of the other.

Cambon's uneasiness during the years of Grey's secretaryship did not arise from any doubt of Grey's integrity. He could no more mistake that than he could doubt his own. The questions that he put to this British Minister, from the time Grey took office in the midst of the dangerous Moroccan flare-up, coalesce into a single terrible question: "Will you fight if we are attacked?" The replies he received were to him a single dread answer, foreshadowing a bitter outcome: "That depends."

But the two men dealt with one another with complete personal confidence. In their conversations Grey spoke in English and the French Ambassador in French. "He spoke his own language so distinctly and with such clear pronunciation that every word could be visualized when listening to him," Grey said in a charming aside. "To listen to him was like reading French." [6] There was no interpreter; after their first conversation they exchanged written records but thereafter dispensed even with that formality. No charge of misquotation arose. And never, even in the most anxious hours of the last days of peace, did Cambon presume to speak to Grey in terms of obligation. His appeal was to British self-interest.

But Brititish self-interest was the interest of an island twenty miles off the coast of Europe. The difference between the French and British approaches to a European alliance was the difference between an inside view and an outside view. An outside view is watching something happen; an inside view is having it happen to you. The "incomparable consequences of sea power" had for two centuries enabled the islanders to hold the scales on the Continent with a minimum expenditure of their own strength; the reserve strength had built the Empire. *Si monumentum quaeris, circumspice,* said Grey proudly in the summing up of his stewardship. This world-wide, loosely governed imperial realm was the British alliance that kept the Continent in balance with Great Britain. To maintain that balance, a policy that might enable Britain to take as much or as little of a Continental war as it saw fit was the primary requisite of imperial security. The skeptical French envoy and the kindly English nobleman were thinking of different systems and different objectives.

Britain had, however, incurred an immense obligation to France, the more dangerous for being unavowed. When war seemed immi-

nent in 1905, Grey's predecessor, Lord Lansdowne, had authorized consultations between British and French naval and army
staffs to devise plans for military cooperation. Grey acknowledged
their existence when Cambon referred to them in their first talk and
authorized their continuance, though by a negative. That is to say,
when Cambon proposed that they be continued, he replied that he
did not dissent.

Then as always, however, he insisted that this planning not be
understood as a pledge by Britain to go to war: "It was to be
clearly understood that these conversations or plans between military and naval staffs did not commit either Government and involved no promise of support in war." [7] The explicit British pledge
was for diplomatic support only. But the staff conversations developed into definite arrangements for the use of the British Expeditionary Force on the left flank of the French army and resulted in
the withdrawal of the French fleet to the Mediterranean. The
French predicament, if war came and Britain decided upon neutrality, was easily imaginable.

Edward Gray imagined it, in colloquies with himself, in words
that he never permitted himself to use publicly. If Germany forced
war on France in order to destroy the Anglo-French agreement and
Britain stood aside, it would be "isolated," "discredited," "hated,"
"despised," he told himself. And he did not think that it would
stand aside. As it happened, a German promise to refrain from any
attack on the open French north coast was the final bid for British
neutrality in 1914. British Ministers did not consider it. Grey
understood his own people.

He did not, however, tell them about the staff conversations. And
he did not bring the military arrangements even to the attention of
the Cabinet until 1912.

That was a serious error and Grey acknowledged that it was. His
explanation was that the first talk with Cambon, in the midst of the
Moroccan crisis, took place during a general election in Britain,
when all other members of the Cabinet were out of London. Several of them, including the Prime Minister, Campbell-Bannerman,

had at once been informed, but none had pressed for a meeting of the full Cabinet. The terms of the Anglo-French agreement made under Lansdowne had been published, and Grey had given no further pledge in oral or written communications with the French Ambassador. In Grey's opinion the unavowed military conversations had not, until 1912, increased the degree of obligation incurred in the known political agreement. The Cabinet, when informed, readily accepted the explanation. It approved one more letter to Cambon restating the British commitment in the same terms that Grey had used from the beginning and approved likewise the continuation of the military staff planning.

After Grey's speech to the House of Commons on August 3, 1914, Britain was at war. Two members of the Cabinet resigned in protest, John Burns and Lord Morley. Morley was bitter about the secret military arrangements. Yet, ironically, he had been informed about them before most other members of the Cabinet, in documents which he received as a member of the Committee of Imperial Defence. He had perceived their significance so little that, in complete good faith, he denied having been shown them.

For the French the lesson of this experience was not that alliances are unsuited to the complexities of international relations but that the British effort to implement this particular alliance was unnecessarily vague and complicated. Instead of larger and even looser arrangements for deterring a possible war-maker, France sought a more precise and binding one. This view also carried to the heart of the planning and administering of the Covenant of the League of Nations.

3. Mackinder's Warning

At Christmastime in 1918, when the trenches across Europe were empty save for the unclaimed dead and Englishmen, Americans, and Frenchmen were preparing versions of articles to be offered as structure for the League of Nations, an individual Englishman, Sir Halford J. Mackinder, was at work on a short book which he hoped would be read by the peacemakers soon to gather at Versailles. The title of the book was *Democratic Ideals and Realities;* its subtitle, *A Study in the Politics of Reconstruction.* The author, a teacher of geography at Oxford and the London School of Economics, favored the League idea. Indeed, he termed it the great political ideal which the twentieth century had added to the eighteenth-century ideal of liberty and the nineteenth-century ideal of nationality. But he noted that the League was faced with a "housing problem." It was to the nature of this problem that he wished to call attention, in new perspective.

Never has genius intervened in practical politics with so beguiling an introductory proposal as Sir Halford's. What he intended to do was to refashion the way of thinking of twentieth-century men about the relationship to one another of the continents, the islands, and the oceans of the globe, and about their own relationship to them. He succeeded, though in the most ironic way imaginable.

The British and American statesmen, whom he warned of impending danger, paid no attention to him, though some of their advisers took heed. Those he tried to warn against—the organizers of tyranny in Germany and Russia—put his strategic insight into practice. Finally, however, those for whom he had originally written also revised their perspective.

Mackinder's housing problem was a metaphor. "Fierce moralists," he explained, allow no extenuation for sin, but practical reformers give thought to the living conditions of the persistently unruly. If the world was to be a safe place for democracies, the League would have to give attention to the influence of environment as well as to the rules of right conduct. Above all, it must give thought to the sources and temptations of power. He asked his readers to perceive how the grouping of lands and seas, of productive resources and "natural pathways," lends itself to the growth of empires, perhaps to a single world empire. "If we are to realize our ideal of a League of Nations which shall prevent war in the future," he said, "we must recognize these geographical realities and take steps to counter their influence." [8]

There is no accounting for genius. Halford J. Mackinder, born in 1861, was the oldest son of a Lincolnshire country doctor. He distinguished himself in his father's eyes at the age of twelve by writing a discourse on Australia; he had been reading Captain Cook's voyages. He distinguished himself at Oxford in natural science and history and was elected president of the Oxford Union. He had been sent to Oxford preparatory to studying medicine; instead he read law. Upon being called to the bar he lost interest in it and turned to teaching. "The new geography"—the study of man's environment—was in the air and appealed to him. He became an extension lecturer in the movement for adult education, also burgeoning in the lively intellectual life of the late Victorians; then Reader in Geography at Oxford, Director of Oxford's first School of Geography, and briefly Director of the London School of Economics. In 1902, at the age of forty-one, he wrote his first book, *Britain and the British Seas*, suggested to him, he said, by the needs of some foreign students visiting Britain. But his career, so far, was simply that of an able scholar.

The flash of genius was to come two years later in a lecture before the Royal Geographical Society called "The Geographical Pivot of History," which disclosed his mature ideas and an originality and farsightedness unrivaled in our time. In a letter written years later he explained himself with the humor which is perhaps the best explanation for his kind of genius: "The author was caned as a boy at school for drawing maps instead of writing Latin prose, and for thirty years afterwards he thought visually and therefore geographically. In the end the impulse to write what he saw mastered him. *Voilà tout.*" [9]

What he saw was not several continents and oceans, but one continent, Europe-Asia-Africa, which he called the World Island, covering one-sixth of the globe; one ocean, blocked to seamen by ice at the poles, covering three-quarters of the globe; and many smaller islands, including North and South America, Japan, and Australia, covering the remaining one-twelfth of the globe. Western Europe was merely a peninsula of the great land mass of Europe, Asia, and Africa.

This was the globe as airmen were presently to see it, though Mackinder did not term his perspective an airman's view. The Wrights had made their flight at Kitty Hawk in December 1903, and he noted the imminence of "winged mobility," as did another brilliant young man, Leopold S. Amery, in the discussion which followed the reading of the 1904 paper. But Mackinder's concern then was not to explore the possibilities of air power but to challenge seamen to take a new look at history and geography. "In the present decade," he said in the lecture, which was published in the *Geographical Journal* in April 1904, "we are for the first time in a position to attempt, with some degree of completeness, a correlation between the larger geographical and the larger historical generalizations. For the first time we can perceive something of the real proportion of features and events on the stage of the whole world, and may seek a formula which shall express certain aspects, at any rate, of geographical causation in universal history."

Mackinder's "Fig. 5," entitled "The Natural Seats of Power," showing what he termed the "pivot area," the "inner or marginal crescent," and the "lands of outer or insular crescent." (From the *Geographical Journal,* Vol. 23, Pt. 4 [1904]. By permission of the Royal Geographical Society.)

The generalization he sought was expressed visually in a little map entitled "The Natural Seats of Power"—the famous Figure 5—which was published with this lecture. Drawn on a global projection, and enclosed within an oval to indicate that he was looking at the world as a whole, his figure was centered not on Europe but on a huge, roughly rectangular "pivot area," slanting down from the Siberian Arctic across Asia and Eastern Europe to Asia Minor and the Dardanelles. This he described as the greatest natural fortress on earth, possessing untold wealth for industrial development, though as yet thinly populated. The coast lands of Asia and Europe, outside this area, were termed the "inner or marginal crescent." North and South America, shown on both edges of the map, were part of the "lands of outer or insular crescent." The three seats of power were this central land mass, inaccessible to ships; its coastal countries; and the outlying islands. Mackinder's thesis was that the way the world was organized in the future would depend on the way power was balanced between the expansive internal forces and the marginal regions. European civilization, he noted, had been molded under the pressure of Mongol and Tartar invasions from the inland area. Even more in the future than in the past, he reasoned, combinations of power were likely to rotate around the land mass, as its population increased and its natural wealth was developed.

In the main, this was the territory of the Russian Empire, which had replaced the Mongol Empire. "The most remarkable contrast in the political map of modern Europe," Mackinder wrote, "is that presented by the vast area of Russia occupying half the Continent and the group of smaller territories tenanted by the Western Powers." But he was not seeking here to read the future in terms of any particular nation. Some new control of the inland areas—by Chinese, organized by Japanese, for instance—would not tend to reduce the geographical significance of the pivot position, he insisted. On the contrary, the strategic importance of the area would in that event become greater, since an "oceanic frontage" would be added to the resources of the great continent. Similarly, the power of the pivot area would become irresistible were the resources of Germany to be combined with those of the inland region. This could happen if Germany and Russia were in alliance, or if one were to conquer the other.

To this conception of the pivot area of the globe he appended another controversial and seemingly paradoxical thesis—the idea of closed space. "From the present time forth, in the post-Columbian age, we shall again have to deal with a closed political system, and none the less . . . it will be one of world-wide scope," he said. There was no paradox involved. Though he asked his audience for a degree of detachment and imagination sufficient to see the geographical features of the round world as a whole, his focus was not outer space but the surface of the earth.

In outline, the geographical knowledge of the earth was complete from pole to pole, he asserted, and claims to ownership of all the dry land had been staked out. "Every explosion of social forces, instead of being dissipated in a surrounding circuit of unknown space and barbaric chaos, will be sharply re-echoed from the far side of the globe, and weak elements in the political and economic organism will be shattered in consequence." He likened the effect of such explosions in the twentieth century to the effect of the explosion of a shell in the rigid structure of a building or ship, as contrasted with the effect of such an explosion in an earthwork.

To avert the great disasters—war and tyranny—he concluded, more accurate estimates of the explosive social forces and of the rigid political structure would be needed. He was tilting here at the political and economic implications of the philosophy of *laissez faire*.

The term "Heartland," the best known of Mackinder's poetic figures of speech, occurred only once in the 1904 paper, and then incidentally. He used it instead of the more technical term "pivot area" when he wrote his book *Democratic Ideals and Reality* fifteen years later, in the hope of reaching a less specialized audience. In some particulars he redefined the area. But the term remained a generalization; no one can say precisely what the boundaries of the pivot area or Heartland are. In the book and in subsequently published papers (which were remarkably few) he sought always for broad political and strategic principles, embodied in vivid metaphors—one reason why his work has been widely borrowed, and tragically misappropriated.

Mackinder was careful, however, to call his elaboration of the original thesis a warning to the victors of the First World War, and the terms in which he formulated the problem of the peacemakers and of the League of Nations were direct. They were also characteristically picturesque. The 1883 eruption of the volcano Krakatoa in the Sunda Straits of Indonesia was used to supplement the illustration of the artillery shell in a tightly knit political system. As the air waves from the eruption had circled the globe to converge in a point in the opposite hemisphere and then diverged to meet again over the volcano, so henceforth would the shocks of political collisions spread, diverge, and meet again. "That, in the ultimate analysis, is why every considerable state was bound to be drawn into the recent war, if it lasted, as it did, long enough." [10] And this conclusion, too, supported the logic of an effort toward world organization.

Mackinder warned the League that its ideals could be applied to international life only if it had power. He distrusted exhortations to justice and peace. "The temptation of the moment," he wrote, "is to believe that unceasing peace will ensue merely because tired men are determined that there shall be no more war." [11] But he reasoned that the peace was no more than a truce between forces which had been generating tension for a century, and that the tension would accumulate again. Estimating that productive forces damaged in the war could be restored within seven or eight years, he held that those few years during which the situation was fluid were the time to forestall the next war.

His view was Paul Cambon's—that to refuse to organize power consciously was to offer total power to an empire of ruthless organizers. Democracies usually think ethically, Mackinder suggested, and that is to their credit; but it is not a virtue for responsible ministers to take pride in the fact that their nations are unprepared for the wars their ideals take them into. In the day of submarines, motorcars, and airplanes, democracies must learn to think strategically. In brief, they must remember that the world is round. "This war has taught us rapidly, but there are still vast numbers of our citizens who look out on to a vivid Western foreground, but only to a very dim Eastern background." [12]

Mackinder's explicit warning to his own countrymen was the famous demonstration of the way land power can conquer sea power by capturing its bases. The word "base," as he used it, did not mean simply a harbor or a coastal fortification, but the whole land area whose natural and human resources enabled peoples to build and maintain their fleets and armies. Basic to naval strength were productive capacity and manpower. (He was the first to use the word "manpower" in this sense.) In contests between sea and land countries, seamen enjoyed the advantage of superior mobility for purposes of commerce and in transporting fighting men—a great asset in days of primitive overland communications. Landsmen possessing a larger base and greater manpower could, however, subdue a naval state the hard way—that is, by roundabout marches to take the seamen in the rear. When successful in such a maneuver, the inland state added the shipbuilding facilities of the conquered country to its land power, and, likely as not, an empire was the product of the merger.

The English geographer went back to the dawn of history for his examples—to Egypt, Crete, Xerxes the Persian, Philip of Macedon, and Alexander the Great, who ended the first cycle of sea power in the Mediterranean by overrunning the bases of the Greeks and Phoenicians and advancing into Asia. Hannibal's long march from Carthage to the Latin peninsula by way of Spain was an instance of the application of the strategy that failed; Carthaginian resources were slender, and the Roman Legions were too strong. Rome "closed" the entire Mediterranean; but though it fought spectacular naval battles, the Legions in reality controlled the sea by holding the coasts.

This illustration, midway in the long story, was to be the significant one for the British naval strategists. The British base was the fertile English plain, "productive and secure," [13] with its adjacent deposits of coal and iron. At the close of the Napoleonic war, Mackinder noted, British sea power encompassed Asia, Europe, and Africa—the "World Island" in his global perspective, though only a great "promontory" to seamen because of the stretch of impenetrable Arctic ice. In the nineteenth century the Indian Ocean, on the far side of the globe, was closed by British power, as Rome had closed its sea. To the Victorians, this Roman position of their own seemed the natural order of things. Mackinder's sharp reminder to the islanders pointed out the difference between Rome's security throughout four centuries and their own precarious position. The difference lay in the fact that, whereas the closing of the Mediterranean depended on the Legions, the closing of the Indian Ocean was maintained "by the long arm of sea-power itself from the home base." [14] As Britain's rivals had grown in population and industrial strength, that base had become dangerously small. The Channel was still there, but not the needed reserves.

Mackinder asked the statesmen and generals at Versailles to reflect not on their victory but on the narrowness of their escape. Had Germany won the war, it would have acquired the shipbuilding resources of the Continent and another cycle of empire would have begun. The Central Powers would have won in 1918 had not American manpower come to the western front in time, he continued, and Germany might have won before that had German generalship not made a fatal error at the outset of the fighting. If the German army had been content to fight defensively on the short western front and to strike its main blow in the east, Russia would probably have succumbed. "It is not improbable that the world would be nominally at peace today," he concluded, "but overshadowed by a German East Europe in command of all the Heartland. The British and American insular peoples would not have realized their strategic danger until too late." [15]

Hence his dramatic trilogy:

> Who rules East Europe commands the Heartland:
> Who rules the Heartland commands the World-Island:
> Who rules the World-Island commands the World.

The pronouncement has been criticized as both oversimplified and unnerving—a fatalistic prophecy that rulership of the world must pass to the state which occupies a particular portion of the earth. The term "commands" is ambiguous, however, implying either peremptory authority or merely a vantage offering the possibility of dominance; we may be sure that Mackinder chose his words deliberately; the range of meanings was intended to preclude fatalism. "The test of the League will come in the Heartland of the Continent," he said flatly.[16] But it was because *nature* offered temptation for the seizure of overwhelming power that *men* had to exercise foresight about political arrangements.

His specific injunction was that the new nations of Eastern Europe—the so-called successor states of the Austro-Hungarian Empire—must be nourished and protected. Independence and strength in that tier of smaller nations was the balancing factor between the Russians and the Germans. The underlying cause of the war, he pointed out, was the revolt of the Slavs against increasing domination by Germans—from both Berlin and Vienna. The task of statesmanship was to forestall another war between Germans and Slavs—a war that could come either as a result of renewed German pressure eastward or through a resumption of the historic Russian expansion from the steppe. He perceived that the Bolsheviks, newly come to power in Russia, were organizers of a new kind, with a doctrine geared for world conquest. "Solid guarantees" were needed in East Europe.

To Americans, North and South, his admonition was set in full global perspective. North and South America lay in echelon, he noted, not in an Atlantic Ocean or a Pacific Ocean but simply in the one ocean of the world. Geographically, they were satellites of the great Continent. Americans, though they may not all have realized it, "must no longer think of Europe apart from Asia and Africa." [17] The Heartland of that great world Continent, he said in one of his most striking figures of speech, was the vast area which, "seen from the moon," would in winter snows appear as a white shield over Euro-Asia. In its northeastern reaches it was separated from North America only by thirty miles of water—the Bering Strait. For the traveler by air, the shortest way from New York to Peking lay across this narrow strait. With new methods of transportation, the physical facts of geography were taking on new meanings.

The story of how Mackinder's political and geographical insight was noted by the German general Karl Haushofer in 1925, applied in his school of geopolitics, and eventually used by Hitler in his bid for *Lebensraum* and world domination is familiar. Less well known is the fact that as early as 1921 Haushofer analyzed Mackinder's theories in a booklet entitled *The Japanese Empire in Its Geo-*

graphical Development. The object of his strategical reasoning was a German-Russian-Japanese bloc to frustrate the Western sea powers. His map showed the lines of a suggested Japanese advance into South Asia and an arrow pointing to Hawaii. *Fas est ab hoste doceri* (it is a duty to learn from the enemy), Haushofer later wrote.[18]

Mackinder died in 1947 at the age of eighty-six, honored as the greatest of geographers and a teacher of general staffs. In an assessment of his thesis, four years before he died, he reasoned that the development of air power had substantiated rather than destroyed the strategic significance of the Heartland area.[19] It had altered the concepts of mobility and security, but the fact remained that air power was based on land. As air power and its weapons went through the familiar alternations of offensive and defensive development, the resources of its bases could be no less decisive than for rivalries of seamen and landsmen, with their ships and legions.

He lived to witness the splitting and harnessing of the atom but not to analyze the variety of weapons of war that this second industrial revolution spawned. But he had lived to see the Soviet Union emerge from the Second World War as the world's strongest land power, and to see its rule established over Eastern Europe up to the River Elbe in Germany. Whereas Germany had been the Central Power of Europe, Russia was now the Central Power of the globe.

II. THE PROSPECTS FOR COLLECTIVE SECURITY

1. The New Machinery

Woodrow Wilson kept his own counsel in preparing his draft of the Covenant of the League of Nations. His Secretary of State, Robert Lansing, was not permitted to read it, nor had the Department of State been asked to comment on the preliminary outlines of the new institution offered by British and French committees. The strange and gifted Colonel Edward M. House was the American President's only confidant. But House was in close touch with British thought on the subject—Lord Robert Cecil's in particular—and there was harmony between American and British approaches. Wilson used the British draft in preparing his own, and a revised Anglo-American draft was adopted as the basic document in the work of the Committee appointed on January 15, 1919, by the thirty-two Allied and Associated governments gathered at the Paris Conference.

In its brief directive to this Committee, the Conference resolved, first, "that a League of Nations be created to promote international co-operation, to ensure the fulfillment of accepted international obligations and to provide safeguards against war;" second, that this League should be created "as an integral part of the general Treaty of Peace, and should be open to every civilized nation which can be relied upon to promote its objects"; third, that the members "should meet periodically in international conference, and should have a permanent organization and secretariat. . . ." Within this ample frame the Committee, of which Woodrow Wilson was appointed chairman, was told to "work out the details of the constittion and functions of the League."

The American President was at the zenith of his power, and this was the authorization he wanted. Its restrictive provision—the second, which tied the proposed organization to the contemplated peace treaty, was there at his demand. He hoped thus to ensure the acceptance of the League in the United States and by European governments whose enthusiasm for it did not correspond either to the breadth of their grant of authority to him or to the passionate hopes of their constituents, and he also hoped that League procedures would correct weaknesses and injustices in the treaty.

Wilson, Cecil, and their aides wrote quickly, compactly and, all in all, amazingly well. The text of the Covenant, laid before the Conference at the end of April, was a product of several revisions of the original draft, including emendations proposed by representatives of other nations. Revisions had also been made to meet objections from critics in the United States; most of those changes are considered to have been improvements.[1] A useful final polishing was given by a special committee.

The dominant idea of the Covenant—its potentially great contribution to the more orderly conduct of international relations—was expressed in Article 11: "Any war or threat of war, whether immediately affecting any of the Members of the League or not, is hereby declared a matter of concern to the whole League, and the League shall take any action that may be deemed wise and effectual to safeguard the peace of nations." The principle of "concern" was not new. It had been stated, in more restricted form, in the Convention for the Pacific Settlement of International Disputes, a product of the first Peace Conference at the Hague in 1899. The former American Secretary of State, Elihu Root who had proposed its inclusion in the Covenant in discussions with Colonel House, likened it to the old principle of the hue and cry against lawbreakers. As the central article of an organized scheme of international relations, however, it was a major departure in world politics. If the threat of war was the responsibility of all nations, there was no longer a valid general principle of neutrality.

By the same token, the decisive step was a modest one—the minimum first step in a turn to a new course. In accordance with the terms of the directive from the Conference, the League would seek simply to find "safeguards" against war. It would do what seemed "wise and effectual" to prevent one; in other words, it would do the best it could in varying circumstances. The Covenant did not attempt to outlaw war; implicit in Article 11 was the admission that there might be no effectual measures to prevent some wars. "The theory was," as a perceptive British scholar has said, "that it is not possible to say before the event in the case of *every* war what exactly other states ought to do about it." [2]

That the principle of concern applied only to international disputes was emphasized in another paragraph of the same article, which declared that each member of the League had "the friendly right" to bring to the attention of the Assembly or Council any circumstance "affecting *international* relations which threatens to disturb *international* peace or the good understanding *between* nations upon which peace depends." (The italics are added.) The League was not a government raised over its members. Under Article 1 they would have the right to withdraw, and, according to other Articles of the Covenant, decisions in both Assembly and Council, with certain exceptions, required unanimous agreement of all members present at the meeting. This respect for the sovereignty of member states was to be assailed as overscrupulous and ruinous to the authority of the League, though the exercise of the veto in the League's work was to prove less serious in practice than it appeared in theory. The assumption was that the League members formed a community within which cooperation was possible. On no other assumption could a beginning have been made.

The tacit admission made in Article 11—that the League would provide security against some international wars but not necessarily against all—was made evident in three succeeding articles, 12, 13, and 15. Under the provisions of these articles, members of the League pledged themselves to submit their disputes either to arbitration, to investigation by the Council, or to a settlement by a Court of International Justice. The award of the arbitrators or the judicial decision had to be made "within a reasonable time." The report to the Council had to be made within six months. The members pledged themselves, further, to wait three months more, after a decision had been rendered, before going to war. They were bound not to go to war with an adversary who accepted the verdict of Council, Court, or board of arbitration. In the event that the other party to the dispute refused to accept the award, however, or if the Council failed to reach unanimity—except for the parties to the dispute, who would not be permitted to vote on their own case— the League's responsibility was ended. Members could then "take such action as they considered necessary for the maintenance of right and justice."

In other words, this series of provisions described the conditions under which war was "legal." This was the famous "gap" in the Covenant, later to be assailed as evidence of hypocrisy on the part of the creators of the League. The charge was unjust, and also beside the point. As it happened, none of the aggressors of the interwar years sought to avail itself of the opportunity thus provided to fight "legally." Defiance of the League system was undisguised—as, indeed, the availability of such procedures for a reasonable adjustment of disputes made virtually certain that it would be. The inclusion of such methods in the Covenant was, of course, the application of what was considered one of the plainest lessons of the drift to war in 1914. Sir Edward Grey's frustrating experience in endeavoring to summon a conference of the powers after Sarajevo was in everyone's mind.

To this carefully implemented idea of a cooling-off period, for use when warlike emotions flared, the Covenant added a pledge of limitation of armaments. That armaments themselves cause war was thought to be the corollary lesson of the prewar years. Members of the League agreed, under Article 8, to reduce armaments "to the lowest point consistent with national safety"; to do so under plans formulated by the Council; to exchange "full and frank information" about arms programs and "such industries as are adaptable to war-like purposes." There was to be a special effort to prevent manufacture of munitions and implements of war by private enterprise, the supposed source of excess armaments. These clauses spelled what was to prove to be the League's saddest illusion.

But the Covenant was not a pacifist document. It foresaw the possibility of a need to fight in behalf of its principles and, in this respect, took a stride in the new direction of collective action. Article 16 was the enforcement clause of the Covenant. It picked up where Article 11 left off, seeking to give practical substance to the responsibility which every member of the League agreed to share in the case of threatened war. The three intervening articles—12, 13, and 15—mentioned earlier had sought to identify the kind of war that the League would, or would not, consider a violation of its basic obligation for the maintenance of security. (The fourth intervening article, 14, authorized the establishment of the Permanent Court of International Justice.) Article 16, the enforcement, or "sanctions," provision, as it came to be called, was the crucial clause of the Covenant.

The first two paragraphs read:

1. Should any Member of the League resort to war in disregard of its covenants under Articles 12, 13 or 15, it shall *ipso facto* be deemed to have committed an act of war against all other Members of the League, which hereby undertake immediately to subject it to the severance of all trade or financial relations, the prohibition of all intercourse between their nationals and the nationals of the covenant-breaking State, and the prevention of all financial, commercial or personal intercourse between the nationals of the covenant-breaking State and the nationals of any other State, whether a Member of the League or not.
2. It shall be the duty of the Council in such case to recommend to the several Governments concerned what effective mili-

tary, naval or air force the Members of the League shall severally contribute to the armed forces to be used to protect the covenants of the League.

A supplementary section specified that members would help each other meet the economic losses they might suffer from interruption of their own trade when such enforcement action was taken and would afford passage through their territory to the forces of members who were "co-operating to protect the covenants of the League." Another provided for the expulsion of a League member who had violated the Covenant. Such a clause was further evidence that the Covenant was not a constitution for a government, from which secession would be out of the question, but only a start at constructing a new system of international relationships for a community in which membership was a privilege. Under the terms of the Covenant, violation of obligations would, nonetheless, bring penalties, including perhaps the heaviest—punishment by force of arms. And countries outside the League could similarly be disciplined, under Article 17, if they resorted to war against a member.

Article 16 was the League's bid for power and contained a large grant of it. Though provided by the members, the power was to be organized by the League, and to organize power is to exercise it. Economic penalties against a state that went to war in disregard of its covenants would be automatic under the terms of Article 16. The council—which was to be composed of permanent representatives of Great Britain, France, Italy, Japan, and the United States, plus temporary representatives of four elected states—could not compel any of the presumably loyal members of the organization to use their economic strength against the state designated for punishment, but once a state had been branded a violator under the procedures of the Covenant as many members—or as few—as wished to ostracize and cripple the offender by the use of their financial and economic strength were authorized to do so "immediately." The League of Nations would use its machinery to make these sanctions as damaging as possible.The way in which the Allied blockade had sapped Germany's strength during the war was fresh in mind and was a reason for supposing that the possibility of such a grim penalty would act as a deterrent upon any future warmaker.

By comparison with the elaborate provisions for economic and financial measures against an aggressor, however, the second paragraph of Article 16, dealing with military measures of enforcement, was sketchy. The Covenant contented itself with saying that "in such case"—meaning the advent of war—the Council would recommend to the governments what forces they should contribute to "the armed forces to be used." The question of how military power was to be organized was left hanging in air.

There was an ample grant of power to members—again, either to all members or to a few, who would obviously be the powerful few—to use their armies, navies, and air forces as they saw fit. But the signal for the collective action was the outbreak of war, and though a well-organized blockade might in time hamper the conduct of war even by a strong aggressor, an inadequately organized collective defense could be overrun within a few months, or even weeks, by a single state in a well-prepared offensive, as had almost come to pass in northern France in the war just ended.

The unified Allied command under Marshal Ferdinand Foch, which snatched victory from apparent catastrophe in 1918, had been agreed upon only after almost four years of seemingly aimless slaughter. But in the prewar years there had at least been the unavowed conversations and arrangements between French and British military staffs. In dispensing even with such a minimum of advance preparation for the use of military force, would not the League make plain in advance that it had no intention of recommending to its loyal members that they engage in any actual fighting? And if so, how effective would the threat of economic sanctions against a violator of the Covenant be? Would not a nation of strength and spirit, subjected to the humiliation and discomfort of these stringent penalties, strike back against one or several of its persecutors, as it would probably consider them? If enforcement under the Covenant was to be taken seriously the terms of Article 16 could be looked upon only as unfinished business.

The French took the lead at the Paris Conference in pointing out the obvious weakness of the machinery of Article 16. They proposed remedies which proved highly controversial, however, and brought the French and Anglo-American views of the requirements of security into head-on conflict. France was not thinking of "every" war, "any" war, or war in general. She was thinking of the possibility of another attack by seventy million Germans against forty million French. The French draft of a scheme for a League of Nations had made the method of enforcement much more precise. The Council was to have troops at its disposal, recruited specifically for the League or composed of national forces put under League command. A military staff, organized by the League, would train these contingents and take responsibility for military planning in advance of the outbreak of war. But the French plan received no serious consideration from Americans or Englishmen. Neither the British nor the American government offered the Bourgeois plan—so called from the name of the chairman of the French group—to their peoples in translation for study and debate, and the Anglo-American draft of the Covenant, in English, ruled the official working paper for the Paris Committee, was offered to the French on what came close to being take-it-or-leave-it terms.

Undoubtedly Wilson and Cecil were correct in assuming that their constituents would refuse to entertain a scheme that would put American and British troops under the control of a staff likely to be dominated by French military men—Marshal Foch in particular. The highhandedness with which French protests were brushed aside, however, caused resentment, and—what was worse—cynicism among the French. On occasion they were lectured like schoolboys. Lord Robert Cecil is reported to have explained, at a stormy meeting of the Committee,

> that America had nothing to gain from the League of Nations;
> that she could let European affairs go and take care of her own;
> and that to a certain but to a lesser extent that was the position

of Great Britain. . . . Accordingly he wished to say frankly to the French delegate that in his view they were saying to America and to a lesser degree to Great Britain, that because more was not offered they would not take the gift that was at hand, and he warned them very frankly that the alternative offer which we have made was an alliance between Great Britain and the United States.[8]

The threat of a separate British-American alliance had no substance, but the cutting words revealed truly enough the nature of the difference between the Anglo-American and French attitudes toward the problem of peace and war on the Continent—the seemingly unbridgeable difference between the outside view and the inside view. To the British, twenty miles off the coast of Europe, and to the Americans, three thousand miles away, French thought was militaristic and reactionary.

At Paris in 1919, the French also insisted on an explicit procedure for the reduction of national armaments contemplated under Article 8. They proposed that this procedure, like the League's troops, be supervised by the international military staff, which would have full power of inspection in all countries, including their own. Wilson and Cecil rejected this plan with the same reasoning with which they had rejected the first. They did, however, agree in a supplementary article—Article 9—that a "permanent Commission" should be constituted to advise the Council on disarmament and on "military naval and air questions generally." To the French, so vague a directive was worse than useless, foreshadowing a game of "Let's Pretend" on dangerous matters.

The French then offered two plain alternatives to their rejected plan for organized enforcement. One was that France take matters into its own hands and prevent another war by detaching the Rhineland from Germany while France was strong and Germany was weak. This was, indeed, a reactionary idea, and France received no support for it, then or later. The peace treaty, however, provided for temporary occupation and permanent demilitarization of the west bank of the Rhine. Since peace treaty and Covenant were intertwined, sanctions under the League would be available for enforcement of the decree, if necessary; but that assurance raised from a different angle the question of the unfinished Article 16.

The other plain alternative was a defensive alliance, linking France, Great Britain, and the United States. France asked for a definite arrangement, limited in scope and geared to a specific purpose, and at the last moment received it. Woodrow Wilson greatly disliked it, however. He felt that it had been brutally pried from him, as indeed, it had. But he himself provided the lever, in the form of two articles—18 and 20—that sought to bind League members to the precepts of open, frank, just, and honorable international dealings that he had stressed in his wartime messages and in the Preamble to the Covenant—the spirit of the "new diplomacy."

The purpose of Article 18 was to prevent such secret treaties as those concluded among the Allies during the war, which were making the territorial settlements at Versailles extremely difficult; it asked that every treaty or international engagement be registered with the Secretariat and published. But Article 20 drove this excellent principle to lengths that could not be fathomed:

> The Members of the League severally agree that this Covenant is accepted as abrogating all obligations or understandings *inter se* which are inconsistent with the terms thereof, and solemnly undertake that they will not hereafter enter into any engagements inconsistent with the terms thereof.

But a document such as the Covenant, which sought to enforce its principles by organizing national power and at the same time to devise institutions capable of transcending national interests, contained unavoidable inconsistencies. Was a defensive alliance inconsistent with its terms? According to the first of Wilson's Fourteen Points, presented in an address to Congress on January 8, 1918, as a statement of American terms of peace, it certainly was. That celebrated first point had demanded, along with "open covenants of peace, openly arrived at," that there should thereafter be "no private understandings of any kind" in international diplomacy. That this meant *no alliances* was made plain by the American President in an angry interchange with the French Premier, Georges Clemenceau, on the subject of power politics at an early session of the Paris Conference. Despite the tartness of the President's rebuke, Clemenceau had replied that France would continue to seek such understandings.

Surprisingly, yet not illogically, help for Clemenceau came from the United States. Whether regional arrangements among friendly states were also inconsistent with Article 20, in particular the written and unwritten understandings known as the Monroe Doctrine, was asked in Washington. Since they certainly could be interpreted in this way, the American President was advised that specific exemption for the Monroe Doctrine should be written into the Covenant. Wilson knew that he had to ask his Paris colleagues for this concession and reluctantly did so. The other powers agreed to the request. A separate Article of the Covenant, 21, granted the Monroe Doctrine special exemption from the provisions of Article 20. But Clemenceau's price for the special favor was the alliance France wanted. Woodrow Wilson suppressed his wrath, and he and Lloyd George agreed to the pact. It took the form of two separate treaties, one between the United States and France and one between Great Britain and France. Both treaties pledged armed assistance to France in the event of an unprovoked attack by Germany; a clause in the British-French treaty provided, however, that it would not become operative until the French-American treaty had been ratified.

"Government is a very rough business," a mid-Victorian adviser once said to the ardent young reformer W. E. Gladstone during a British political crisis. "You must be content with very unsatisfactory results." Woodrow Wilson's temperament never allowed him such contentment (nor, indeed, did W. E. Gladstone's). That was one source of Wilson's power, and also of his destruction.

2. Organizing Mankind

In his emphasis on "open diplomacy" Wilson had more in mind than the expression of ideals of political behavior. His object was to harness the power of public opinion for enforcement of the central clauses of the Covenant. This was a clue to the sketchiness of Article 16. He was confident that if the people of the world knew what was going on while the machinery of Articles 11 to 15 was being employed to delay an incipient aggressor they would support League principles with such intensity that no violator could hold to his course. There would then be no need for harsh economic and military penalties, let alone the more pointed arrangements that France desired.

Even before the days of radio and television Wilson had demonstrated how effectively this seeming abstraction, "opinion," could be marshaled and used in world politics. With skillful command of language, yet with utmost naturalness, he had addressed himself not to the presidents of other states, not to generals, prime ministers, ambassadors, or, least of all, to the legal counselors of foreign offices, but simply to mankind. "What we seek is the reign of law, based upon the consent of the governed and sustained by the organized opinion of mankind," he said in midsummer of 1918, the most anxious days of the war, when the armies on the western front had swarmed out of their trenches for the climactic battle. The words had helped powerfully to hearten the peoples of the Allied and Associated Powers and to undermine the will to resistance of the Central Powers.

The Fourteen Points evoked a vision of peace and justice for the weak and the vanquished no less than for the strong and the victors. Though some were statements of absolute principles, such as "the impartial adjustment of colonial claims," whereas others were qualified by "as far as possible"—the removal of economic barriers and equality of trade, for example—their appeal was irresistible. Observers of the reception given Woodrow Wilson in December 1918 by the people of London, Paris, and Rome believed that had he gone on to Vienna, Berlin, Prague, and Warsaw, the excitement, which approached worship for him as the embodiment of this vision, would have been the same.

The need for public awareness of the basic issues in future questions of war and peace also explains Wilson's insistence on what turned out to be the most controversial provision of the Covenant, the famous Article 10. This read:

> The Members of the League undertake to respect and preserve against external aggression the territorial and existing political independence of all Members of the League. In case of any such aggression or in case of any threat or danger of such aggression the Council shall advise upon the means by which this obligation shall be fulfilled.

It offered obvious dangers in interpretation since it apparently promised to keep the national boundaries of 1919 forever unchanged, even after a war. The French, eager to make the territorial settlement permanent, especially in both Western and Eastern Europe, thought the general affirmation excellent, provided the Council were given power to make it good against strong opposition. Lord Robert Cecil and his colleagues were unenthusiastic about the range of it but were willing to go along. For Wilson, it was the heart of the Covenant. He cared little about French strategic principles, but he cared greatly about the freedom of small nations. He had proposed this pledge for the protection of the weak against the strong in 1916, in one of his earliest speeches on international relations. The crossing of a national boundary by foreign troops is the plainest of acts of aggression, and there was no lack of logic in the reasoning that led him to place this yardstick in the Covenant before the provisions setting forth the machinery of enforcement. There was, however, a sad failure of perception on his part with regard to the response it would evoke in his own country.

The kind of cooperation required to translate general precepts into the specific provisions of treaties offered for signature and ratification by governments depended upon an understanding, not between the American President and mankind, but between him and other presidents, prime ministers, cabinet members, chiefs of staff, and lawyers in Paris and other capitals of the world, including Washington. These men, too, held positions of responsibility in organized governments, and few of them were unaccomplished in oratory or unaware of the rapidity with which the public mood can change and be changed. The compact between the American President and mankind left their contribution out of the reckoning.

An example of what was to come occurred at Paris when Wilson tested his authority by appealing to the Italian people, over the head of their Prime Minister, Vittorio Emanuele Orlando, in the matter of Italian occupation of Trieste, at the head of the Adriatic, and found the magic gone. The Italian people made plain that their claim—of dubious validity—to the territory was more important to them at the moment than the claims of mankind. By going to Paris in person, the American President had come down from the mountaintop. In losing his temper in such altercations as that with Clemenceau, he had also revealed very human defects of character.

Neither human weaknesses nor inconsistencies between precepts and practice in particular provisions of the Covenant, however, invalidated the practical need for enlisting the support of the people of the world in behalf of the new organization. With its great-power majority, the Council was a league of the victors, an extension of the prewar idea of a concert of the powers. Even so it was an institution, and therefore assumed to be permanent. The democratic Assembly was entrusted with large and vague tasks in which it would be influenced by the governments composing its membership. Through these tasks, however, it might, in its collective capacity, develop an influence over governments. Woodrow Wilson conveyed the idea in a dazzling phrase: the Assembly was a place "where the moral judgment of mankind can sway the opinion of the world." The sound of that made men march, but the meaning was hard to pin down.

Forty-two states were signatories to the Covenant, and the door was left open for Germany and Russia, the two major powers omitted. The important question of membership in the League was put wholly in the hands of the Assembly. "Any fully self-governing State, Dominion or Colony not named in the Annex," Section 2 of Article 1 declared, "may become a Member of the League if its admission is agreed to by two-thirds of the Assembly, provided that it shall give effective guarantees of a sincere intention to observe international obligations, and shall accept such regulations as may be prescribed by the League in regard to its military, naval and air forces and armaments."

The Covenant, unlike the Charter of the United Nations, gave the permanent members of the Council no veto over the admission of new members, and the League Council had no authority to make recommendations on the subject of membership. Although it was foreseeable that major powers would exercise influence on this question behind the scenes, the idea of the concert was thus open to significant enlargement. Interpretation of such ambiguous terms as "fully self-governing" would be made by the Assembly.

In Wilson's view, "self-governing" meant that members would have democratic institutions. His message to Congress of April 2, 1917, asking for the declaration of war, had stated, as the American object, the following.

> To vindicate the principles of peace and justice in the life of the world as against selfish and autocratic power and to set up amongst the really free and self-governed peoples of the world such a concert of purpose and action as will henceforth insure the observance of those principles.
>
> . . . the menace to that peace and freedom lies in the existence of autocratic governments backed by organized force which is controlled wholly by their will, not by the will of the people.

As F. P. Walters notes, however, the term "self-governing" could also be understood in the sense of the French phrase *qui se gouverne librement*—a state "free to make its own decisions, i.e., not forced to act under the instructions of another state." [4] And it was, in fact, so interpreted by the Assembly: though a member state of the League might be ruled by a despot, it was expected to be an independent despotism. Yet the League was by no means intended to be a "universal" organization in the sense that any government in control of national territory was automatically eligible; qualifications for membership were exacting. Whether there was any possibility that a powerful despotism would accept them "sincerely" was yet to be revealed.

The Assembly was also authorized (in Article 3) to "deal at its meetings with any matter within the sphere of action of the League or affecting the peace of the world." "Deal with" was a wonderfully ambiguous phrase. It meant merely "discuss"; but it also meant that the Assembly might, if it could, bring to bear on the great powers that were permanent members of the Council—and on other members of the League—the new force of world opinion. What that would turn out to be and where it would come down no one knew.

In Article 19 the Assembly was given a broad commission to rectify injustices in the Treaty of Versailles, or what would certainly be considered injustices by those whom the settlement had deprived of territory and power: "The Assembly may from time to time advise the reconsideration by Members of the League of treaties which have become inapplicable and the consideration of international conditions whose continuance might endanger the peace of the world." The provision had been included at the suggestion of Lord Robert Cecil, who had sought to define its terms in plainer language. His objective was to supply an escape clause for the rigid guarantee of Article 10. But the diverse nations and interests represented at the Conference could not agree on language that plainly unsettled the practical political and economic problems of the Peace Treaty, while they were still endeavoring to settle them. The compromise wording of Article 19 was thus another abstraction; the yardstick for an "inapplicable" treaty was "the peace of the world"—a phrase borrowed from the general definition of the responsibility of the Assembly, as stated in Article 3.

The Covenant also included a series of articles, some intended to make the League the center of various international activities, some of them presumably uncontroversial. National Red Cross groups, for example, were encouraged, though, as it happened, the Soviet government looked with suspicion and hostility upon the idea that voluntary organizations could cross international boundaries, even on errands of mercy. Article 24 suggested that international bureaus already in existence be placed under League direction. The Committee had the Universal Postal Union particularly in mind, but American refusal to join the League was to frustrate its intention.

A second section of Article 24 instructed the Secretariat of the League to collect and distribute relevant information "in all matters of international interest" that were regulated by general conventions. Nevertheless, even so small a grant of authority to the Secretariat was circumscribed; the Secretariat would exercise this power only "subject to the consent of the Council and if desired by the parties." Lord Robert Cecil, looking ahead in this particular area, envisioned the Secretariat as the efficient international civil service it became and foresaw that a Secretary-General of ability and tact would have a great deal to say about the policy of the League. But, knowing the limitations of bureaucracies, he felt that "it was of the utmost importance" that responsibility for policy not be allowed to drift altogether into the Secretary-General's hands, since the result would be "an exaggerated tendency to seek the line of least resistance." [5]

In contrast to the modest objectives and cautious tone of Article 24, an ambitious program of social, economic, and political activity was set forth in Article 23. Members of the League would

(a) endeavor to secure and maintain fair and humane conditions of labour for men, women and children, both in their own countries and in all countries to which their commercial and industrial relations extend . . .

(b) undertake to secure just treatment of the native inhabitants of territories under their control;

(c) entrust the League with general supervision over the execution of agreements with regard to the traffic in women and children, and the traffic in opium and other dangerous drugs;

(d) entrust the League with the general supervision of the trade in arms and ammunition with the countries in which control of this traffic is necessary in the common interest;

(e) make provision to secure and maintain freedom of communication and of transit and equitable treatment for the commerce of all Members of the League . . .

(f) endeavour to take steps in matters of international concern for the prevention and control of disease.

Opinions differed as to whether this dispersal of effort would strengthen or weaken the League. One important point of view, written between the lines of this article, was that of the complex statesman and mystic General Jan Christiaan Smuts, former guerrilla leader of the Boer War and in 1919 Prime Minister of the Union of South Africa, who had made his peace with the British and was influential in imperial councils. In a famous pamphlet, *Practical Suggestions,* he had said of the League of Nations, "It must function so strongly in the ordinary peaceful intercourse of States that it becomes irresistible in their disputes; its peace activity must be the foundation and guarantee of its war power." His eloquence matched Wilson's. He believed that there could be a transformation of international conditions and institutions: "The very foundations have been shaken and loosened. The tents have been struck, and the great caravan of humanity is once more on the march."

That the League had to develop as an international center if it was to have vitality could be doubted by no one. That the clash of nationalisms had to be regulated, and if possible harmonized in its earliest manifestations, was sensible and logical. But did the emphasis placed on "peace activities" by Smuts and those who shared his vision mean that the enforcement function of the organization was secondary to these activities? In theory there did not have to be any conflict between the two views of the League's mission, but in practice loyal members of the League were to split disastrously in interpreting it. In the era of so-called pacific settlement of disputes Smuts' thesis was to be used as the rationalization for the avoidance of the hard and disagreeable task of preparing for possible war against a powerful aggressor. At Paris in 1919, however, those who expected much and those who expected little from Article 23 joined hands, and it was accepted with less controversy than almost any other clause of the Covenant.

The other important article which sought to center international activities in the League was 22, governing the disposition of former Turkish provinces and conquered German colonies. General Smuts was also foremost among those who devised these arrangements. They provided for a system of mandates, classified as A, B, and C according to the supposed readiness of the inhabitants of the territories for self-government. This was a remarkable blend of some of the worst aspects of the old politics and the best of the new. France and Britain had provided for the division of the Turkish spoils by secret agreement during the war, and Britain was declared the mandatory power for Iraq, Transjordan, and Palestine, while France was made mandatory for Syria. These were A mandates. Other Turkish provinces received their independence. In Central Africa, German colonies were divided among Britain, Belgium, France, and Portugal as B mandates. South-West Africa went to the Union of South Africa as a C mandate, and German islands in the Pacific were assigned to Japan, Australia, and New Zealand in the C category. Article 22 provided that the mandates were to be exercised "on behalf of the League." The mandatories were named in the treaties of peace, however, not in the Covenant, and the territories were ceded by Turkey and Germany to the Allied and Associated Powers, not to the League. As E. H. Carr has said, "Where the sovereignty over the mandated territories resided was an insoluble legal conundrum." [6]

All this was a great deal less than the "free, open-minded and absolutely impartial adjustment of colonial claims," with the interests of the populations concerned given equal weight with the claims of the governments, demanded in the fifth of Wilson's Fourteen Points. Even so, it was not only an ingenious solution of a baffling problem but a forward-looking arrangement. The conquered territories were not formally annexed by the victors, but held in "trust." The effort to distinguish between the territories that were capable of "standing by themselves" and those that were not, according to the stages of development of their inhabitants, their economic resources, their geographical situation, and the size of their population, represented an intelligent approach to this complicated question. Mandatory powers were made responsible in various ways for conditions within the territories they administered and were required to submit annual reports to a Mandates Commission of the League "in reference to the territory" committed to their charge. Japan refused to submit such reports about its mandated islands in the Pacific, which were being secretly fortified, and the commission could not hope to control such intractable political problems as the conflict between Arab and Jew in Palestine or the general Arab dissatisfaction with the appropriation of former Turkish provinces by the victors in the war. Yet, working selflessly and expertly, the Mandates Commission gained the confidence of administrators in the "backward" African territories, and its criticism and recommendations were received with respect and, indeed, appreciation. The key word in matters of progress toward self-government at the time was, of course, "gradual."

3. The American Lawyers

The newness of the problems embedded in the Covenant and the degree to which they remained unsolved are dramatized by the gulf that opened between the American President and his Secretary of State, Robert Lansing, during this period of drafting and revising the document and debating the question of ratification. Where League questions were concerned, the two men ceased to be on speaking terms. Sometimes they communicated through Colonel House, and on occasion the Secretary of State addressed letters to his chief elucidating his views. The letters were unanswered and perhaps unread.

In Lansing's view, Woodrow Wilson was "wholly wrong" [7] in his understanding of the functions of a League of Nations, not to speak of the fundamental principles of the Constitution of the United States. Understandably, the President suggested to his subordinate that he devote himself to matters other than those of the League, accompanying the request, unfortunately, with a personal and petty comment on "lawyers."

Robert Lansing, born in 1864 in Watertown, in upstate New York, was an experienced and able lawyer and a founding editor of *The American Journal of International Law*. His marriage to the daughter of John W. Foster, Secretary of State under Benjamin

Harrison (and grandfather of a boy who was to become a still more eminent Secretary of State, John Foster Dulles), had drawn him into cosmopolitan life and an international legal practice. He had entered the Wilson Administration in 1914 as Counselor of the Department of State and was appointed by the President to succeed William Jennings Bryan as Secretary in June 1915, after Bryan had resigned in protest against the firm line Wilson wished to take in regard to the sinking of the *Lusitania* by a German submarine.

Lansing and Wilson worked harmoniously during the period of American neutrality. Though Lansing favored the Allies, he was aware that the German use of the submarine to further the recognized right of belligerents to interrupt and destroy enemy commerce was "by no means a one-sided question." [8] The submarine was a new weapon and had changed conditions of naval warfare. From the point of view of the Wilson Administration, the problem was to bring the belligerents to agree upon concessions that would protect the lives of noncombatants on merchant ships. Lansing proposed that the Allies agree not to arm commercial vessels and that the German submarine commanders give passengers and crews an opportunity for safety. The agreement did not hold for long, but Lansing's search for a solution was the serious effort Wilson wanted. Similarly, Lansing sought to uphold the American claim to neutral rights against some of the sweeping injunctions of the British blockade.

"Freedom of the seas," emphasized by the President as a pillar of American policy, was already a lost cause, as was his hope of being accepted as mediator in a negotiated peace between the Allies and the Central Powers. But the Secretary's willingness to subdue his own emotions in behalf of Wilson's objectives earned him the confidence of his chief. His comments on the drafts of diplomatic correspondence that the President liked to tap out on his own typewriter were helpful and tactful—he was by disposition polite and sociable, not at all the gray-cardboard character that legend has made of him—and he saved Wilson from mistakes. His estimates of the hesitant American and Latin American moods at the time were also sagacious and modestly offered.

In 1917 Woodrow Wilson's mood changed and, with it, the country's. With America at war, the need to crowd on sail made an anchor, as represented by Lansing, seem an annoying impediment to the President. Wilson was eager to get beyond the war to the "great consummation"—the new international order—without which the American acts of war could not, he felt, be justified. By instinct and training, Lansing distrusted great consummations, especially when put in terms of duty to mankind—the very ideal Woodrow Wilson, a Presbyterian clergyman's son, by instinct and training eloquently invoked. "Nations do not respond to the impulse of self-sacrifice," the Secretary noted.

Robert Lansing's assumptions about the League were those that came to be termed isolationism. They are especially interesting because Lansing was a Democrat, and whatever the differences in temperament that made his break with Wilson irreparable, partisan animosity had no bearing on it. Lansing's point of view, that of most educated men of the prewar years, represented a high ideal—the assumption that progress under law was the normal condition of things, that a stable international order existed, in which rights and responsibilities were generally acknowledged. It was assumed, further, that these were embodied in an established doctrine applying to the relations between citizens of states and also, though less plainly, to the relations between sovereign states as well. It was normal for treaties not to be flagrantly violated, normal for international law to be reformed where necessary through revision of treaties and for its province to be extended. It was considered normal, moreover, for both parties to a dispute to desire a settlement; that being so, the dignified and objective forms of judicial inquiry would make adverse decisions more palatable to the losing side than would political settlements based only on political power. "There are different ways of being right," the French legal philosopher Louis Renault said, in words carrying the flavor and the wisdom of the old order, "and the form should not aggravate the displeasure caused by the substance." [9] By the careful process of judicial interpretation, particular decisions could be generalized and used to provide fairly predictable results in the conduct of international affairs.

Such assumptions were strengthened for Americans by the grand example of the acquisition of authority by the Supreme Court of the United States. The United States had also been a leader in the development of the special Hague tribunals for arbitration of international disputes, and the results seemed evident and heartening. In the closing years of the nineteenth century and the early years of the twentieth, some ninety controversial cases had been settled through such semijudicial procedures. Robert Lansing had appeared before such bodies more often, perhaps, than any other American lawyer.

This was the foundation on which he proposed to build. His recommendation was simply that the method used for relatively minor international disputes be applied to all conflicts between states. All states would be asked to agree to put their disputes in the hands of a court, which would be "an independent international judiciary, whose decisions would be final." [10] In his view, a court was the primary, perhaps the only essential, agency of the proposed League. Since the ideal court was free of political influences, the problem, he said in a speech at Boston in 1919, was to remove disputes from the processes of diplomacy and prevent the influences which enter into diplomacy from affecting their consideration.

This was not as naïve as it appears in an age when totalitarian states have made all law seem merely a cynical struggle for political power. Lansing knew that his ideal was honored in the breach as well as the observance, and not by wicked European nations only. The United States had refused to accept the decision of an arbitral tribunal in 1911, for example, in the dispute with Mexico over the boundary of the Rio Grande River in the area of El Paso, Texas. Moreover, there had been no American effort to seek arbitration of the conflict that resulted in the Spanish-American War, though the question of the alleged blowing up of the battleship *Maine* by a Spanish mine in Havana Harbor, turning as it did on an issue of fact, might have been supposed to be well suited for judicial inquiry. Other aspects of the Cuban problem were obviously political, in the broadest sense of the term, and not justiciable. But it was true, too, that responsible Americans—particularly those concerned with the development of international law—had deplored the part that American yellow journalism played in the Spanish-American conflict. The episode strengthened, rather than weakened, the ideal at which Lansing aimed.

His conscientious internationalism became in practice a retreat to a world of abstractions, however, when, in offering proposals for international organization, he sought to ignore the question of power and rejected on principle answers to it that others gave. "The basic principle of [Wilson's] plan," he noted with dismay, "was that the strong should, as a matter of right recognized by treaty, possess a dominant voice in international councils." [11] It was true that they would be dominant, but the restrictions on the exercise of national power contained in the procedures of the Covenant were, nevertheless, actual. To Lansing, the dominance of the great powers within the Council of the League was an abandonment of the principle of the sovereign equality of states, and, at the same time, the machinery of enforcement was a violation of the sovereignty of the United States. This was a conception of national sovereignty so perfect, and so abstract, that it was paralyzing.

The idea of a supplementary alliance with France at first seemed to him not only unconstitutional but likely to endanger the safety of the new small states of Eastern Europe by tempting France to use her military power for conquest. He corrected his position, however, when he learned that the successor states of Eastern Europe not only did not fear a strengthening of French power but desired it, since France would be their natural protector against the power of a revived Germany.

In response to the question of what would be done under his

EUROPE AND
THE MIDDLE EAST,
1914

plan for "strict judicial settlement" when a sovereign state refused to accept the jurisdiction of a court or refused to abide by its verdict, he also went so far as to suggest that the offending nation should be outlawed and isolated economically. This suggestion took him halfway toward the actual proposals of Article 16 of the Covenant, but he recoiled from the thought of enforcement of any kind. His conclusion was that nothing was possible or desirable beyond a promise by states not to attack one another; they could not promise to defend one another. This principle, in effect, was that of the nonaggression pact, later to become the favorite device of the powerful dictatorships for anesthetizing the states they intended to destroy. It was also the principle of the Kellogg-Briand Pact, made under a frankly isolationist American administration a decade later, which outlawed war on paper.

Woodrow Wilson shared Lansing's ideal of a community of states under law, but he was realistic in appraising the significance of his own failure to keep the nations of the Western Hemisphere out of the war. He knew that the waters of the ocean were a conductor of electric currents from the European storm, not insulation from them. He had received the shock. "We have seen the last neutrality in such circumstances," he said briefly, in the message of April 2, 1917, asking Congress for the declaration of war.

His objective in the Covenant was not an ideal system of law that would exclude all political influences but a system of international politics that would enforce such law as there was. His early plan for the League contained no provision for a formal court, nor did he show interest in the development of the Hague procedures for arbitration. As was his way, he was concentrating on the main point. The old order had broken down. The cause of the breakdown was not the incompleteness of the machinery for arbitration or adjudication of national quarrels but the lack of any curb on "arbitrary might." The needed remedy was political, not legal.

He was right; but, as was also his way, he was overconfident of the completeness of his own solution. The remedy he envisaged was to put law and politics in the hands of one body—the Council of the League. As Sir Alfred Zimmern has pointed out, "he considered that the Council of the League, through the jurisdiction which was given it to deal with disputes, was in fact, in this aspect of its activity, a Court of Arbitral Justice." [12] There was consistency in Wilson's view. What could be more solemn or more binding than the oath of a *covenant*—the Presbyterian word that he insisted upon having repeated again and again in the articles of the new organization? What could be more dignified or more suitable as witness of the moral judgment of mankind than such an assemblage of great powers and chosen small nations as he envisaged, met in the spirit of the Covenant to safeguard the peace of mankind?

But here too the word did not have the ring for all that it had for the President. Wilson had found himself opposed by most of his supporters as well as by his critics in his desire to dispense altogether with a formal court and to rely wholly on the Council. He yielded and accepted the provision establishing a Permanent Court of International Justice, building upon the foundation of the old Hague system. The knotty problem of a method of choosing judges was solved by Elihu Root in a plan by which candidates were nominated by nongovernmental national groups and elected by majority votes of both Council and Assembly.

There was no possibility that the hard-shelled American isolationists—the group of a dozen or so Senators of whom the Republican William E. Borah of Idaho and the Democrat James A. Reed of Missouri were leaders—could be won over to American participation in an international political organization of any kind. In the battle for ratification of the Covenant, these were the so-called irreconcilables; the shock of another world war was necessary to shatter the assumptions they held about North America's immutably privileged position within space and mankind. The possibility of United States membership in the League depended upon Woodrow Wilson's willingness to work with men who were very different from himself, yet who did want a League of Nations equipped with machinery for enforcement.

They were the men who had launched the society called the

League to Enforce Peace in 1915. Most of them were Republicans. President William Howard Taft, Elihu Root, Chief Justice Charles Evans Hughes, and A. Lawrence Lowell, President of Harvard, were among the leaders of the group. Senator Henry Cabot Lodge was a member, though he diverged on a narrow partisan line. Elihu Root was the key man. He had been brilliantly useful to Theodore Roosevelt as Secretary of War and then as Secretary of State. His ambitions were more than satisfied, but he wanted to be used at the Paris Conference. It had been generally supposed that he would be appointed to the American delegation as the best-qualified Republican. When Wilson, compounding his error in asking the country for a Democratic Congress in 1918 to support his leadership in foreign policy, revealed his unwillingness to have any Republican of stature on the delegation, leading Democrats, as well as virtually all Republicans, hoped that he would at least use Root in a special advisory capacity. Both Colonel House and Robert Lansing recommended this to Wilson. So did Wilson's son-in-law, William Gibbs McAdoo, the Secretary of the Treasury. Labor leaders were opposed to Root, however, and Wilson used Root's reputation as a conservative in domestic affairs as the excuse for rejecting him. His appointment as special counsel would weaken the Delegation, he said.

As Philip C. Jessup writes in his biography of Root, there is every reason to believe that he would have served Woodrow Wilson with complete loyalty, especially since the obligation of lawyer to client was the cornerstone of his code. Root was not only an able lawyer but a great one, capable into his old age of adapting himself to new tasks and widening old views. He had been a Senator from New York, but by appointment; he was not a man for elective office and knew that he needed a client if he was to use the full range of his ability in public affairs. A letter he wrote to Charles Francis Adams in 1915 gives the flavor of his mind and character. Adams had written him to note what seemed to him an irresistible trend toward Tennyson's "Parliament of Man, and Federation of the World." Root replied:

I agree with you about the tendency. It is incredible that after this war the world should go on to do precisely the same things in precisely the same way. . . . To put a better scheme of things into operation, however, will involve solving difficult practical problems. My moral nature is being ruined by habitual anger at a lot of fools who think that difficulties can be solved by refusing to see them. We must have a court, that is certain; but if it is to be really a court and not some new form of arbitrary government by plot and counterplot, the court must have a law which it is bound to apply. In order that there shall be an adequate law, there must be agreement upon the rules of conduct. In order that the judgments of the court applying this law shall be respected, there must be sanctions for its enforcement, and here we come to the international police force. When an American thinks of that he must consider how far the United States is willing to abandon its policy against entangling alliances and interference in the affairs of Europe. Close, discriminating and instructed thought ought to deal with that subject, always remembering that the most generous sentiments are the most dangerous when the people of the country are going to stand up to them. It is going to be a business for experts who combine technical knowledge with imagination, and the abundant vocabulary of the well-meaning pacifist will not be very useful.[13]

The cutting edge of this statement was directed, we may guess, at such manifestations of the antiwar spirit of the time as the Ford "peace ship." Root was not so much angry at such foolishness as amused. Appreciation of the comedy in things was not among Woodrow Wilson's great talents, however. Root could never have had the close relationship with Wilson that he had with Theodore Roosevelt, who admired him enormously and yielded with delight to Root's pungent banter even when it was directed at him, as it sometimes, affectionately, was. But Root's practical imagination would have been at Wilson's service and of inestimable value to him.

The might-have-been in regard to American membership in the League of Nations turns on the possibility that Root could have opened Wilson's mind to three ideas. The first was that the case for the unqualified guarantee of political independence and territorial integrity of League members as offered in Article 10 was weak. The article challenged credibility. To have modified it, or to have omitted it altogether, would not have harmed the prospects of the League. A willingness to use the procedures of Articles 11 to 16 was the practical test of faithfulness to the principle of collective security. Article 10, though cited by the Assembly in the conflict with Japan over Manchuria, was never invoked, and at the next try at world organization no such "Article 10" was written into the Charter of the United Nations.

Root's second idea was that the solution to the special problem of French security, on which reconciliation with Germany depended, lay in the defensive alliances linking France with Britain and the United States. Root perceived this and undertook to get the Franco-American treaty through the Senate. He says he had won a promise from Lodge and other Republican leaders to support it if Wilson would submit it separately to the Senate and delete a reference to the League Council. Such a separate consideration of this particular arrangement was a legitimate request—necessary, indeed, for a full understanding of so unprecedented an America obligation. He also obtained Lansing's promise to urge this upon Wilson, but "nothing further was heard of it." [14] Since Wilson never submitted the treaty, Lodge's support for it must also remain conjectural.

Root's third idea was that reservations to the Covenant providing for Congressional consent to American action under its procedures were not merely inescapable, in the swing back from the wartime aggrandizement of Presidential power, but desirable. The mysteries of the constitutional relations of President, Senate and House of Representatives in American foreign relations, though often expounded, remain mysterious. But "the fact remains," as Edwin S. Corwin, one of the foremost authorities, has said, "that no presidentially devised policy can long survive without the support of Congress." [15] In 1945 the constitutional problem was to be solved, or at any rate satisfactorily sidestepped, by the United Nations Participation Act, passed by majority vote of both houses of Congress.

The Lodge reservations to the Covenant in 1919 anticipated this executive-legislative collaboration. Some of the reservations were extreme in their statements of Congressional power, and the one supposedly protecting the United States against the multiple votes of the self-governing parts of the British Empire, on the assumption that they would all vote the same way, was beside the point. But the British Commonwealth was then only in bud, and who could understand its mysteries? An American legislative imprint on the Covenant was the way in which the new international organization could be made to belong to America.

Elihu Root's view was that the original form of such an institution was not too important, provided there was capacity for growth. The scholar in the White House who had written the book *Congressional Government* agreed in principle. Indeed, he and Cecil had prided themselves on having taken just such an approach. But Wilson was outraged by the opposition he met when he returned to Washington. He expressed a willingness to accept some of the reservations, but he would never assent to Congressional restrictions on Article 10. And he would accept no reservation that would require formal amendment of the Covenant.

No one knows whether other signatories would have accepted such changes, but the likelihood is that they would. Edward Grey, hoping to ease the President's path, ventured to send a message to Wilson saying that he believed they would; the only result of Grey's intervention was that the name of this modest man went on the list of those to whom Wilson would never again speak and whom he would not forgive.

Caught in questions that only the experience of international life could simplify and assailed by demagoguery from opposite sides, public opinion in America was helpless. Audiences cheered Woodrow Wilson when he promised that if they would "make good their redemption of the world," the Covenant would lead them "into pastures of quietness and peace such as the world had never dreamed before." They cheered Senator Lodge, too, when he begged fathers and mothers, sisters, wives, and sweethearts, "to think, think well," lest "the hope of their families, the hope of this nation, the best of our youth," be sent on the errand of war through the League.

One of the coolest of American observers, Harvard's President A. Lawrence Lowell, deduced from all this that a large majority desired a League, but that the majority also desired "some reservations, and neither knows or cares very much what those reservations are." [16] Lowell himself wanted the League, with reservations or without, with Article 10 or without, perceiving that little depended on that furiously controversial clause. He also thought that, since the primary responsibility for leadership rested with the President, so too did the primary responsibility for conciliation. "The fact is," he said, in a letter to Colonel House, "that the President and the Republican majority in the Senate are not very far apart; they are such a little distance apart that the ordinary man can hardly see the difference."

This was the voice of reason. Like Woodrow Wilson, A. Lawrence Lowell had for a short time been a practicing lawyer with small practice. He once ran successfully for public office, as a candidate for the Boston Public School Committee, but after one term was denied renomination by both Democrats and Republicans and defeated as an Independent. As he later wryly remarked, his voice did not always add strength to a cause. But Lowell's heart no less than his mind was given to the cause of the League. He wrote letters to everyone he knew, Republican or Democrat, urging all to forgo partisanship, and he went so far as to make speeches from the rear platforms of trains, analyzing the structure and possibilities of the League for the populace whose comprehension he had estimated so coolly. He even mounted the stage of a Boston hall and entered into public controversy with Henry Cabot Lodge in an effort to convince the Senator that Article 16, not Article 10, was the significant clause of the Covenant.

But the orators prevailed. Lodge knew that Wilson could not obtain a two-thirds majority for ratification unless the word *Congress* was written into certain clauses of the Covenant and the Versailles Treaty in reservations—we may note again—by no means unjustifiable and in some cases clearly advantageous. But he made the act of concession as humiliating as possible for Wilson by making the issues as personal as possible, choosing sarcastic words in reports on the floor of the upper house. The President rose to the bait, and, in thrall to his own character, sought satisfaction in martyrdom. In the western speaking tour in the autumn of 1919 he destroyed himself physically. After the stroke and the paralysis, he destroyed his own handiwork.

The last act of the drama, as performed in March 1920, is so incredible that it tends to be slurred over in summaries of the League battle. It is generally said that the United States rejected the League by act of the Senate. But that is not quite the real story. The final vote in the Senate *favored* ratification, with the reservations, by a majority of forty-nine to thirty-five. Seven more votes would have brought the needed two-thirds majority. They were withheld at the insistence of the President.

Among the thirty-five Senators who voted against ratification were twenty-three Wilsonian Democrats. Had Wilson urged these loyal supporters to vote for ratification, it is virtually certain that the United States would have accepted membership in the League. Had he merely set them free to follow their own judgments, as some begged to be allowed to do, it is extremely likely that a sufficient number of them would have voted with the Senate majority to bring ratification. The escapist mood of the American people and of the Congress of the United States, all too evident in later years, was forming; it had not yet crystallized. The fateful vote of March 19, 1920, crystallized it. Had it not been for Woodrow Wilson, there probably would have been no Covenant of the League of Nations; but, Wilson being Wilson, the United States could not belong. The deeper meaning of the shattering experience remains obscure, except as it may be illuminated by the truism that the material of politics is people—much more diverse and refractory than the concept "mankind."

III. WITH BENEFIT OF HINDSIGHT

1. The European Society

The life of the League of Nations began officially on January 10, 1920, when the Treaty of Versailles came into effect. The first meeting of the Council was held six days later. The Council gathered for the last time on December 14, 1939. That was the wartime meeting at which the Soviet Union was excitedly expelled for its attack on Finland. It marked the end of the League's actual existence—a period of almost an even twenty years—though the organization was not formally disbanded until April 18, 1946, by vote of thirty-four members.

During the two decades in which the League was in operation every "fully self-governing" state in the world except the United States was a member at one time or another—a total of sixty-three. The customary approximation of the size of the membership during most of the period is only some fifty, however, since there were seventeen resignations, and three member states were conquered and annexed—Ethiopia and Austria in 1936 and Albania in 1939. The number of members was largest in 1932, when fifty-seven states were represented at Geneva. Up to that time only two members had resigned—Costa Rica for financial reasons in 1925, and Brazil from wounded pride in 1926. The wave of withdrawals began in 1933, when Japan and Germany gave notice of resignation in May and October respectively.

The Japanese defiance of the League's authority was a psychological blow and must have influenced the timing of Hitler's withdrawal. It cannot be supposed to have caused it. German elections had brought one hundred and seven of Hitler's Nazis into the Reichstag in 1930 for the avowed purpose of smashing the Peace of Versailles, and Hitler established his dictatorship three years later. Japan took advantage of the German insurrection against the League and Europe but did not bring it about.

It is evident that the strength of League members was never sufficient to coerce a great power in the Far East. Japan's Manchurian adventure brought the United States to the Council chamber at Geneva, and though the American representative attended only as an observer, the League took its cue from the United States in its policy of nonrecognition of Japan's conquest, on the principle of the Kellogg Pact for the renunciation of war. Whether the strength of the United States would have been used with the intelligence and determination needed to give the Japanese story a happier ending had the United States been a member of the League is unknowable.

Nor can hindsight tell us whether American participation in the work of the League would have brought to American policy the wisdom needed to maintain peace in Central and Eastern Europe, where the Second World War began. Here the strength of League members—or of only two of them, Britain and France—was ample to enforce collective security at least through the year 1937, had there been the will to use it. If it was the American rejection of the League and of responsibility for the Eastern European boundaries, which Americans had done so much to determine at Paris, that undermined the collective will, then the fatal turning point in this first effort came in Washington in 1920.

Speculation on this theme is tempting; yet it is a game played with abstractions: some things being different, how different would other things be? With the United States outside, the League was essentially a European system. It is as such that it can profitably be studied.

"Europe" lives and changes—a political idea no less than a geographical location. In 1932, the year of the League's largest membership, the League system embraced the Continent of Europe in its most familiar aspect. This was not *the* continent as a geographer such as Mackinder saw it—the land mass of Europe-Asia-Africa, encircled by the one ocean of the world—but the Continent that begins at Calais, as French or Germans or Italians on one side of the English Channel, and Englishmen on the other side, know it and speak of it. Britain may "go into" Europe, or "stay out" of Europe, or be "in but not of" Europe according to the nature of the policies of the day. On the far margin of the area, Russia's relationship with Europe is similarly fluctuating. This Continent ends where Eastern Europe merges with Asia, and where Asia begins depends upon what Russia is politically at the time. In 1932, Britain was half in and half out. Bolshevik Russia was outside but was soon to enter briefly. France and Germany were deeply engaged at the center.

In the moment before it dissolved, the European society as represented by the League of Nations was a community of twenty-eight free countries. This is the list:

Albania	Lithuania
Austria	Luxembourg
Belgium	Netherlands
Bulgaria	Norway
Czechoslovakia	Poland
Denmark	Portugal
Estonia	Rumania
Finland	Spain
France	Sweden
Germany	Switzerland
Greece	Turkey
Hungary	United Kingdom of Great Britain'
Irish Free State (Eire)	and Northern Ireland
Italy	Yugoslavia
Latvia	

Of the other twenty-nine members of the League at this high-water mark, seventeen were from Latin America. In addition to the two Latin American states that had already resigned, eight more were to leave. Three others absented themselves from meetings of the Assembly for long periods, though without formally resigning. The twenty republics were ill at ease within the European system, though individuals from Central and South America made valued contributions, especially to the work of the Court.

The four British Dominions—Canada, Australia, New Zealand, and the Union of South Africa—and the Government of India, were original members. The degree of their sovereignty was indefinable: imperial Britain signed for them, and they also signed for themselves. Persia (Iran) in the Near East was also an original member. The Irish Free State (Eire) gained independence in 1922 and joined the League the following year. Iraq, a British mandate, achieved nationhood and was accepted in the League in 1932. Besides the Soviet Union, three more countries joined after 1932: Afghanistan, Ecuador, and Egypt.

There were never more than five Asian members of the League —Afghanistan, India, Japan, China, and Siam (Thailand); and there were only three states from non-Mediterranean Africa— Ethiopia, Liberia, and the Union of South Africa. The problems of the group of European countries supplied the Council, the Assembly, and the Court with their major business, except for the Manchurian affair.

What hindsight suggests is that the League of Nations was not exceptionally ill-favored by circumstances of birth and formative years, as is generally assumed, but on the contrary was relatively fortunate. Though there was serious trouble for Britain in India and Egypt, the League was spared the disruptive colonial problem as its successor, the United Nations, was to know it, and it had a breathing space of ten years before it was challenged by a powerful dictatorship. The United Nations was riven from the start by its implacable enemy, the Soviet Union, an ominous shadow in the east during the League's years, but weak and preoccupied with its domestic massacres during most of the period.

Nor was the Great Depression of the 1930s responsible for the destruction of the League. An unmistakable turning point in the League's fortunes came midway during the first decade, a time of increasing economic recovery in Europe. The failure was political. The cluster of treaties arranged at Locarno, Italy, in 1925 by a group of seven European states—Great Britain, France, Germany, Italy, Belgium, Poland, and Czechoslovakia—reaffirmed the League's guarantee of frontiers in Western Europe but opened the frontiers of Eastern Europe to German adventure. The arrangements brought Germany into the League, but under their terms the League was doomed. They were, however, hailed at Geneva as a triumph of peaceful settlement. The attempt to understand the *why* of these things is the effort to read the major lesson of the League experiment. The years of opportunity are the interesting years.

2. The Nonpolitical Agencies

The League rallied from the American retreat to isolationism and tackled its assignment with intelligence and courage. By organizing themselves in interacting political, nonpolitical, and legal bodies the original members created a new system for the conduct of international affairs. It was sometimes something greater than the sum of its individual members, at times less, but always something different from a mere aggregation of states. The League had a personality; it was loved, hated, condemned, and beseeched. The government of the United States even went to the trouble of treating it with elaborate discourtesy for a year or two.

The system was a businesslike one, in the old-fashioned sense of that term. How old-fashioned it was can be seen from a glance at the League's finances. The annual budget, covering all expenditures for administration and operation including the costs of the Permanent Court of International Justice, the International Labor Office, the Secretariat, the subsidiary political and nonpolitical organizations, and, indeed, the expense of building the Palace of Nations at Geneva and buying office furniture, averaged about $5,400,000. The League was never looked upon as a center for the distribution of funds.[1]

Great Britain and the Dominions bore the largest share of the

League budget, twenty-six per cent. The original scheme of apportionment was based on the national shares of the costs of the Universal Postal Union, but this proved unrealistic and percentages were revised more in accordance with ability to pay. Most shares were paid punctually, and only a few small countries, along with China, whose finances were chaotic, were constantly in arrears. the League borrowed no money.

The Secretariat, organized by Sir Eric Drummond, a former British Foreign Service official, drew up the budget on British civil-service principles. The watchwords were professional competence and strict economy. The Secretariat correlated the proposed expenditures of every League agency in a single estimate, giving attention to the smallest items. Sums available for printing by various agencies or for traveling expenses, for example, were scrutinized and pared down. If a country wished the technical assistance of a League commission, it was expected to pay the steamship fares and hotel bills. Experts of the Secretariat did the preparatory work for international conferences, and under such section leaders as Jean Monnet and Sir Arthur Salter did it superbly—but the host country was asked to meet the expenses of any conference invited. The idea of the free "field trip" for students of international relations had not yet been imagined. Lord Avon tells in his recent book of having been invited by Sir Austen Chamberlain, British Foreign Secretary, to accompany him on a trip to Geneva in 1926 on condition that he pay his own expenses, "for the rules were very strict. A Parliamentary Private Secretary could not pass muster as a necessity." [2] This was also the spirit of the League budget.

When the budget had been drawn up it was triple checked, first by a supervisory commission, then by the national treasury of every member, then by the Finance Committee of the Assembly. Finally it had to be approved by the Assembly as a whole, where each member theoretically held the right of veto. No veto was ever cast. Dissenting members abstained. The precedent was established that an abstention was not a negative vote, but occasionally a veto was threatened.

It is easy to imagine the heartburnings of the officials of the Secretariat, full of plans for expanding the League's work, when subjected to such financial stringency. Their suffering was compounded, as F. P. Walters, a Deputy Secretary-General, notes in his *History of the League of Nations,* by the bitter and persistent charges of reckless extravagance brought against the League by its enemies. In perspective such accusations seem comical, but they could harm not only morale at Geneva but also the League's political work. The Commissions sent by the Council to report on the fighting between Bolivia and Paraguay in the Chaco, and between Japan and China in Manchuria, for example, were delayed while the Secretariat wrestled with the problem of funds. The warring states finally agreed to pay the costs.

As compensation for the penny-pinching, the League was spared a multitude of distractions. There were only ten nonpolitical organizations, and only two of them were autonomous—the Permanent Court of International Justice and the International Labor Office. In providing a procedure for electing judges that was acceptable to large and small nations, and by underwriting expenses, the League made possible the creation of the Court—the League's finest achievement. The judicial body was familiarly known as the World Court, but though a number of its judges came from non-European countries, including the United States, neither the United States nor the Soviet Union subscribed to its statutes. Almost all the disputes brought before it originated in European or Mediterranean lands.

The cases included none of the major disputes of the interwar years, but the body of international law which the Court interpreted and began to develop was respected. It rendered more than sixty judgments and advisory opinions, all of which were obeyed. The respect paid to the Court was witness to the actuality of a European society. Though the work of the Court came to an end when Hitler achieved dominance over both League and Europe, it opened a window on a future that civilized men long to enter.

The International Labor Office, under the direction of a forceful and ambitious French trade unionist, Albert Thomas, foreshadowed the course of a variety of United Nations nonpolitical agencies. It came under the aegis of the League through the Preamble to the Covenant, which expressed the desire of the "high contracting parties" "to promote international cooperation," and again through the first paragraph of the omnibus Article 23, which specified that "fair and humane conditions of labor for men, women and children" were a particular League objective.

The ILO had its own constitution, drawn up by a special commission at the peace conference, which provided that the Office should be "part of the organization of the League" but gave it a general mandate which overlapped that of virtually every other agency. Moreover, in asserting the right of the ILO to impose penalties on member states for violation of its labor codes and even to regulate their economies in behalf of wage-earners, the constitution went further theoretically in the direction of international legislation than the League itself ever dreamed of going. All League members were automatically members of the ILO under Article 2 of the Charter, but the ILO wrote its own membership rules. Some states were admitted to the agency before they joined the League; the United States was admitted without joining the parent organization; and some states that resigned from the League retained membership in the Labor Office. Its Secretariat was originally envisioned as a group of international civil servants, on the order of Sir Eric Drummond's Secretariat. Under the powerful leadership of Albert Thomas it swelled to a staff of five hundred—Sir Eric had less than one thousand for all the League's work—which unblushingly engaged in propaganda for the agency's objectives.

These objectives ranged from protection of children and women in industry to far-reaching changes in the economic and political structures of all the countries of the world, under one of those magnificent slogans that silence those whom they do not automatically convince: "Social justice is a necessary prerequisite to peace." In principle, the Labor Office, subsidized by the League, was the League's political rival. In fact, however, though the ILO referred some of its jurisdictional puzzles to the Court, it never tested its claim to the power that would have been needed to achieve its more far-reaching aims and never possessed such power. Its pioneering work in the field of industrial relations was expert and practical and was highly regarded by management as well as labor. The model Conventions, covering such questions as health of workers, social insurance, hours of labor, and so on, that it offered for governmental signature were indirectly influential, though they received only limited formal acceptance. Since the businesslike Council insisted that even this independent agency coordinate its requests for appropriations with those of all other agencies, the problem of overlapping programs was kept manageable.

Of the other eight specialized agencies, only three—the Health Organization, the Committee on the Traffic in Women and Children, and the Committtee on the Traffic in Opium and Other Dangerous Drugs—were essentially nonpolitical. International programs in all these fields had been organized before the League was established. The work of the Health Organization was directed especially against the postwar epidemics of typhus and cholera in the borderlands of Eastern Europe and Russia. Though certainly in this case unduly limited in funds, the organization won universal acclaim—literally universal, since both the United States and the Soviet Union gave support—and was extended to the Middle East and Far East, mainly by technical advice and sanitary services. Here was the prototype of the United Nations' great World Health Organization.

The activities of the Committee on Drugs skirted the edge of the indefinable zone of international affairs termed "political," since the export of narcotics was a source of revenue for several Far Eastern countries and colonies, and the raw drugs were processed in Western factories for legitimate as well as nefarious uses. But the lands producing opium—China in particular—were less intransigent then than now, and sagacious conduct of the campaign against the underground narcotics traffic won a commendable measure of national cooperation. The agency operated under a mixture of unofficial and governmental direction, restricting the export of raw drugs by issuing certificates and later exercising control through inspection at the factories. The general principle was to determine the amount of the drugs necessary for medical and other scientific purposes and to limit the distribution to these legitimate needs.

It is interesting that the relative success of this effort led to an attempt to adapt the same principle to the problem of the reduction of national armaments when every other approach to that question had failed. "Look upon arms as if they were opium," it was suggested, the note of hope being especially marked in voices three thousand miles across the Atlantic, "and distinguish between necessary and nefarious quantities." This new version of an abandoned effort to differentiate between offensive and defensive weapons quickly evaporated for the same reason for which the earlier one had failed. There was no yardstick, not merely because no nation, large or small, would willingly put its destiny in the hands of a disinterested commission but also because the experts themselves could not find criteria. National policy could not be contained in a test tube. The nature of submarines, for example, changed with the policies that employed them; France and Italy thought them defensive, but Britain sought to abolish them. Under Hitler's totalitarian policy, even concrete became an offensive weapon, as he used it to immobilize France for the attack on Poland after the occupation of the Rhineland. But the attempt to equate arms with opium did provide a memorable illustration of the difference between political and nonpolitical problems.

"Useful work in matters of secondary importance" is a fair verdict upon the accomplishments of most of the League's specialized agencies. The work of the Committee on the Traffic in Women and Children—later called the Committee on Social Questions—came plainly under this heading. It offered Conventions raising the legal ages of consent and marriage and drew up a General Declaration of the Rights of the Child. Because of the nature of its major topic—white slavery—this Committee received a gratifying measure of publicity and approbation. "Be thankful for fallen women," was a wintry comment to be heard at Geneva in the years when there was little else in the League's work that the public relations section thought wise to emphasize. The cynicism was prompted by the awareness of undue optimism about the effectiveness of the League in the hard political tasks that the Council and Assembly were established to perform.

Committees on refugees and on slavery occupied intermediate zones between political and nonpolitical. Under the valiant leadership of Fridtjof Nansen, the Refugee Committee was instrumental in returning more than four hundred thousand former prisoners of war to their own lands, and it aided several hundred thousand displaced people, in particular emigrés from Bolshevik Russia, in finding havens. Improvised and entirely unofficial "Nansen passports" were honored throughout Europe. The activity of this Committee declined as the war years receded, however, and as efforts to find new fields of work inescapably collided with the primary responsibilities of governments in matters of citizenship.

The Committee on Slavery amounted to little. It promulgated an Anti-Slavery Convention and issued a report on slave-trading in Liberia—a League member—and in Ethiopia—a prospective member. Both countries promised reform. Incidentally—though it is most interesting—these two, along perhaps with Albania and— finally and fatally—Germany, were the countries for whose benefit the League painfully strained its membership qualifications. Neither Liberia nor Ethiopia was an organized state. Liberia, a neglected American responsibility, was an original member of the League, but only because the United States paid the expenses of a delegation which lived in Paris during the Peace Conference. Britain advised against the admission of Ethiopia, which took place in 1923, but France and Italy, suspecting British self-interest in the region, insisted upon its inclusion.

The International Institute for Intellectual Cooperation, the forerunner of UNESCO, did not get fully under way until 1930, after a period of reorganization. France, proud of her traditional hospitality to the arts, was its foremost early sponsor, envisioning the agency as a cultural center for individuals and groups, free from political pressure or obligation. It was also a useful clearing house for the concerns of professional educators. Imperceptibly, its control expanded in all directions. An effort to exert an "influence for peace" by inspiring teachers to rewrite history text books became its major—or, at least, its best-known—objective, mercifully circumscribed by limited funds.

The two economic organizations that complete the list of the League's specialized agencies were the most important of them. The Economic and Financial Organization is noteworthy because of the work it actually performed, whereas the Organization for Communications and Transit is noteworthy chiefly for its unrealized potential. The activities of the former deserve separate examination among the instances of the League's major work. The record of the Organization for Communications and Transit is mainly one of frustration. Its province was the enormous territory casually traced in Article 23 (e) of the Covenant—"freedom of communications and transit and equitable treatment for the commerce of all Members." To achieve these goals on a global scale was out of the question, and after one world conference, at Barcelona in 1921, which drew up a Convention on Freedom of Transit and International Waterways, the Committee resigned itself to acting mainly as a clearing house for technical aspects of European problems of ports, roads, and railways. Accomplishments ranged from the determination of port dues to such things as road signals and international automobile licenses.

The Organization for Communications and Transit did not resign itself to such ineffectiveness without a struggle. It sought autonomy—a free hand in tackling the commercial problems for which, it knew, coordinated national policies were the only remedy —and pleaded for the "depoliticalization" of such matters. But the Council and Assembly held the agency on an ever tighter rein, since the solution of commercial problems required more, not less, emphasis on politics. The experts of the Organization for Communications and Transit could, for example, give the League's High

Commissioner for the Free Port of Danzig sound advice about transport by rail and ships through the city and harbor, and the Commissioner would apply as much of it as he could. But efficient use of the Free Port involved the whole range of German-Polish relations. The League had inherited a peace settlement. The question before Europe, upon the answer to which all other problems depended, was whether the political settlement was going to hold.

3. The Heart of the Settlement

However just or unjust the provisions of the Versailles Treaty under which Germany was deprived of its colonies, most of its merchant marine, and all its warships, sunk by the Germans outside the British naval base at Scapa Flow, they gave no immediate trouble to the victorious countries. The Treaty also forbade Germany to possess tanks or planes and restricted her to an army of one hundred thousand men; understandably enough, the government of the new German Reich soon took steps to evade these restrictions. Payment of the huge assessment for reparations was a matter of almost instant trouble; it was scaled down after Germany and France had fought a nine-month war—what we would now call a cold war—over it.

The League, however, was not responsible for enforcement of these aspects of the Versailles settlement. The Supreme Council had entrusted immediate supervision of the execution of the Versailles Treaty and the subsidiary treaties with defeated Austria, Hungary, and Bulgaria to a standing committee outside the League —the Conference of Ambassadors, composed of envoys of Britain, France, Italy, Japan, and the United States. (The American ambassador attended as an observer after 1920.) There was also a separate Reparation Commission; the victorious great powers always kept the related questions of their own war debts and credits and of reparations from Germany in their own hands.

At the heart of the peace settlement were the decisions on national boundaries, for these, with their losses and gains, then as always touched the most sensitive popular nerve. "There is a profound psychological difference between a transfer of territory and a change in a trade treaty or pact of international cooperation," a great American geographer, Isaiah Bowman, Chief Territorial Specialist of the American Commission at the Paris Conference, has written.[3] "Territory is near and evokes personal feelings and group sentiments. To a people conscious of its individuality, 'how sweet the silent backward tracings.' Such people endow the land itself with a mystical quality, hearing revered ancestors, the authors of past grandeurs and doers of heroic deeds, speak from their graves in its soil. To all classes, landscape is an essential part of home. Enshrined in every national literature are the changing moods and compositions of river, mountain, plain, forest and shore. All the familiar techniques of living are involved in the complex of feeling, remembered experience and imagination surrounding place and home." It is title to such things that is transferred in a change of boundaries.

In Western Europe, Alsace and Lorraine were returned to France under the Versailles Treaty; title to the coal mines of the German Saar region were vested in the French in compensation for the destruction of French mines, and the Saar was put under League administration for fifteen years, its final disposition to be determined by a plebiscite. The Rhineland was to be demilitarized and occupied by Allied forces, which were to be progressively withdrawn from stated zones in five, ten, and fifteen years. Eupen-Malmédy, a corner of German territory with sixty thousand inhabitants, was claimed by Belgium as a frontier rectification, and Schleswig, a Danish province annexed by Bismarck in the first of his wars, was divided between Denmark and Germany on the lines of a plebiscite which revealed that the northern part was strongly Danish in sentiment and the southern part German. Viewed in the perspective of the Second World War and its aftermath, the astonishing aspect of these rearrangements seems to be their moderation.

In the same perspective, the remarkable aspects of the redrawing of the boundaries of Eastern Europe were the conscientiousness of the effort and the fact that the territorial experts and their masters, the statesmen, came so close to the ideal of a just settlement. Four absolutisms—Russian, German, Austro-Hungarian, and Turkish—which had ruled sectors of this inner frontier, running from the Baltic Sea in a long curve to the Adriatic, had collapsed from internal and external pressures. In earlier centuries, kingdoms which these empires obliterated had themselves warred and ruled, advanced and retreated along this frontier—Poles, Lithuanians, Bohemians, Magyars outstanding among them—engulfing and abandoning pockets of ethnic, religious, and national minorities. The problem of the statesmen at Paris in 1919 was, as Bowman put it, "to fit the intricate patterns of speech, folk groupings and sense of nationality" of the more than one hundred million people of this region to the requirements of contemporary politics.

The political ideal was, more specifically, self-determination—the principle that "well-defined" national groupings should live under governments of their own choosing. The ideal was modified by some stern actualities: the immediate need for order, the longer-term need for economic viability among the successor states of the dislocated empires, and the still longer-range requirements for strategic safety, not only for the states in this borderland but for Europe as a whole. Every noun and adjective in such a catalogue of requirements—which could be almost infinitely enlarged and subdivided—was susceptible to varying interpretation and emphasis. That the interpretations would be made from the point of view of the powers that had triumphed on the battlefield was the only obvious constant in the complex calculation.

Seven nations emerged, new or reborn: Finland, Estonia, Latvia, Lithuania, Poland, Czechoslovakia, and the Kingdom of the Serbs, Croats and Slovenes (Yugoslavia). Finland and the three Baltic states—Estonia, Latvia, and Lithuania—won their independence after relatively brief fighting with the Russian Red Guards who attempted to maintain the old imperial rule. Lithuanian claims to the seaport of Memel and to the ancient capital city of Vilna brought painful conflicts of rights with Germany and Poland respectively; Lithuania maintained a state of war with Poland until 1927.

The Allies at Paris needed only to accept, by recognizing the new governments, the Estonian and Latvian boundaries as agreed upon by these states and the Russian Bolshevik government when the fighting ended. These newly sovereign countries, and Finland as well, had homogeneous populations; all had circumspectly refrained from any effort to push their boundaries beyond the evident limits of their ethnological groupings at the expense of disorganized Russia, and all devoted themselves henceforth to minding their own business, political and economic—and did it intelligently and well.

On the southern end of the Eastern European crescent, Yugoslavia was created out of subject peoples of the Austro-Hungarian Empire and built around the Kingdom of Serbia. Here the peacemakers had to struggle with the problem of the secret treaties which had promised Italy territorial rewards in return for the wartime decision to break its alliance with the Central Powers and fight on the Allied side. After the Allied victory made the fulfillment of a contrary set of promises unnecessary "villainous" was the word for such pledges. Where now did justice lie? Those responsible for deciding were, moreover, assailed from another flank. A closer approximation of justice, ethnically, might have been achieved by dividing the area into three states (or four, since the former Kingdom of Montenegro was also embedded in the new Yugoslavia). This solution was strenuously recommended by groups of Croats and Slovenes. Statesmen and their advisers labored over such questions for eight months—maps, population charts, and documents in their hands, volleys of passionately contending pleas echoing in the rooms in which they sat.

In the end, all the south Slavs were denominated one state. Italy gained an implicit protectorate over Albania, all the Italian population of Austria-Hungary, some Slovene areas in the north, and the German-speaking South Tyrol—the latter acquisition claimed as strategic protection for the Brenner Pass, though the transfer was a plain injustice to the two hundred and forty thousand inhabitants of the region and to Austria. This was much less than Italy hoped for. Critics of the Paris settlement predicted a brief life for the composite state of Yugoslavia. Though never able to manage parliamentary government, it is very much in existence, however, thanks to its own determination to maintain its independence and to Western protection from Soviet Russian imperialism after the Second World War.

Where Magyar, Austrian, and south Slav populations were mingled, Yugoslavia got the benefit of any doubt. So it was everywhere in the Balkans: territorial settlements followed the main lines of ethnic groupings, but where peoples and nationalities were inextricably mixed—as, for example, in Macedonia, "the variety of whose populations has given French cooks a word for fruit salad," in Hugh Seton-Watson's phrase—verdicts were weighted in favor of the system the winners sought to construct. Rumania, which had wound up in the Allied ranks after twice changing its mind, profited at the expense of Hungary and Bulgaria, and Bulgaria lost territory to Greece and Yugoslavia as well. The over-all settlement in this troubled region tended to confirm the results of the two Balkan Wars which had touched off the World War. The remarkable fact here is not that there was dissatisfaction with details of the arrangements but that the Balkans began to settle down.[4]

By strength and location Poland and Czechoslovakia were the key Eastern European states in the Versailles structure. In its strategic aspect, emphasized by the French, that system was intended to achieve stability on the Continent by setting the limits of German expansion eastward and Russian expansion westward. Its more general political objective, emphasized by British and Americans, was a degree of justice that would permit the settlement to last by making it endurable to the mixture of nationalities and peoples concerned. That the areas of Poland taken by Prussia, Austria, and Russia in three successive despoilments of the eighteenth century—the last of which obliterated Poland as a state—should be restored was a measure of long-overdue justice. It was also highly expedient, if ever there was to be an end to the Polish question, over which the powers of Europe had quarreled, intrigued, and warred.

The settlement imposed on Germany at Versailles was, in the main, in accord with the Prussian-Polish boundaries before the Prussian conquests. It has been estimated that it brought a transfer of 3,855,000 people from Germany to Poland. Of them, 1,364,000 were German-speaking.[5] Restoration of territory which held something like a two-to-one majority of Poles after more than a century of German colonization was not an injustice. Perfect justice for all the inhabitants of this area of the earth was not within human reach.

German anger at the settlement was exacerbated by the arrangement made for the city of Danzig, at the mouth of the Vistula River. Poland passionately desired it as a Baltic port that would give access to the sea, though the city was populated largely by Germans. Historically Danzig had been an autonomous city under Polish suzerainty, but its special privileges were extinguished by Prussia in the first partition of Poland. Under the Versailles settlement it was restored to its former status as a free port serving the commerce of Poland and Prussia. This was a reasonable answer to the economic problem as well as to the prickly political problem of associating a city preponderantly of one nationality with a hinterland preponderantly of another. The majority of the inhabitants of the "corridor" that connected this port with the main body of Poland were Poles.

As it happened, the economic arrangement was to fail because of German intransigence, and Poland built her own port, Gdynia. What the Germans could not bear was the idea that, for them, symbolized the whole territorial readjustment—in a word, that some Germans should be governed by *Poles*. We may note, incidentally, that the alternative solution to this complex question of interwoven

Polish-German nationality groups—mass deportation of the minorities—was not considered in the relatively humane era in which the Versailles Treaty was drawn up.

Plebiscites in the Allenstein and Marienwerder districts of East Prussia, where there was a strategic railway, showed heavy German majorities, and these areas were refused to Poland, to the great dismay of the Poles. A negotiated German-Polish settlement of boundaries was out of the question. Poles saw the full text of the Treaty only one day before it was shown to the Germans.

In the east, Poland recovered Galicia from Austria and so-called Congress Poland from Russia, plus a disputed area of the vaguely defined territory known as White Russia. This was less than Poland's territory before the partition and less than the Poles hoped for. Historically and ethnically this whole area—a plain with few natural dividing lines—was especially scarred by old marches and countermarches, migrations and colonizations. The Polish-Russian boundary was determined only after the Russians had repulsed a Polish effort to seize all the Ukraine (the appetites of lesser as well as greater powers grow by eating), and after Poles had in turn routed a Soviet offensive that almost reached Warsaw. The territorial experts and their superiors at Paris had recommended that Poland be content with the so-called Curzon line, coinciding roughly with the boundary of Congress Poland, but the Poles pressed one hundred and fifty miles further eastward.

Lenin's government, which had with fanfare renounced imperialism and all its works, signed a treaty with Poland at Riga, in 1921, recognizing the latter frontier. The Soviet Ambassador, Adolf A. Joffe, declared that the treaty left no problems unsolved, and the Foreign Minister, Grigori V. Chicherin, repeated that it settled "all questions of interest to these two states." The terms of peace that Lenin had offered Poland when Russian troops were at the gates of Warsaw were, however, more meaningful than these declarations. By those terms Poland, granted a boundary at the Curzon line, was to reduce her army to fifty thousand men, dismantle all war industries, and agree to the formation of a Polish "worker's militia" equipped by the Russians, to police the country.[6] This meant a Communist Poland and the quick extinction of Polish independence. The Poles knew it. Their desire for additional territory eastward for the protection of Warsaw was intensified by this experience.

The only part of the whole Russian frontier that the Russians refused to validate in treaties was the one with Rumania, which had repossessed the former Turkish province of Bessarabia. This had once also been under Czarist sovereignty. Joachim von Ribbentrop and V. M. Molotov—and their masters—were to quarrel fatally over the control of this area at the end of the 1930s; for both it was an avenue to the achievement of ambitions on the Persian Gulf and at the Dardanelles.

With all its imperfections, the eastern settlement after the First World War traced a decent middle ground, literally and figuratively, between German and Russian imperialism. It is necessary to remember that German war aims, as revealed in the 1918 Treaty of Brest-Litovsk with the Bolshevik government, envisaged a German-satellite kingdom of Poland restored at Russian expense, and, indeed, a chain of satellite states running from Finland to the Black Sea, embracing the Ukraine and Georgia. Given the opportunity in 1945, Stalin was to change the direction but not the nature of the aggrandizement and to press his advantage even more ruthlessly.

That the Allied and Associated Powers blindly or vengefully dismissed an opportunity in 1919 to set Europe on the road to a more stable future when they permitted the break-up of the Austro-Hungarian Empire is the most persistent of the myths of the iniquity of Versailles. They could have saved the Dual Monarchy only if they had possessed the attribute of omnipotence, for its salvation depended upon unending life for the Emperor Franz Josef. The dam that had held the national, ethnic, and social currents of three-quarters of a century in check was the principle of monarchy, symbolized by the seemingly timeless figure of the Emperor and maintained, as C. A. Macartney has observed, by the force of habit. When Franz Josef died in November 1916 at the age of eighty-seven, the dam burst.

His successor, his grandnephew Karl, offered concessions to the nationalist movements and feelers for peace. But even if he had been willing to make peace without his ally, Wilhelm II, and even if Germany had been willing to make concessions—neither of which was the case—the material of the old dam was too rotten for use in rebuilding. The realm held together for another year, "saved partly by the complexity of its own problems (which excluded the possibility of any generally acceptable solution of them) partly by the continued successes of its armies and Germany's." [7] Suddenly there was nothing left but the bureaucracy in Vienna.

The London, Washington, and Paris governments had early refrained from making the destruction of the Dual Monarchy one of their war aims and had kept open minds about future arrangements in the region. All had put specialists to work on the intricate problem, and all were aware of the desirability of maintaining as much economic unity as possible in the Danube River area. They were also well aware of the usefulness of as strong a state as could reasonably be hoped for in south-central Europe, as counterweight to renewed German expansion. The French, indeed, seem to have considered the possibility of a Danubian grouping built around Hungary after Hungary itself had broken away from the Dual Monarchy.[8] But that came to nothing, for one reason because Hungary was rent by three revolutions, the second one being a period of terror under the Communist Béla Kun.

The Allied and Associated Powers backed the claim of the Czechs to organize the area as the most reasonable answer to the problem. Essentially it was a claim to the recovery of nationhood by the three provinces of the historic Bohemian kingdom—Bohemia, Moravia, and Lower Silesia—and the constitutional union of these with Slovakia, long ruled by Magyars as a province of Hungary. As a result, the prewar German-Austrian boundary would become the Czechoslovak boundary with Germany. Stretching around the rim, on the Czech side of the mountains that demarcated the frontier, would be some three million German-speaking Austrians. This was a large minority—the now-famous "Sudeten Germans"—who, however, had never been part of the German Reich. Inclusion of these in the new nation-state of Czechoslovakia occasioned little interest in Germany at the time.

The most contested boundary of the new state was the Slovak frontier with Hungary, drawn to give the victors in the war the benefit of the doubt. There was also a grievous conflict between Czechs and Poles over the small city of Teschen, an area with railroads and coal fields desired by both; a compromise to the advantage of the Czechs was reached, under pressure from the powers. In the controversy, the Polish government was handicapped by internal dissention.

Czechoslovakia was a favored state at the Paris Conference, especially by the Americans, but not simply because there was a large contingent of Czech, Moravian, and Slovak immigrants in the United States; there had also been heavy emigration to America by Poles and Hungarians, for example, and American feelings toward them and their homelands were no less friendly. Nor was it because the Czech representatives, Thomas Masaryk and Eduard Beneš, and Karel Kramář, the Slovak leader, were gifted spokesmen. It was because they spoke for an orderly government that they persuaded Englishmen and Frenchmen no less than Americans at Paris to back their claim to statehood.

Thomas Garrigue Masaryk, who married an American and incorporated her name in his own, was a professor of philosophy at the University of Prague, and also a man of exceptional political insight. In 1914 he had shrewdly estimated the significance and probable outcome of the war and went to work to raise sizable armed forces—from deserters from the Austrian army and prisoners of war in Allied hands—who fought stoutly on the Allied side. In due course a provisional government was set up in Paris, with Masaryk as President, Kramář as Vice President, and Beneš as Foreign Minister. It was the first new government to be recognized.

Moreover, the government-in-exile made the journey home, usually so hazardous a transplantation for provisional wartime regimes, with celerity and success. It was not challenged and instituted an effective government almost immediately. Czechoslovakia became one of the most prosperous democracies in the world, and, along with the Scandinavian countries, exhibited the highest degree of social justice in Europe and probably in the world. Hitler found it intolerably in his way and whipped up the Sudeten crisis as a pretext for the war he wanted.

The question of self-determination, Masaryk once wrote, is not whether every minority shall have complete autonomy but "whether nations, conscious of their nationality and proving the possibility of political independence by their economic and cultural progress, and by their claims and effort for liberty, can be independent." [9] In sum, the validation of the abstract right to self-government was the ability to make good the claim. No wonder Americans listened; this was their yardstick when Edmund Burke was their spokesman.*

Every Eastern European state, new or already established, was obliged to sign a treaty with the Allied and Associated Powers, pledging in detail that there would be no discrimination against racial, religious, or linguistic minorities. The League was made guarantor of the agreements, a responsibility it accepted with reluctance, since the Covenant forbade it to interfere in the domestic concerns of its members.

This effort to give special protection to the minorities in certain countries was the expression of an ideal rather than a practical program. Since the pledges were embodied in formal treaties, the Permanent Court of International Justice had a legal basis for assuming jurisdiction over disputes, and it ruled with fairness and

---

* When Woodrow Wilson was asked during his first term in office whether the Philippine Islands would be given independence he replied, "How can freedom be *given?* It can only be earned." He sent emissaries to the Islands to report on the readiness of the Filipinos for self-government, and later took the first plain action to open the door through which the peoples there might move to independence. Throughout the wartime years he seldom used the phrase "self-determination" without qualification.

restraint in a number of cases, most of them involving German minorities in Poland. A conscientious and hard-working committee of the Council also devoted itself to the problem, examining hundreds of complaints referred to it through the Secretariat and doing its best, by friendly advice behind the scenes, to ameliorate abuses. But the opportunity of petitioning the Council for redress of grievances was also abused, not only by individuals with trivial complaints but also, toward the end of the 1920s, by organized German efforts to use this privilege as an instrument for undermining the entire settlement. The Council eventually found itself in the humiliating position of aiding revisionist propaganda, presented in the name of German minority rights in Poland and Czechoslovakia, while unable to take notice of persecution of Jews within Germany.

Woodrow Wilson and many others, aware of imperfections in the Versailles settlement, had emphasized the presence in the Covenant of the provision for reconsideration of any "inapplicable" treaty—Article 19, which embodied the so-called principle of peaceful change—and hoped much from it. Failure to make use of this article was a source of bitter comment on the League, and on the follies of men and nations, during the interwar years. But peaceful change itself is a product of stability. No one has stated the truth that underlies the paradox as wisely as J. L. Brierly, in a review of the League's work:

> Peaceful change has been too often recommended to us as if it were an alternative to power in the organization of security, a sort of 'soft option,' for why, it is argued or implied, should states want to fight if they can get their just grievances redressed by peaceful procedure? Of course the answer is that whereas peaceful change would give them what it is just that they should have, war, if it succeeds, will give them what they want, and it is a dangerous self-deception to suppose that these two things coincide.[10]

Those who drew the boundary lines at Versailles succeeded in fitting them to patterns of language, folk groupings, and sense of nationality more closely than ever before in modern history. The territorial settlement provided the only basis for something corresponding to peace in Europe that our century has seen. What Europe needed in 1920 was not an intensified search for a more perfect justice but time to settle down. That the settlement would be difficult to maintain was doubted by few who took the responsibility for recommending it. That was the reason for the effort toward collective security.

IV. THE YEARS OF OPPORTUNITY

1. Law through Peace

Europe and the League were fortunate in the circumstances of the early postwar years, not only because no powerful outlaw state challenged the new system until a decade had passed but also because the spasms of warfare on the periphery subsided relatively quickly. Fighting in the eastern borderlands drew to an end in 1921. By the close of 1922 Kemal Atatürk had established his revolution in the Turkish homeland of Anatolia, and to everyone's astonishment the new Republic of Turkey began to emerge as a stabilizing influence in southeast Europe. In the west, there was bloodshed in the Ruhr when France attempted to collect reparations; preconditions of peace did not exist there until the end of 1923. Scholars of the period who looked back one hundred years to the Congress of Vienna for their ideal of peacemaking thought the pace shockingly slow, though it seems an enviable achievement compared to the twenty-two-year search for a treaty of peace in Europe after the Second World War.

In 1919 neither Clemenceau nor Wilson would entertain the suggestion that Germany be accepted as an original member of the League of Nations; they asked for evidence of Germany's intention to observe international obligations as a precondition of membership. Under Article 1 of the Covenant, "guarantees" were required of all applicants, but the Allied note emphasizing this requirement greatly affronted the German delegation at the peace conference. After the Statute of the Permanent Court of International Justice had been adopted, however, and the Covenant amended by the First Assembly in October 1921 to include provisions for judicial settlement of disputes, the Weimar government subscribed to the statute. It accepted the decisions and opinions of the Court, unfa-vorable and favorable, and used its procedures for the amelioration of minor grievances. This was a testimony of respect for the new system that the United States, ironically, refused to give. Through-out the years of opportunity of the League, the Permanent Court, above all other agencies of the system, was witness to the existence of a European society embracing victors and vanquished, and thus to the possibility of a stabilized Europe.

The first interesting case to come before the League was the dis-pute between Finland and Sweden over the Åland Islands in the summer of 1920. These small islands in the Baltic Sea, occupying a location of military importance at the mouth of the Gulf of Finland and also commanding the Gulf of Bothnia, northwestward along the Swedish and Finnish coasts, had been part of the Duchy of Finland under the Czarist empire. With independence, Finland had taken sovereignty over them. Sweden contested Finnish possession, partly on the ground that the title to sovereignty was not clear but mainly because the population, almost entirely of Swedish stock, had made plain its desire for tranfer to Swedish rule. Agitation for a plebiscite and self-determination had resulted in the imprisonment of some of the Ålanders by Finnish authorities.

There was strong support for the separatist movement in Sweden and some sentiment for a solution by force of arms. Though the wartime mood still prevailed throughout Europe, it is unlikely that these neighbor states would have come to blows, even without an international authority to mediate the quarrel. As it was, the dis-pute was brought to the attention of the League by Britain, and a special meeting of the Council was held in London. The Permanent Court had not yet been organized, but the Council, adopting a semi-judicial approach, appointed a special committee of lawyers to study the conflicting claims.

Naturally, the committee of lawyers pointed out that the case was more complicated than laymen realized; two other countries—Russia and Britain—had interests in the matter. These two had signed a treaty with Sweden in the midnineteenth century which provided that the strategic islands not be fortified or put to any military use. Time for reflection thus having been gained, the Council appointed a commission to visit the islands and examine the particulars.

This commission did not report to the League for about a year. During the interval Finnish sovereignty was more plainly established by a treaty of peace with Russia, and Ålanders imprisoned for separatist activity were released. The commission found no abuses and no practical grievances. It proposed that things remain as they were, and so they did remain, Finland retaining sovereignty and the League retaining the right of investigation which it had successfully asserted. Sweden argued vigorously against acceptance of the commission's recommendations for the settlement but accepted the formal verdict of the Council. A new Convention barring fortification of the islands was subsequently concluded.

This apparently mild imbroglio had significant aspects. One was the good sense of the League's ruling on the demand for self-determination by a tiny national minority. The Council held that the minority had a right to fair treatment but insisted also that it could not be permitted to separate itself from the country of which it was a part simply because it wanted to do so: that was the road to international anarchy. Recognizing Finland's sovereignty, the League concluded that the nationality of the islanders was a Finnish domestic matter. In other words, the abstract right to self-determination was subject to practical tests; there was no rule of international law requiring "self-determination."

This, incidentally, was an example of the use of the Council as a court, as Woodrow Wilson had imagined it in his early outlines of the Covenant, and proceeded as that strange man expected. The Swedish argument was put with eloquence and dignity by Sweden's Prime Minister, the great internationalist Karl Branting. First Ministers of other nations heard his case. Their judgment rendered, the stronger power yielded to the weaker. It was early in the morning of the League; and, of course, the political aspects of the dispute were minor.

Even so, some later commentators found the political nature of the ruling unfortunate. Had the Permanent Court been organized at the time, the case would undoubtedly have been referred to it rather than to the Council. Nevertheless, though it would be rash to guess what the Court's response would have been, it is noteworthy that the Court drew upon an aspect of the Åland Islands case in support of a subsequent decision of its own. This was in 1922 in the Court's fourth advisory opinion, relating to a dispute between France and Britain over decrees that France had promulgated in her protectorates of Tunis and Morocco converting certain British subjects into French citizens.

The Court's opinion in this instance was one of those wonderfully intricate compositions, of balanced negatives that looked to the establishment of a positive principle in international law. It also illustrates both the hazards of interpretation by laymen of judicial reasoning and the charm such reasoning—like half-understood poetry—can hold. Since the political question of self-determination was not at issue, the Court did not refer to that aspect of the Åland Islands decision in citing the useful precedent it found in the earlier hearings. It concentrated on the legal point of the British-French dispute, which was whether the French decrees were a matter of domestic jurisdiction—that is to say, whether the Court itself could properly hear the dispute.

What it cited from the reasoning of the earlier committee of lawyers was an opinion to the effect that a dispute does not "achieve an international character merely as a consequence of its being brought before the Council of the League of Nations, nor as a consequence of appeals by a party to the dispute to engagements of an international character". [1] But this was only a way of clearing the ground.

In the Court's words:

> The question whether a certain matter is or is not solely within the jurisdiction of a state is an essentially relative question; it depends upon the development of international relations. Thus, in the present state of international law, questions of nationality are, in the opinion of the Court, in principle within this reserved domain.

This much-quoted pronouncement referring to the possible diminution of the scope of state sovereignty and saying, in effect, "Not now, but some day perhaps," was then refined and particularized by the Court for the purpose of a practical estimate of the business in hand. There could be no question, the Court said, but that a state possesses exclusive jurisdiction in regard to questions of nationality in its own territory. But did such exclusive jurisdiction extend over protected territories? No, or, at least, not necessarily, said the Court. And furthermore, the question whether certain treaties, relied upon by Britain to protect her subjects in Tunis and Morocco had lapsed (as France believed) was clearly a question of international law. In sum, the Court concluded that it did properly possess jurisdiction over the dispute and was prepared to hear the case on its merits.

Whether Woodrow Wilson, with his disesteem for lawyers and his impatience to get to the point, would have thought the legal minuet overelaborate and unnecessary is also beyond guessing. But the Permanent Court of International Justice had not only pointed to the door marked "Rule of Law," but had given it a push. In this particular case, the upshot of the circumspect judicial approach was an anticlimax. France offered to submit the case for a judgment on its merits, but Britain, thinking possibly of problems in its own protectorates, now hesitated, and the dispute was compromised out of court. It was prosaically agreed that the nationality laws would not apply to the present generation of British subjects in Tunis and Morocco but would apply to the next generation.

The Court never accepted a case without painstaking examination of its legal right to do so; questions of jurisdiction were paramount in some thirty cases. In a notable instance it refused to give an advisory opinion requested by the Council of the League—in the Eastern Karelian dispute, in which Finland sought clarification of the status of territory presumably granted autonomy by the Bolshevik government in a Declaration appended to the 1920 Treaty of Dorpat.

The Russians held that the Declaration was not a contract but had been made "merely for information." The degree to which such an annexed Declaration was binding upon states that signed a treaty was an interesting field for judicial investigation, but the Court felt that it must decline the League's request for an opinion. Lenin's government was not a member of the League and had not subscribed to the Court's statutes, and the People's Commissar for Foreign Affairs notified the Council of the League by contemptuous telegram that he considered the proceedings "without legal value either in substance or in form." Lacking Russian cooperation, the Court could not obtain the needed evidence.

Since the Court had been brought into existence by a formal international treaty, not by an act of the League of Nations, nonmembers could accept its jurisdiction if they wished to, but neither nonmember nor member could be brought before the Court against its will. The justices stated the principle that guided them in a famous sentence. It is "well established in international law," the Court said, "that no State can without its consent to compelled to submit its disputes with other States either to mediation or arbitration, or to any other kind of pacific settlement."

All the Court's powers were conferred upon it by the sovereign states, and the Court constantly reminded itself of its limitations. When the statutes of the Court were being drawn up, many lawyers —Elihu Root prominent among them—were extremely doubtful of the wisdom of including among the Court's duties the novel task of formulating merely advisory opinions. They felt that the Court might be subject to abuses that would injure its reputation and perhaps destroy its usefulness. That would happen if one party to a dispute were permitted to air its case without the full procedure of a legal trial; in brief, if it were permitted to use the Court for propaganda. The refusal of the justices to give any opinion in the Eastern Karelian dispute meant that the Court intended to apply legal rules to this function of adviser to states just as strictly as it did to its function as a court of justice that issued judgments and orders. The practical result was that the Court heard no case, issued no order, and gave no opinion unless it was confident that its words would be heeded and its orders obeyed. For about a decade they invariably were—a record of success in adjudication of disputes between states never approached before or equaled since.*

The Permanent Court of International Justice was effective in its carefully circumscribed task of applying legal standards to international disputes, not because it sought to exercise compulsion but because it spoke for a relatively peaceful community. There was power behind the "old" Court—the power of the states that led the

* One judgment and five of seven advisory opinions of the International Court of Justice have been flouted: a judgment in the case of Albanian reparation due to Great Britain for damages done by mines laid in the Corfu Channel (1949); an opinion interpreting the peace treaties with Bulgaria, Rumania, and Hungary (1950); an opinion invalidating bloc voting in the admission of new members to the United Nations (1950); an opinion on the status of the South African mandate over South-West Africa (1950); and supplementary opinions (1955 and 1956); and an opinion on assessments for peacekeeping forces (1962).

The tangled South-West Africa case defies classification. There was a judgment in 1962 supporting the unheeded advisory opinions and ordering contentious proceedings. South Africa duly appeared before the Court, but a judgment of 1966 reversed the judgment of 1962.

The case is profoundly political, and both judgments were rendered by a Court divided eight to seven. The majority opinion in the crucial 1966 judgment, written by the President of the Court, Sir Percy Spender, found that the Court lacked jurisdiction. A strong dissenting opinion was written by Judge Philip C. Jessup. An authoritative summary of majority and minority opinions can be found in "Issues Before the 21st General Assembly," *International Conciliation*, September 1966, pp. 60–67.

League; but the Court did not pretend that it could do with words from the bench what the members of the League were unwilling to do with ships and armies through the enforcement machinery of Article 16.

The range of the Court's activity was extended by a Convention called the Optional Clause, attached to the Protocol of Signature of the Statutes of the Court, making more explicit the types of disputes over which the justices would be granted jurisdiction. This was signed by some forty states—the first general treaty in history for judicial settlement of international disputes. The United States Senate would never accept it, though two Presidents advocated it. This Optional Clause is often described as conferring "compulsory jurisdiction" upon the Court, and the phrase has introduced an exaggerated notion of the Court's actual power; the countries that subscribed to the clause specified in various reservations the kinds of disputes they would not consider suitable for adjudication as well as those they would.

Such reservations seemed at the time less sweeping than was expected; indeed, some of them today seem surprisingly unguarded. As Hugh McKinnon Wood, Legal Adviser to the Secretariat, has noted, Great Britain, for example, reasoning mistakenly that under the Covenant of the League the lawfulness of her naval action could never be tested before the Court, abandoned a traditional claim to shape the laws of naval warfare.[2] In 1939 she found herself liable to suits for damages by other parties to the Optional Clause for measures taken in the course of her blockade against Germany. Since Hitler had repudiated German membership in League and Court, he could act at sea with legal impunity. Britain hastily and unilaterally denounced the relevant section of the Optional Clause that she had signed.

Only once, unwillingly, did the Court become mired in a decision so controversial as to bring into question its own objectivity. That was the episode of the Austro-German Customs Union in 1931, when an advisory opinion of the Court found the proposed *Anschluss* contrary to a provision of the Treaty of St.-Germain and a subsequent protocol under which Austria promised to take no action that would directly or indirectly "compromise" its "independence." In the eight-to-seven opinion the justices divided in every direction in an effort to interpret the legal significance of these high-powered political words. Their resulting estimate of the threat to Austrian independence was, in common sense, sound enough, but the retreat from legal reasoning to political and economic forecasting on which it was unavoidably based, somewhat tarnished the Court's fine reputation. By then the era of peace that had made possible the development of law was almost over. None of the major disputes of the prewar period was brought before the Court—in retrospect, a blessing, for the Court, spared the disrepute that desperate and unheeded pronouncements would have brought upon it, remained as a model for later attempts.

Though international law could not maintain peace, the brief interval of peace did bring a development of international law—how much of a development most scholars hesitate to say. As Professor Oliver J. Lissitzyn notes, "No scientific technique has yet been found to measure the growth of the law." Teachers of international law who expounded the significance of the Court's work in the early 1930s tended to be sanguine about the growth of the law; then the tone changed.[3] At least the work of the Court marked an advance beyond the system of special tribunals for arbitration. At most it served to start habits of resort to international law for the settlement of disputes between states. The complete failure of a conference held in 1930 to codify the rules of international law relating to nationality, territorial waters, and the responsibility of states for injuries to aliens indicated how much time and how much greater a degree of political confidence were going to be needed before such habits could take firm hold. Even this relatively homogeneous group of states tended to withdraw previous concessions when the "law" was to be written in black and white.

To lawyers, the Court's interesting cases were for the most part the minor ones—"nonpolitical" because little was at stake—in which the justices could develop technical points useful as possible precedents. The Permanent Court could, however, be bold even in matters of major political importance when it knew that the disputants wished to see authority asserted. An instance was the settlement of the long-standing quarrel between Norway and Denmark as to the ownership of Eastern Greenland, vexatious to both countries. The Court found that sovereignty lay with Denmark, and did so partly on the ground that a Norwegian Foreign Minister had conceded the Danish claim in a verbal answer to a question put by the Danish government. "The Court considers it beyond dispute that a reply of this nature given by a Minister of Foreign Affairs on behalf of his Government in response to a request by the diplomatic representative of a foreign power is binding upon the country to which the Minister belongs." That a Foreign Secretary's spoken words were in honor and law to be considered binding was, indeed, an advanced concept in international relations. Lawyers at the time wondered if this ruling would establish a precedent for dealings between foreign ministries.

It was the afternoon of the League, 1932, when the Danish-Norwegian dispute came before the Court; but the disputants were friendly neighbors, both anxious for a settlement. There is a certain contrast between the Court's boldness in this instance and its refusal even to consider the question of the binding force of the written Declaration of the Russian government in the dispute with Finland over the status of Eastern Karelia. Scrupulously and wisely legalistic in the performance of their duties as were the justices, they were not without political sensitivity.

For the layman, the political implication of the group of cases in which the countries that had been victors in the war and the countries that had been losers appeared together before the black-robed judges at The Hague is the significant part of the Court's story. The significance is that these cases were decided by the procedures of peace. There was again a European community. In the first four years of the Court's existence every case that came before it dealt with European problems, most of them with interpretations of the various peace treaties. States that had been wartime enemies paid each other the compliment of accepting the old battlefield adversary as a normal litigant under the law. The Court paid both states the compliment of treating them with equal formality, courtesy, and consideration. When there was no citizen of a contending state on the bench, a national of that country was appointed temporary judge; if necessary, two extra judges were appointed. Dissenting opinions were published—an adoption of the Anglo-Saxon practice which, incidentally, somewhat shocked Continental jurists; even so, the problem of combining the principles and procedures of common law and Roman law turned out to be less formidable than many jurists had feared.

No one can say precisely how many times vanquished and victors appeared together before the Court, for some of the cases came up several times in different form; at least two dozen cases can probably be put in this category. A few may be listed for the pleasure of recalling the last brief era of freedom and peace in Europe.

In the case of the SS *Wimbleton,* brought by the British, French, Italian, and Japanese governments against the German government in 1923, Germany was directed to pay damages for refusing free access of this ship to the Kiel Canal under the terms of the Versailles Treaty. Germany did not contest the Court's jurisdiction and paid the damages.

In interpretations of the reparations clause of the Treaty of Neuilly, resulting from a dispute between Greece and Bulgaria, judgment was rendered in one instance in favor of Greece, in another in favor of Bulgaria.

In three separate cases, too technical for summaries, one between Hungary and Yugoslavia, one between Czechoslovakia and Hungary, and one between Bulgaria and Czechoslovakia, the decision in the first favored Yugoslavia, and the decision in the second favored Hungary. In the third instance Czechoslovakia, which had brought a claim against Bulgaria, withdrew it before a decision was rendered.

A German-owned nitrate factory at Chorzów, expropriated by

Poland, became famous—in textbooks of international law—because the resulting dispute between Germany and Poland came before the Court five times. It involved a significant assertion by the Court of its right to assume jurisdiction, and the case was eventually decided in favor of Germany. So were half a dozen cases involving rights of German minorities in Poland, some decided by way of formal orders and judgments, some by advisory opinions. Poland acquiesced in all instances.

The question of Danzig was before the Court four times in issues complicated by Polish and German nationalisms. In a significant advisory opinion in 1928 the court upheld the jurisdiction of local courts of the Free City of Danzig against a Polish challenge. Eventually, this issue was also brought before the Council of the League of Nations, which was prepared to consider action to enforce the Court's advisory opinion, but the Polish and Danzig governments reached an agreement which made action by the Council unnecessary. A few years later the Nazis were in control in Danzig, the Council of the League was helpless, and the Court's important work was over.

2. Peace through Power

The peace that made possible the growing acceptance of international law by European states in the years of opportunity of the League was established and maintained by international political power. For some years that power was formally represented by the Conference of Ambassadors set up by the Supreme Council of Allied and Associated Powers to supervise the carrying out of the peace treaties; what is more important, it was expressed in the normal diplomatic interchanges of the major governments. The League system was supplementary to this unorganized "concert," but it modified the old procedures and now and again exercised leadership.

The Versailles Treaty did not seek to destroy the unity of Germany, and despite much internal dissention the Reich remained a single state under its republican central government. Though Germany was outside both League and concert, it was certain to enter one and rejoin the other. The question "when?" was the question "on what terms?" That basic issue did not come explicitly before the League for about five years, but it was in the background of every important controversy in which the political agencies of the League were involved. Half a dozen instances may be chosen to indicate what such a political institution as was established at Geneva could usefully do. The episodes are related through the interaction of the old system and the new. The scene, we may note again in rough summary, was a Continent weary of war, after a treaty of peace whose European territorial settlements were in the main reasonable and moderate, but with the major defeated Central Power shocked in disbelief at the fact of defeat and potentially stronger than any combination of Continental states that could be brought against it. The corollary was that maintenance of peace depended upon whether additional enforcement power would continue to come from outside the Continent—in the circumstances, from the British Isles.

UPPER SILESIA

Of particular interest among the political activities of the League of Nations was the part played by the League's Council in the quarrel over the disposition of Upper Silesia. This began as a contest between Germany and Poland and became a more dangerous conflict of policy between Britain and France.

The province of Upper Silesia on the extreme eastern borderland of Europe, with the tangled history of invasion and counterinvasion common to the region, had been snatched from the Empress Maria Theresa of Austria by Frederick the Great of Prussia in the middle of the eighteenth century. It was then populated almost entirely by Poles, though it had not been part of the Kingdom of Poland since the twelfth century. Frederick sought it as a military stronghold for offense or defense against Russia or Austria and because of the deposits of coal and other minerals in its mountains. He retained it by desperate fighting through the Seven Years' War which followed the usurpation. The successful raid marked the beginning of Prussia's rise to the rank of a foremost military power and provided resources for further conquest; after an influx of German settlers and under German management, Upper Silesia became one of the major industrial centers of Europe and a source of about a quarter of Germany's coal. On the eve of the First World War there was a population of more than two million, mostly Germans and Poles, in what proportions no one knew.

To the Poles after the war, possession of this industrial district seemed an issue of life or death for their reborn and economically retarded state. German ability to grant or withhold access to the resources of the area would put Poland at Prussian mercy, economically and strategically, the Poles reasoned. Monopoly control of this Upper Silesian arsenal was essential to Germany if it planned war—but essential only for that purpose, they insisted, pointing to the availability of the coal and iron for normal peacetime trade. Was it not the Allied object in the war just ended to put limits to Prussian expansion? The terms of the Treaty of Brest-Litovsk, from which Eastern Europe and Russia escaped only because of the eleventh-hour appearance of American troops on the western front, revealed the scope of the ambitions of contemporary Germany and the power behind them. It also underscored the strategic relationship of eastern and western fronts. Dimunition of German power in the east was wise and just; transfer of some industrial ingredients of it to Poland was necessary if Poland were to play a role in stabilizing the new Europe.

At the Paris Conference, experts of the American advisory group reasoned as did the Poles. British advisers in the historical section of the Foreign Office shared the view. So did their French and Italian colleagues. The recommendation of the Commission on Polish Affairs was unanimous: Upper Silesia should go to Poland.

In the Council of Four, Clemenceau frankly emphasized the strategic meaning of the issue: Continental and, most definitely, French security required a Poland—and a Czechoslovakia—strong enough to face a resurgent Germany with the risk of a two-front war if Germany advanced east or west. Wilson supported the French Premier and his own advisers, though rather on the ground of fairness to Poland, so long subjugated, for he did not like the vocabulary of "power politics," * and Orlando concurred. Lloyd George, however, dissented strongly, to the confusion of his advisers and to the alarm of Clemenceau.

In a written statement (the so-called Fontainebleau memorandum) the British Prime Minister advanced the principle that the Polish-German frontiers should be determined "irrespective of strategic or transportation considerations"; in other words, territorial decisions in this area should be made solely on ethnic grounds. This was a puzzling pronouncement. As Clemenceau noted, Britain certainly had not disregarded considerations of strategy and transport in making sure that the German fleet would be surrendered into British hands, the German mercantile marine virtually wiped out, and the largest share of the German colonies transferred to the Empire.

* How Upper Silesia figured in Prussian stategic thought and in power politics is suggested by a passage in Bismarck's memoirs referring to a conversation with the King of Prussia at the time of the Crimean War, in which Russia fought France and England:

> During the discussion of the treaty of April 20 [an offensive-defensive alliance between Austria and Prussia, signed in 1854] I proposed to the King to utilise this occasion for raising Prussian policy out of a secondary, and in my opinion unworthy, position; and for assuming an attitude which would have won for us the sympathy of and the lead among those German states which desired, with and through us, to preserve an independent neutrality. I considered this practicable if, when Austria should call upon us to bring up our troops, we should at once acquiesce in a friendly and willing manner; but should station 66,000, and in point of fact more men, and not at Lissa, but in Upper Silesia, so that our troops should be in a position whence they could with equal facility step over the frontier of either Russia or Austria, especially if we did not trouble ourselves about overstepping without saying anything about it, the figure of 100,000. With 200,000 men his Majesty would instantly become the head of the entire European situation, would be able to dictate peace, and to gain a worthy place for Prussia in Germany.

(*Bismarck, the Man and the Statesman: Reflections and Reminiscences* [New York: Harper, 1899], Vol. I, pp. 106, 108.)

This incident occurred during Bismarck's most headstrong, early days, and the King of Prussia rejected this particular advice, with the reply, "My dear boy, that is all very fine, but it is too expensive for me."

The dismay of the French and the Poles was profound and genuine, and Lloyd George's further explanation had an even more ominous sound. He observed that the danger in Europe no longer lay in the likelihood of renewed German expansion, but in attacks on a weakened Germany by her neighbors. Was this a signal for a British effort to ensure stability on the Continent by moving away from France and toward Germany?

That is how it was to turn out, in the most disastrous misjudgment of Continental forces that British statesmen ever made. But Lloyd George's memorandum was a signal only, not a settled policy. Settled policies were not Lloyd George's specialty. Throughout the conference, as in his whole career, he improvised, with the genius that led him in all directions from greatness to chicanery. He had wisely dissuaded the French from their design to annex the Rhineland, perceiving that France could not hope to hold this indisputably German territory, and the compensating suggestion for a joint American-British alliance with France, so distasteful to Wilson, originated with him. He did not wish to trample a beaten foe and he had the humane, if sometimes shortsighted, island instinct to get on with the healing business of trade. Yet he stood triumphantly for re-election on the degrading slogan, "Hang the Kaiser." He was never far out of touch with the British mood, but he manipulated it to his partisan advantage; and he was singular in the rapidity with which his own mood changed. Small wonder that everyone was puzzled by his moves, including the Germans, who came to believe that Britain was firmly behind them on the Upper Silesian issue.

The controversy was to swirl for two years more before it reached the League of Nations. The complexity of the problem highlights the League's constructive achievement. Neither Wilson nor Orlando was swayed by the Fontainebleau memorandum, and the Treaty of Versailles provided for the cession of Upper Silesia to Poland. However, when Count von Brockdorff-Rantzau, chief of the German delegation sent to Versailles to receive the terms of peace, protested against this part of the settlement with extreme vehemence, Lloyd George insisted that the decision be reconsidered. He suggested a plebiscite in the area as a compromise.

German reasoning about Upper Silesia ran diametrically opposite to Polish reasoning. Germans reminded themselves that their revered ancestor whose voice spoke from the grave was, by an uncontested verdict of history, "the Great." How could he be disowned? How could the clock be set back? By what reckoning, moreover, was Frederick's conquest of an Austrian province an injustice to Poland, to be righted six hundred years after Upper Silesia had ceased to be part of a Polish state? Moreover, what injustice for Germany to be deprived of these resources just as it was presented with a huge bill for reparations after a lost war!

These were normal reactions to the painful fact of the loss of a degree of power; but the Germans were driven to total intransigence—we must again unhappily note—by the imagined degradation of losing power to "uncivilized" Poles, as Brockdorff-Rantzau insultingly described them in his formal, public reply. The sum of this unmeasured hostility to the reborn Polish state by the emissary of the Weimar Republic amounted to insistence that Polish national life, which had been forcibly suppressed, should never exist again. It was evident that though concessions in regard to Upper Silesia might help the German people and their new leaders accustom themselves to the actuality of a Poland, any "compromise" would certainly have to be imposed on both sides and maintained for some time by power superior to German power.

After angry argument in the Council of Four between Lloyd George, as champion of Germany, and Clemenceau, as champion of Poland, Wilson changed his position for the sake of peace between the two major allies. The Treaty was amended to provide for a plebiscite in Upper Silesia, Clemenceau agreeing with great reluctance. As amended, the Treaty specified that voting in the plebiscite would be by communes and that geographical and economic factors would also be taken into account in the final award. Every man or woman over the age of twenty residing in Upper Silesia was eligible to vote, and all who had been born there and moved away might, if they wished, return to cast their ballots. Two adjacent areas, not strictly part of Upper Silesia and not claimed by Poland, were included in the plebiscite area. The plebiscite was to be held within eighteen months of the ratification of the Treaty by Germany; it was hoped that the postponement would permit orderly voting. German troops were to be withdrawn and replaced by Allied contingents, and a new Commission was appointed to supervise the election.

The danger of a resort to plebiscite for the settlement of territorial disputes, in which emotions are inflamed and the margin is likely to be narrow, is that both sides seek forcibly to anticipate the verdict; the intensity of the contest renders acceptance of the settlement more difficult. The period of declared uncertainty in Upper Silesia brought every kind of pressure, economic, financial, and military, upon Poles and Germans within the plebiscite area and outside it. Since the future of all Europe would be affected by the outcome, the plebiscite became the central issue of European politics, and rivalries came close to getting out of hand.

When the Allied troops arrived—mainly French, with some British and fewer Italians—disorders in the province gradually subsided. The plebiscite, held in March 1921, was conducted in an orderly manner, and an astonishing 97 per cent of adult Upper Silesians went to the polls to cast secret ballots. But this was the calm before the storm, for the results were anything but clear, as was inevitable under the terms of the French-British compromise.

By totals the vote was 707,605 for Germany, 479,369 for Poland—56 per cent as against 40 per cent. This was a sizable margin, but it had been gained mainly by an outpouring of Germans who had been born in the province and moved away; a campaign to get them to the polls had brought 180,000 to Upper Silesia for the day. Polish "outvoters" numbered only 10,000. The populations of Neustadt and Leobschütz, outside Upper Silesia, added 90,000 German votes to the total, but only 5000 Polish. The votes of people actually living in Upper Silesia were divided nearly fifty-fifty, the advantage slightly with Germany.

There was no question of the validity of the ballots cast by the outvoters, which weighted the plebiscite in the German favor. But the terms of the Treaty as amended provided that the vote should be counted by communes. This could mean nothing but partition. The communal vote in the northwest revealed a clear German majority of four to one, and in the south a Polish majority of two to one. The center zone returned five to four for Poland, and the mining and manufacturing district—the so-called industrial triangle—five to four for Germany. Where would the line be drawn?

The deadlock now became menacing. The German press and people, who had convinced themselves that the stipulation for a vote by communes was irrelevant, demanded Upper Silesia in entirety and the government pledged itself to resign if any part of the area were severed from the Reich. Lloyd George, reinterpreting his compromise with Clemenceau to suit his mood, called the result "overwhelming" and supported Germany in strong language in the House of Commons. The statesmen's quarrel was now a public feud. Under refurbished slogans, parliamentarians and sections of the press in Britain and France resumed the old sport of cross-channel baiting that they had denied themselves for a number of years—"Back to Prosperity and Down with French Hegemony," "For Security and Against British Selfishness"; and other spirited war cries even less polite. In Upper Silesia, French and British members of the Commission meeting to draw a line of partition found twenty miles of deep water between them. So did the French and British representatives on the Surpeme Council in Paris.

The Polish contribution to a solution was a revolt in Upper Silesia and seizure of points of vantage for a showdown with force. The commander of the French occupation troops turned his back on the uprising; and the excited British Prime Minister brought the confusion to a climax by proposing that the German army be directed to re-enter the area and subdue the Poles. This would have meant the resumption of the war, and no party to the quarrel stood to gain by that, least of all Germany, which if it renounced the Treaty of Versailles, risked cancellation of the enormous, fundamental concession of the Armistice—the unity of the German state. The German government massed regular troops on the Upper Silesian border, but contented itself with the infusion of "volunteers." These *Freikorps* were better trained and armed than the Polish irregulars and, after sharp scrimmaging, dislodged them. British and French troops held aloof lest they find themselves firing on each other, but Italians were killed in efforts to restore Allied control. Then everyone paused, as if by signal.

What happened next was so logical that it was foreseen by no one. The riven concert of the powers passed the problem on to the larger and more formal organization it had recently created. As F. P. Walters relates, "When the journalists, waiting outside the Quai d'Orsay in the expectation of some dramatic break between France and Britain, were told that Briand (who had succeeded Clemenceau as Premier) and Lloyd George had agreed to appeal to the League, they broke into incredulous laughter." [4] But the Council of the League (itself somewhat incredulous at this development) brought order out of chaos within six weeks.

The move that insured success was taken before the dispute was submitted to the Council. It was a pledge by Britain and France—made, of course, behind the scenes—to accept the League's decision in advance. A. J. Balfour was probably mainly responsible for it, with essential help from Léon Bourgeois. Balfour was British representative on the League Council and, as former Prime Minister and leader of the Conservative Party, very influential in Lloyd George's coalition government. When Balfour chose to act he was as steady as Lloyd George was erratic, and he knew far more about European politics than Lloyd George's Foreign Secretary, the hapless Lord Curzon, former Viceroy of India. Balfour knew that Britain and France had divergent interests on the Continent but were not enemies: the nonsense had gone far enough.

The League succeeded where the concert had failed because the grant of full political power enabled it to call in impartial economic experts, under the chairmanship of a Swiss engineer. This Commission reported that partition of the industrial complex was economically feasible. It suggested a line of division through the two zones in which the communal vote was close, linking German and Polish sectors with the zones where the plebiscite had shown clear ethnic majorities. It supplemented this proposal with a detailed scheme for the continued operation of the industrial area as an economic unit, crossing the national frontiers—in effect, a steel and coal community, a "Schuman Plan"—forty years ahead of time.

But was this plan ahead of its time? It was, in fact, adopted by the League and ratified by the Supreme Council of the Allied Powers. Neither the Poles nor the Germans received as much territory as they wanted, and the German Cabinet did resign, with angry words for everyone, the League of Nations especially. But Chancellor Joseph Wirth reconstituted his Cabinet within a few days, and German industrialists came forward, under League auspices, to help negotiate with the Poles an elaborate convention of more than six hundred clauses to implement the plan. One provision was the guarantee of German access to coal in the Polish sector without import duties.

For fifteen years the area was administered as an economic unit under a League Commission and prospered. During the Depression it operated more effectively than any other major industrial area in Europe. Most of the factories remained under German management; others were ably managed by Poles. There was always more coal available than Germany used.

The precious gift of time for Germans and Poles to practice cooperation ran out in 1937, when the fifteen-year agreement expired. In the circumstances then prevailing there was no possibility of renewal. After the next war Stalin decreed that all Upper Silesia should go to Poland, but all Poland was captive.

THE FRONTIERS OF ALBANIA

While the League of Nations was seeking to untie the Upper Silesian knot, it was drawn into a dispute over the frontiers of Albania. By comparison the episode is only a footnote in the League's story, but it holds some prophetic lines.

The German prince whom the prewar concert of six powers, in its final effort of peace-keeping at London in 1913, established on the Albanian throne sagaciously fled the country a month after the declarations of war in 1914. Albanian independence and frontiers alike became fictions. A defeated Serbian army took refuge in the northern mountains and stayed. A secret pact signed in 1915, under British auspices, by Serbia, Montenegro, and Greece provided for partition of the country among them but was later annulled. Another secret treaty in London gave Italy the port of Valona, and in 1917 Italy declared Albania a protectorate and sent in troops. The Albanians fought Serbs, Montenegrins, Greeks, and Italians with impartial enthusiasm and with sufficient success to cause the Italian government to withdraw its infantry from the free-for-all, though it kept a wary eye on the goings-on.

Economically the land was not worth all the attention, the tangle of peaks and gorges of the North Albanian Alps being among the wildest in Europe and the coastal swamps and abutting wastelands —ruined by deforestation and grazing goats—among the most dismal. Charming valleys yielded a subsistence agriculture, with a little left over—or subtracted—for trade. The million or so inhabitants were a collection of clans, many of them living in a prefeudal social relationship and fragmented further by religious rivalries— Catholic, Moslem, and Greek Orthodox. Pleased enough to fight one another when no more interesting enemy offered, the tribesmen were, nonetheless, fiercely aware that they wanted no foreign ruler. But the two-hundred-mile coast lay around the Gulf of Otranto, off the heel of the Italian peninsula, commanding the Adriatic Sea on the north and the Ionian Sea on the south, and with ports susceptible of development as railheads for Balkan commerce. Nature, taking with one hand but bestowing with the other, had made the strip of land a prize.

In 1920 an assemblage of Albanians sent emissaries to Geneva to ask membership in the League of Nations. Under the Covenant, the admission of new members was entirely in the hands of the Assembly, with a two-thirds majority required for election. Fifteen states, or areas which hoped to be nation-states, offered themselves as candidates. Of them, this first Assembly rejected, or held over, eight: Azerbaijan, the Ukraine, Georgia, Armenia, Latvia, Estonia, Lithuania, and Liechtenstein. The first two of these had, in fact, already been reconquered by Russia, and Georgia and Armenia were soon to be reabsorbed, the former by Russia, the latter by Russia and Turkey. Liechtenstein, with a population of two hundred thousand, was rejected as too small; the three Baltic states were asked to wait. (They were voted in the following year.) An application by Montenegro was not considered. Six candidates were accepted: Austria, Bulgaria, Luxembourg, Costa Rica, Finland, and Albania.

The quick acceptance of Albania was the questionable action. No one knew what or where the frontiers of Albania were, or, indeed, how to reach unmapped parts of the territory that had thus been put under League protection. The question of the frontiers was the responsibility of the Conference of Ambassadors, authorized by the Treaty of Versailles to complete the postwar territorial settlements. The League had no legal power to draw the boundaries and no physical power to eject the Yugoslavs and Greeks from the mountains and valleys, since it lacked a specific grant of authority from members prepared to send soldiers for the purpose. The Assembly had put the cart before the horse. Further progress could be made only by backing up, and this the League did. It dispatched a message requesting the Ambassadors to hasten their decision.

When the second Assembly met in September 1921 no decision about the frontiers had been forthcoming, however. The Assembly, with Lord Robert Cecil as prime mover, then reached for a lever of power. It was a new one in world politics—the power of institutionalized democratic propaganda. Wilson and Cecil had fashioned it, in the Covenant, when they instructed the representatives of the nation-states—one nation, one vote—to "deal with" any matter "within the sphere of action of the League and the peace of the world." The representatives had smoothed the lever to their hands by the decision to meet in annual Assemblies instead of at intervals of several years, as was expected by the architects of the Covenant. And the Assembly tipped the new lever directly under the source of great-power strength in the League itself by dealing with the formal reports of the Council as material for their democratic approval or disapproval. Perforce, the delegates of the powers had to explain and defend. That made for interesting reading, as spread abroad by the new means of communication, which were improving with lightning speed—in contrast to conditions in Albania, for example.

Lord Robert Cecil used the occasion for a dramatic denunciation of the wicked ways of the powers, his own country included. The Ambassadors were bargaining secretly, he said indignantly. "We have no right to play with the lives and happiness of the peoples in order to serve the methods of old-world diplomacy." The Assembly, with which Cecil had much influence, as he had also with the large body of supporters of the League idea at home, echoed his indignation at the dilatory Ambassadors. There had been sufficient schemes for carving up Albania (as there were to be in the future) to give the charge carrying power, though neither Britain nor France sought any of this rocky terrain. Their problem was an accommodation between Yugoslav and Italian rivalries, and behind that the question of policies toward Germany and her former allies, to which every political issue, new and old, inescapably led. The Ambassadors were also aware of the sharp edge of the local problem that Cecil's oratory rounded off. When their hands traced these frontiers, they would not be brushing an abstraction called "the peoples"; they would be touching Albanians where they lived. Neither Europe nor language itself could offer a more pointed illustration of the difference between the general and the particular.

But the concert took in good part the League's admonition to grasp the nettle, and announced a decision. The frontiers would, in the main, be the frontiers as understood in 1913; survey parties would be sent to define them where they were unmarked. Slight rectifications in the north were announced to please the Yugoslavs. The award also included a balancing statement that preservation of Albania's territorial integrity was essential for Italy's security. All of this, including the ambiguous suggestion of an Italian protectorate, was about as expected—and all that could be expected, given the nature of the problem.

The conclusion of the award (or bargain) was, however, punctuated by an unforeseen exclamation point. One day before the decision was formally made public, the Secretary-General of the League received a telegram, signed with David Lloyd George's name, demanding an immediate meeting of the Council of the League of Nations for the imposition of economic sanctions on Yugoslavia if Yugoslav soldiers were not instantly withdrawn from Albania. The surprised Secretary-General dispatched his notices to the Council members informing them of this communication, and the members duly responded. It took ten days for all to come together. But even before that, the Yugoslavs were on their proper side of the frontier, and the sensation was over.

The background of Lloyd George's action remains obscure. It was said that he had evidence that the Yugoslavs were planning a military offensive, aimed perhaps at the small city of Scutari. Yugoslavia certainly wanted the port and was disappointed in the terms of the settlement. That the League would have, or could have, set the machinery of Article 16 in motion so haphazardly is much to be doubted; nevertheless, whether or not the bluff was needed, it worked. Most interesting of all was the evidence that the new lever of power at Geneva could be manipulated from the abode of the great powers on the Council as well as by the smaller states of the Assembly and that minds less idealistic than Lord Robert Cecil's had taken note of its availability for their purposes.

CORFU

The Albanian frontiers provided dramatic news again in August 1923, though this time only as a backdrop for a new actor on the European stage—Benito Mussolini, who had established his Fascist dictatorship some ten months earlier. His bombardment and occupation of the Greek island of Corfu in reprisal for the assassination, on Greek soil, of General Tellini and his staff, Italian members of the Boundary Commission, was a gesture of contempt for the principles of the League. The outcome was not, however, the disgrace for the League or the triumph for Mussolini that it is commonly supposed to have been.

The unlucky Italian commissioner, his interpreter, and two other assistants were carrying out the hazardous task of marking an Albanian-Greek boundary, as instructed by the Conference of Ambassadors. They were ambushed while motoring some twenty-five miles beyond the line, on a road running through indisputably Greek territory. The murderers were never identified.

Whether the crime had a political motive or was an act of routine banditry, the Greek government was in principle accountable. The Conference of Ambassadors immediately asked for an investigation, punishment of the criminals, and compensation for the families of the victims. The Duce, however, could not forgo the opportunity to get into the act. Before the Athens government could reply he dispatched an ultimatum demanding apologies, giving Greece five days to find the murderers, and setting the sum of fifty million lire (the equivalent of perhaps of two million five hundred thousand dollars) as reparation, to be paid directly to the Italian government.

The Greek replies to both the Conference of Ambassadors and Mussolini were apologetic. The regrets were certainly sincere, for Greece was in a miserable predicament, the impotence of Greek police in this wild area of Northern Epirus being matched by the weakness of the Greek army and of the state itself—a result of the recent collapse of a reckless effort of conquest in Turkey. But the notes were equivocal, disavowing responsibility for the crime and, in effect, asking the Conference of Ambassadors to solve the mystery by catching the criminals. The search for them should take place on both sides of the Greek-Albanian frontier, the Greek government suggested.

Mussolini's response was the military occupation of undefended Corfu, preceded by a senseless shelling of medieval fortifications in the harbor, in the course of which civilians were killed. This disproportionate reprisal created the sympathy for Greece, among all the small nations of Europe, that had hitherto been lacking. Greece renewed the appeal to the Ambassadors and asked for justice from the League. The Italian dictator, having gained the attention he desired, shouted his defiance: if the League interfered, he would withdraw Italian membership.

It is revealing, however, that Mussolini at once qualified his belligerence by stating that the punitive action was not intended as a declaration of war. By granting that a solution lay within the competence of the Conference of Ambassadors he also, in effect, canceled his ultimatum. Willingness to accept such mediation prevented a Greek appeal to Article 15 of the Covenant, from which sanctions could follow, and though the brutal Italian action was certainly sufficient to warrant discussion of the episode under Article 11—the principle of concern—the Council of the League was content to leave the problem in the hands of the Ambassadors. It refused, in particular, to recommend the case to the attention of the Court. International law on the subject of reprisal was—and still is —vague to nonexistent, and though in theory it would have been opportune to use the episode as a means of illuminating the cloudy question with some clear legal principles, the plainest aspect of the affray was that every ramification of it was sensitively political.

The Assembly of the League, in session at the time, was far from content with what many members considered an abdication of the League's political responsibilities, but it withheld debate. The restraint of leaders of the Assembly, such as Eduard Beneš of

Czechoslovakia and Paul Hymans of Belgium, stemmed in part from the alarming possibility that here was another Sarajevo: if it were, verbal castigation of offenders might well wait upon a clearer understanding of what the next step would be. And, indeed, the terms of a solution were obviously the responsibility of the Conference of Ambassadors, as Greece had acknowledged by her initial appeal to this agency of the concert, which would cease to exist as a formal body when it had completed the tasks assigned to it under the Versailles Treaty and its unenviable role as demarcator of boundaries was nearly played out. There was little point in an effort by the new Geneva organization to challenge its competence on grounds that could scarcely be sustained. The new lever of power to Geneva—the appeal to "opinion"—was, however, power in reserve. The possibility that the Assembly would use it exerted an influence throughout the episode.

Quickly it became apparent that Balkan disorders of the 1920s did not follow the pattern of 1914. The assassination was not the signal for a desperate confrontation of great powers. Bolshevik Russia showed no interest in the affair, and there was no nervous and imperious Austria-Hungary to be affected. Such confrontation of powers as there was in August 1923 lay in the Ruhr; that, not the Balkans, was now the supersensitive area. There, disarmed Germany, in the throes of its cold war with France over reparations, was using the weapons of passive resistance, which included the deliberate destruction of its own currency. Mussolini's intervention in the Balkans was a great embarassment for France, for, however legal or illegal it might be interpreted to be, it was malodorous behavior. By the end of August 1923 it was evident that France was winning the contest of wills with Germany, but the terms of a settlement were altogether obscure. As in the Upper Silesian quarrel, Britain had separated itself from France and was occupying a position of ostensible neutrality between French and German policies. That again, in effect, brought Britain down on the German side and encouraged German resistance. On the Reparation Committee, Belgium voted with France; Britain stood in opposition to the two allies. The vote of the Italian representative, the fourth member of the Commission, could thus be decisive in a settlement.

Mussolini was very well aware of this split between France and Britain on the future of Germany and the fate of the Versailles Treaty. But once more, as in the Upper Silesian quarrel, it was a break between friends, not a clash of enemies. Mussolini strutted through the gap but retreated when it was closed.

It was closed, so far as Corfu was concerned, when Mussolini, emboldened by the support he was receiving from France within the Conference of Ambassadors, intimated in a press campaign that Italy would resuscitate the ancient claims to Corfu of the Venetian Republic and would maintain the occupation of the island. This projection of an Italian military base at the foot of the Adriatic was aimed not merely at Greece but even more directly at Yugoslavia, whose existence no Italian government had yet fully accepted. The nations of the so-called Little Entente—Yugoslavia, Czechoslovakia, and Rumania—and Belgium as well, all close allies of France, were now truly alarmed at Italian pretentions and besought France to call a halt to the Fascist adventurer. France perceived the danger and a common French-British position was achieved within the Conference of Ambassadors.

In the upshot, the Ambassadors ruled that reparation should be paid to the Italian government in the amount demanded by Mussolini. Other demands of the Italian ultimatum were dropped, and Mussolini withdrew his expedition from Corfu. Significantly, he then backed away from the quarrel he had been pressing with Yugoslavia over an unratified commercial treaty. The ensuing accord left Italy in possession of the disputed city of Fiume but gave Yugoslavia the trade relations with Italy essential to its economic development. To the relief of the Yugoslav government, Mussolini also discontinued efforts in Rome to stir up trouble among foreign elements, particularly Montenegrin exiles, unreconciled to the Kingdom of the Serbs, Croats, and Slovenes.

The fundamental lesson of the unsavory episode was that, though the Fascist Caesar could be expected to seek to profit from any French-British division on the German question, he would remain within bounds if that problem were in hand. The League had been warned that it must be prepared to withstand a measure of ill will from an important member. There could be no answer to the abstract question, "How much ill will could the League endure?" Whatever collective security might turn out to mean in practice, it would almost certainly never mean a unanimous response by all members in any serious crisis. But when France and Britain worked together the League could survive and prosper.

MOSUL

Paradoxically, an adverse decision by the Council of the League, in December 1925, on the Turkish claim to the province of Mosul, for centuries part of the Ottoman Empire, signaled the accession of Mustapha Kemal's revolutionary Turkey to the European society. Whether the decision was just or unjust remains an unanswerable question, but the settlement endured, and the Republic of Turkey became a force for stability and peace in the Balkans and the Near East. This was perhaps the most constructive major political development of the League's years, and certainly the most surprising.

No one foresaw the exceptional nature and objectives of the Kemalist revolution until events disclosed them. When the armies of the Sultan surrendered unconditionally in 1918, it seemed unmistakable that Turkey, the "sick man of Europe," had at length died. No one grieved. As Ernst Jäckh, former Carnegie Professor at Columbia University, a perceptive German student of the old and the new Turkey, has said, "The very name [Turk] had been a byword of dread or of contempt among the civilized nations of the West." [5] The Ottoman Empire was a synonym for corruption and for misrule of subject peoples. The Turks themselves were a subjugated people, legally members of the "slave household" of the Sultan, possessing no family names. The Anatolian peasants, hardy, loyal, brave, illiterate, and abominably mistreated, were the core of Turkish military power. They could not know their own possibilities until the word "Turk" was given a new meaning.

Mustapha Kemal Atatürk—"father of the Turks"—accomplished this political and educational miracle. He was one of the Young Turk army officers of the reform movement of 1908 which had overthrown the "unspeakable Turk," the Sultan Abdul Hamid, and had shown himself a resourceful fighter and a commanding leader in the defense of the Gallipoli Peninsula in the First World War. The Young Turks were, however, imperialists, seeking governmental reform for the purpose of maintaining Ottoman conquests. Yet Kemal was to lead a revolution in Anatolia, marked by the abolition of the caliphate (along with the symbol of Ottoman nationality, the fez), secularization of the state, the emancipation of Turkish women, and adoption of western dress, the Latin alphabet, and the Swiss civil code, that brought Turkey surging into the modern world. That such a Republic of Turkey would, moreover, accept the limits of the Turkish homeland as the essential bounds of the territorial ambitions of the revitalized nation could have been perceived in 1920 only by statesmen with clairvoyant powers.

The Treaty of Sèvres, imposed by the Allies on the government of the Sultan in 1920, was conceived with perfect naturalness, if uncommon unwisdom. It was intended to achieve an effect that the Treaty of Versailles with Germany never envisaged save in the minds of those who created the myth of its iniquity—dismemberment and destruction of the defeated enemy state. There had been four secret wartime treaties among the Allies for division of the sick man's estate after his death. The first of these, sardonically divulged and renounced by the Bolshevik government, promised Constantinople and the Straits to Russia. Other agreements gave zones of influence and colonies in Anatolia to Britain, Italy, France, and Greece. Sèvres was an amalgam of these arrangements, and of others covering the disposition of the Arab provinces of the Ottoman Empire. Istanbul (Constantinople), the Dardanelles, and an adjacent area around the Straits were to be "internationalized" and occupied by Allied troops. There would be a puppet government under the Caliph in Istanbul, but no Turkish representative on the governing Allied Commission. There was to be an Armenian state, and a "Kurdistan" formed of the wild, nomadic tribes of the borderland mountains along southeastern Anatolia—"Albanians," as it were, only more so—a device for driving a splitting wedge into Turkey. The corner of Anatolia that was to be left to Turkey would be under occupation and rigid tutelage, which included complete control of economic, financial, and legal institutions.

This was, indeed, a vengeful peace. Yet even the relatively disinterested American King-Crane Commission, sent to the area by President Wilson to study and report, could perceive no future for the Turks consonant with "order, peace and development" other than an indefinitely long period of tutelage. This commission proposed that the United States assume the responsibility for the future of the Turks, under a League mandate which would include Palestine and Armenia; as an alternative, it recommended Britain as mandatory power. When the idea of such an American mandate dissolved, Britain refused the honor; but Lloyd George then rashly chose Greece as an instrument of British policy in Anatolia.

Kemal's nationalists shattered all this with rough blows, aided with arms supplied by the Soviet Union, which saw in Turkish nationalism, intolerant of Communism as it was at home, much the lesser evil at the Dardanelles. Italy and France, perceiving the impracticality of an enforcement of their paper claims against the resurgent Turks, made separate arrangements and withdrew their troops from Anatolia. But the Greeks, urged on by Britain, plunged from Smyrna (Ismir) into the interior of Anatolia.They were repulsed and driven into the sea. When Kemal and his lieutenant, General Ismet Inönü, turned with their army toward Istanbul, where a British fleet was in the harbor and a ring of British troops lay around the city, war with Britain seemed imminent; astounded Dominion governments around the world received telegrams from London requesting them to send reinforcements for the second round against the Turks. The telegrams, however, did not herald the beginning of war but the end of Sèvres and of Lloyd George's policy. The British coalition government fell, and Britain and Turkey turned to negotiation at Lausanne.

The outcome of the negotiations was a new treaty of peace, signed by seven of the Allied Powers with the Republic of Turkey on July 24, 1923. Supplementary conventions provided for freedom of transit through the Straits for all nations and full jurisdiction for Turkish courts. No more was heard of partition and tutelage, or of occupation of the Straits. Though Kemal had begun to build a new capital at Ankara on the Anatolian plateau, symbol and safeguard of the reorientation of the new nation he had created, the new treaty restored Istanbul to Turkey, along with the European region of Eastern Thrace, north of the Sea of Marmora to the Maritsa River, desired by Greece. (This area provides a protective belt for the Straits and was to be of incalculable value, in Turkish hands, for the protection of the Near East against the Axis Powers.) The formerly Ottoman area of Western Thrace was ceded to Greece, and Turks and Greeks made their own peace, which included a large-scale exchange of nationals—Greeks in Turkey and Turks in Greece—and a Turkish indemnity to Greece for damage to Greek property in Smyrna, a far-sighted act of conciliation. These concessions and arrangements marked the beginning of a fruitful period of cooperation between the two ancient enemies.

At Lausanne, skillful Turkish negotiations were, as General Inönü has written, "accommodating on matters that could be postponed." [6] Such items of unfinished business were, in particular, a provision barring fortification of the Straits and Turkish acceptance of the retention of the city and hinterland of Alexandretta (Hatay) on the Mediterranean by the French, as part of the French Syrian mandate. The Turks, confident of their own peaceful intentions, knew that time—and European self-interest—could be counted on to correct both encroachments on Turkish sovereignty. As it turned out, restrictions on fortification of the Straits were removed in negotiations among the signatories of the Lausanne Treaty at the Conference of Montreux in 1936, and France met Turkish wishes at Alexandretta in 1939, on the eve of the Second World War.

The pledge of Turkish good faith at Lausanne and of the revolutionary change in the concept of Turkish self-interest was the complete renunciation of any claim to the vast Arab possessions of the old Empire. Complete, that is, with one exception—the Ottoman province of Mosul, on the southeastern boundary of Anatolia, populated by some eight hundred thousand Arabs, Turks, and Kurds. Mosul was rich in oil. For this and other reasons, Turkey wanted it very much.

Under the Treaty of Sèvres, Mosul had been incorporated in the new state of Iraq (Mesopotamia). Since Britain was mandatory power for Iraq under an "A" mandate—that is, until Iraq was "able to stand alone"—the contending parties were Turkey and Britain. In August 1924 the case was referred to the Council of the League, as provided by an article in the new treaty, after further negotiations between Britain and Turkey had proved futile. British troops occupied most of the contested area, and it was evident that, in contrast with Britain's uncertain response to the Kemalist challenge at the Straits, the British government intended to stand its ground. Concessions for undeveloped oil resources in the region were held by a British consortium (in which, at the insistence of the United States, Americans had been allowed a minority interest when the new state of Iraq was created). Even so, there was more to the problem of the conflicting claims to Mosul than a scramble for oil. Mosul was the area of the desert war, wrested, and, in truth, rescued from Turkish misgovernment by Britons and Arabs. Britain was aware of obligations and responsibilities, aware that in Arab minds the mandate system was a sad anticlimax to wartime hopes, and aware also that events had not as yet demonstrated the pacific intentions of this revitalized Turkey but, on the contrary, its ability to fight back against its enemies. Mosul in Turkish hands could be a tempting springboard for the reconquest of Mesopotamia, where there was much more oil and a virtually defenseless government. Lord Curzon, as chairman of the conference, had, reasonably enough, stressed this aspect of the question at Lausanne.[7]

With British troops occupying most of the contested area and the state of Iraq an actuality, Turkey could hope to repossess the entire province only by reopening the desert war against the Arabs and Britons. Since much else had been salvaged quickly from the wreckage of 1920, that obviously was not in Turkey's interest. What the Council of the League had to determine was where the boundary of a divided Mosul would be drawn. Underlying both that decision and an advisory opinion of the Court which facilitated it was the question whether both Turkey and Britain had agreed, when submitting the dispute to the League, to accept the verdict of the Council. Britain had plainly given that advance assurance. Turkey seemed also to have pledged itself, by signing the treaty of which Article 3 specified submission of the dispute to the League. Statements by various Turkish representatives in the course of negotiations at Lausanne were, however, ambiguous in this regard, and it was evident that Turkey expected to get more than it finally received.

Even so, Turkish behavior was correct throughout the heated wrangle. As soon as the question of the location of a boundary was put before the Council, warmth was, of course, intensified on both sides of the barbed wire that separated Iraqis and British from Turks in the area. Each sought to anticipate the verdict by seizing more ground, and there was a crisis. An emergency meeting of Council members at Brussels called upon both sides to accept the line upon which they stood as a temporary boundary; both acquiesced, and the scrimmaging stopped. The Council thereupon appointed an impartial commission, headed by Count Paul Teleki, who had been a Prime Minister of the former enemy state of Hungary, to investigate, with special attention to the wishes of the inhabitants of the area.

The final term of the instructions was a counsel of perfection. The Arabs and Turks hated one another. The Kurds, estimates of whose numbers ran from a third to half of the population, hated both. A plebiscite among these illiterate and roving people was out of the question; they would have voted with their guns. Should the Kurds nonetheless be counted as Turks? Turks insisted that the Kurds certainly were Turkish nationals, a claim very important to Turkey in principle and practice, since there were perhaps one million more Kurds in Anatolia, the restless element in an otherwise homogeneous population. The Kurds had retained ethnic purity through Xenophon's march across their lands in 400 B.C. and ever since, and they had their own language. Once, in the tenth century, there had been a Kurdish kingdom but it lasted only during the lifetime of the chief who established it. Moreover, the Kurds spilled down into Iraq almost to Baghdad, over into neighboring Iran, and westward into Syria—a mobile and turbulent minority, noted for "a prediliction for shooting at moving objects," as Professor Westermann has said.[8] The principle of "historical rights" offered no help in the problem of drawing a boundary in Mosul.

Count Teleki, a distinguished geographer as well as statesman, sought counsel from an American who had wrestled with such problems as a field man for Woodrow Wilson—the now legendary Archibald Cary Coolidge of Harvard. Professor Coolidge gave a sage, if general, answer: "In practice one has to make such a compromise of conflicting considerations as one best can and hope for luck on the outcome." [9] That is about what the commission did. It suggested that the temporary boundary might well be made permanent, for lack of a better; and so the Council of the League decided. The virtue of the decision was that it was plain. It gave the Turks about ten per cent of the oil of Mosul and deprived them of the Kurds—not too bad a bargain, since Anatolia had oil, and an ample supply of Kurds, of its own. The Council also denied to Britain (and Iraq) a further slice of Mosul that they had sought for added strategic protection from Turkish efforts at reconquest— quite unneeded protection, as things luckily turned out.

The Council's decision was interrupted by a noteworthy advisory opinion by the Permanent Court. Though the appeal to the Court was made by Britain, it was, in effect, a final effort by Turkey to escape, through a technicality, from an adverse ruling. The Court was asked to answer two prosaic queries:

> (1) What is the character of the decision to be taken by the Council in virtue of Article 3, Paragraph 2, of the Treaty of Lausanne? Is it, for example, an arbitral award, a recommendation, or a simple mediation?
>
> (2) Must the decision be unanimous, or may it be taken by a majority? May the representatives of the interested parties take part in the vote?

The Court's answers to the two questions were severely, indeed abstrusely, technical. In their advisory opinion, the justices declined to characterize the decision of the Council as an arbitral award or a "recommendation," as the term was used in Section 4, Article 15 of the Covenant. Were it either of these, it might have been taken by a majority vote of the members of the Council—(among them, in this instance, a representative of Turkey, although the Republic of Turkey was not a member of the League).

The decision, the Court declared, was simply a "decision"; the case stood by itself. Under the provisions of the Treaty of Lausanne and Article 15 of the Covenant it was, however, something more than that, the Court continued: it would be a "binding" decision, despite a Turkish vote against it. Though in such a body as the Council—composed of "persons delegated by their respective governments, from whom they receive instructions and whose responsibility they engage"—observance of the rule of unanimity was "naturally and even necessarily indicated," the justices explained, it was not so in this instance. Section 7 of Article 15 permitted an exception; the rule of unanimity did not require the assent of parties to a dispute. Thus representatives of both Turkey and Britain might vote, but their votes would not be counted. That is to say, Iraq, represented by Britain, and not Turkey, would have Mosul.

It was a very interesting judicial opinion, following a line of reasoning along curves that caused eyebrows to be raised among lawyers. But what was even more interesting, for present purposes, is the fact that Kemal's government acquiesced. It did so reluctantly; but the dispute was ended and eventually Turkey applied, successfully, for admission to the League. Thus the Court registered the dramatic extension of the community to include the Turks, the ancient enemy of Christian Europe, and by this act of witness helped create a new community.

And thus the League of Nations recorded an instance of "peaceful change" under the Covenant, though Article 19, which empowered the Assembly to take the lead in the reconsideration of inapplicable treaties, was never invoked and had no bearing on events. It could have had no bearing, since no general clause of any covenant, charter, or treaty could have fitted the particulars of the case. Kemal used force to gain a negotiated peace, but in negotiations he accepted limits. That is why the peace endured. This extraordinary dictator did not get what he wanted in Mosul, but his acceptance of territorial limitations, as defined by Court and Council, brought him what he wanted even more than territory and oil. That was the opportunity to turn his back on frontiers and travel through the villages of Anatolia, a blackboard under his arm and a piece of chalk in hand, to prepare the Turkish people for self-government. "This form of headgear is called a hat," he would write on the blackboard, in the letters of the new alphabet. He gave new meanings to the words "nationalism" and "revolution," as well as to the word "Turk," though the instance remains unique in our time.

THE LAST BALKAN WAR

The significance of the Greek-Bulgarian "war" of 1925 is that it was not fought. The spark was struck by a frontier shooting incident in October 1925, just as the Council of the League was bringing the Mosul quarrel to its end. Quick and decisive action by France and Britain, in close association, extinguished the small flame. But they used the League as instrument, discarding the Conference of Ambassadors, and the proof of the efficacy and suitability of the Geneva organization gave the League a modest but pleasing triumph.

The fight between Greek and Bulgarian soldiers guarding the boundary in the lawless Macedonian region north of Salonika began by spontaneous combustion. There had been a series of such affrays, the result of congenital hot blood and of rivalry between the two states—allies in the first Balkan War, enemies in the second and in the World War. The last two wars had left Bulgaria reduced in territory and especially angry at Greece because of loss of an outlet through Thrace to the Mediterranean. The earlier frontier incidents had sputtered out as unaccountably as they had flared. This clash, however, built up to the proportions of a crisis. When a Greek officer with a flag of truce was shot, Greek troops advanced in some strength across the frontier, bringing up artillery. Bulgarian outposts retreated five miles or so to the nearest town, Petrić, where they were reinforced to meet the Greek invasion. Greece, at the moment, was ruled by the disreputable General Theodoros Pangalos, who had established a dictatorship a few months earlier (it was soon to be disestablished) and seemed eager to win honor on the battlefield. Balkan tinder appeared ready to blaze.

Bulgaria, however, sought to avoid a war It had had enough of slaughter in the three wars (the second of which it had initiated with a treacherous surprise attack on its Balkan allies of the first) and in postwar massacres by terrorists of the left and right. The Bulgarian government appealed to Geneva by telegram under Article 11 of the Covenant, asking the Secretary-General to call a meeting of the Council and citing the threat to peace. Both Bulgaria and Greece were members of the League.

The Covenant obligated the Secretary-General to call the meeting, but, it is interesting to remember, limited his authority to that duty. There was no pretense that the Secretariat itself was an executive agency. Sir Eric Drummond, the Secretary-General, notified the members of the League Council, and peremptory telegrams were at once dispatched to the governments of Greece and Bulgaria. The telegrams demanded an immediate cease fire and withdrawal of combatants to their proper sides of the frontier. But they were signed not with the name of the Secretary-General but with that of the President of the Council, Aristide Briand, who was then the Premier of France; he spoke also for the British representative on the Council, Sir Austen Chamberlain, the Foreign Secretary of Great Britain. There had, of course, been consultation, and there was assent by other Council members—and, notably, no dissent by the Italian representative, though Mussolini was suspected, probably correctly, of surreptitiously supplying Macedonian terrorists with arms, for what profit he might gain by that.

In sum, the President of the Council spoke with the voice of power as well as good sense; whether or not there was authorization in the Covenant for this Presidential way of jumping the gun in advance of the formal meeting of the Council, Briand's telegrams did literally that. The combatants dropped their guns. Formal Council procedures, at a special meeting in Paris, then disposed of the matter. General Pangalos withdrew his troops and the Council sent a Commission of Inquiry, and, in the subsequent regular session, levied a small indemnity against Greece for damage done in the incursion. A noteworthy innovation was the appointment of two neutrals, one chosen by Greece and one by Bulgaria, to act for two years as arbiters in any further frontier incidents.[10] It was a rudimentary "Peace Observation Corps"; and peace was preserved.

In addition to the Bulgarian appeal to Geneva and the forceful political response of France and Britain, acting through the standing machinery of the League, two other factors contributed to this smothering of the last threat of Balkan war in the 1920s. The first factor was positive and constructive. Both Greece and Bulgaria needed money for stabilization and development. Greece had received one loan to help with the settlement of refugees from Turkey and wanted another, which it received. Bulgaria was granted two loans in the next two years. All were arranged under the auspices of the League.

The negative factor was political, and of greatest underlying importance: neither Russia nor Germany attempted to cast weight in the scales. Lenin had died in 1924, and Stalin was busy spinning his web of power in Moscow. Bolshevik efforts at revolution in Bulgaria had been bloodily defeated, and though the Comintern was ready enough to make trouble for ideological pleasure or profit, Russia was not seriously interested in expansion. German policy depended upon the effect upon Germany, and on all Europe, of the Locarno Treaty, which Briand and Chamberlain had signed with Gustav Stresemann, the Chancellor of Germany, just before the telegram from Sofia reached Geneva. Conditions in the Balkans were ripe for peace. "Given ten years of real peace," a perceptive American foreign reporter, Hamilton Fish Armstrong, had noted even earlier, "and a new picture would not be slow to appear on the old botched and disreputable canvas." [11]

RECONSTRUCTION IN AUSTRIA

We must reverse the chronology of our story to include the financial reconstruction of Austria in 1922 as the final example of significant accomplishment by agencies of the League. It was planned and carried out by the experts of the Economic and Financial Section, headed by Sir Arthur Salter, in collaboration with an Assistant Secretary-General of the League—a young Frenchman named Jean Monnet. What is most significant is that their achievement was made possible by a wise and firm initiative taken by their political masters on the League Council, working closely with key governments of Europe.

It was perceived everywhere before the First World War was over that reorganization of the Austro-Hungarian Empire must be "total and thorough" (in the words of the last Minister of Finance of the Dual Monarchy). No reconstruction, political or economic, was possible during the flood that followed the final crumbling of the imperial structure, under the pressure of war and revolution.

When the waters receded, Austria was isolated and Vienna a ruined metropolis. About half the total population of six million six hundred thousand lived in this capital city of the vanished empire. Management of imperial business (and pleasure) had been their reason for existence. Neither the civil servants of the bureaucracy nor the inhabitants of the provinces could think of themselves other than in relationship to the old Dual Monarchy of fifty million or more German-speaking Austrians, Magyars, and Slavs who were now the citizens of six independent states. Of these, the new Republic of Austria, embracing some thirty-two thousand square miles, was the smallest and weakest, though it occupied one of the most vital strategic positions in central Europe.

The first act of the successor states, taken, as it were, by reflex action, had been to wall themselves off by tariff barriers from the imperial center from which the lines of trade, communications, and control radiated. Three of the new, or enlarged, states—Czechoslovakia, Rumania, and Yugoslavia—reached over and around Austria and Hungary with a series of alliances, intended primarily to guard against a Hapsburg restoration, which was attempted in Hungary. By 1921, conventions covering commercial and political relations had been exchanged among these countries of the Little Entente and extended, in varying terms, to include Italy and Poland. Hungary was still outside the group, but Czechoslovakia had moved to draw Austria into the new pattern through a treaty of friendship, made explicit by a lowering of trade barriers and a loan. Eduard Beneš of Czechoslovakia and Count Carlo Sforza, the Italian Foreign Minister, were architects of this design for cooperation among the sundered parts of the old empire. Economic conferences held in Italy in the spring and autumn of 1921, attended by representatives of these states, were marked by a diminution of political fears and signs of returning economic health.

Austria, however, was still prostrate and Vienna an abode of wretchedness. The area now denominated "Austria" had produced only about a third of the food consumed by its population, and, though agricultural—and, indeed, industrial—resources were to prove capable of unexpected development, the shock of defeat and collapse had reduced the Viennese to hopelessness. The corresponding mood of the provinces was indifference to the plight of the city. A new national consciousness had to be created.

For three years, as Sir Arthur Salter has written, Austria was "the beggar of Europe." [12] The role offered the Viennese only the promise of slow death by starvation, despite loans of more than one hundred million dollars—by France, Britain, and Italy, as well as Czechoslovakia—and large amounts of private charity. Demoralized Austrian governments sought to maintain the imperial bureaucracy unreduced in numbers and to finance loans for schemes of social welfare and housing that were recklessly large in the circumstances by printing money. By June 1922, the value of the crown was about one-hundredth of a cent—less than the cost of the paper and ink. In August of that year the Allied Powers, meeting in London, refused Austria further financial assistance and referred it to the League of Nations for advice and help. Though the experts of the Financial Section had quietly been preparing for such an eventuality, the response of the powers was generally taken to be an expression of cynicism. Monsignor Ignaz Seipel, the Austrian Chancellor, interpreting it this way, made a round of visits to Prague, Rome, and, ominously, Berlin for conversations, much to the unease of all Europe. The Germans were then in the depth of their currency inflation and could give Austria no economic help; but political collaboration between Germany and Austria would challenge the entire Versailles settlement, with Italian intervention in Viennese disorders an immediate possible consequence.

When the Austrian government did turn to the League, it found the Council, the Assembly, and the three major powers of Europe, prepared for serious work. Msgr. Seipel was made a temporary member of the Council, as was Beneš; and a strong committee of five, consisting of these two; Balfour; Gabriel Hanotaux of France, a former Foreign Minister; and the Marquis Imperiali, an Italian ambassador, was formed to direct the rescue operation. The Financial Committee of the Secretariat reported to this political steering committee. The plan was completed and the project launched within five weeks.

The basis of the reform of Austrian finances was a protocol, signed by Great Britain, France, Italy, Czechoslovakia, and Austria, containing a declaration that the signatories would, in sum, "respect the political independence, the territorial integrity and the sovereignty of Austria; that they would seek no special or exclusive economic or financial advantage which would compromise Austria's independence, and that if any such question arose they would refer the matter to the Council of the League and comply with its decision." [13] By signing the protocol, Austria made the same commitments. That is to say, Austria repeated in strengthened form the pledge it made in signing the Treaty of St.-Germain, disowning any effort toward union with Germany, and received in return remarkably disinterested and effective financial help.

Why the insistence upon this pledge? The "natural" desirability of an Austro-German customs union was a favored theme of the revisionist historians of the interwar years, when they expatiated on the stupidity of statesmen and the wickedness of the *status quo* (the shorthand symbol of the Versailles settlement). In fact, Austria's essential economic links were in the Danube basin. In 1922, and still more plainly in 1931, when—as unfortunately happened— efforts to form a customs union were made by the foreign ministers of Austria and the doomed Weimar government, the supposed economic benefits were merely a cloak for political merger. As Erich Eyck has said, "Not many Germans had any clear idea of the economic benefits that either country would drive from a simple customs union, but they were enthusiastic about its political future." [14] That future was the Great Germany envisaged by Hitler, and the effort to steal his thunder, though abortive, had the effect of bringing down the Viennese *Credit Anstalt* bank (its short-term loans were called in for political reasons) and sending sky-high the tariffs of Austria's neighbors, who read in the episode, correctly enough, the notice of approaching war.

Why an Austria independent of German control was a prereq-

uisite for Austrian—and European—reconstruction after the First
World War had been most authoritatively explained by Bismarck
some thirty years earlier. Writing retrospectively in the mid-1890s,
after his dismissal by Wilhelm II, Bismarck explained why he had
rejected the tempting possibility of an organic union with Austria
after his own wars had been won. Germany, in his view, was then
"satisfied." He desired peace and stability in Europe. For that, an
Austro-Hungarian Empire secured from danger of Russian attack
was essential, he reasoned, but so also was a Germany free from
the obligation to make her own the needs and claims of that Empire
in south central Europe and the Balkans. He wrote in his memoirs:

> The future of Austria, regarded in herself, cannot be reckoned
> upon with that certainty which is demanded when the conclusion
> of durable and, so to speak, organic treaties is contemplated. The
> factors which must be taken into account are as manifold as is
> the mixture of her populations. . . . Not only Panslavism and
> the Bulgarian or Bosnian, but also the Servian, the Roumanian, the
> Polish, the Czechish questions, nay even to-day the Italian ques-
> tion in the district of Trent, in Trieste, and on the Dalmatian
> coast, may serve as point of crystallisation not merely for Aus-
> trian but for European crises, by which German interests will be
> directly affected only in so far as the German Empire enters into
> a relation of close solidarity with Austria.[15]

This master of statecraft had concluded that a strictly defensive
alliance with Austria-Hungary, limited to the single contingency of
a Russian attack and, as he coolly noted, as expendable as any
other treaty if circumstances changed, was the suitable answer to
the problem of securing "a peaceful and conservative policy" for
Austria. A reinsurance treaty of friendship with Russia was the
other pillar on which Bismarck based his policy for a European
equilibrium. The burden of his veiled but bitter charge, in retirement, was that his successors in the chancellorship—and the young
Emperor—had destroyed the foundation of his policy by abandoning the treaty with Russia and tacitly extending the scope of the
Austrian alliance to provide German support for all Austrian

claims and needs in the Balkans and the East—"an idea to which our own press has already succeeded in giving practical shape." [16]

Bismarck's policy was as mortal as Bismarck, and inherent in the statecraft, as in the man, were the seeds of destruction. What policies might have prevented the "crystallization" he foresaw are still beyond knowing. This extension of German claims to embrace Austrian claims was, at any rate, the major reason why—in Barbara Tuchman's sparkling phrase, "swords were piled as delicately as jackstraws" [17] in Europe in 1914, and why the guns of August sounded. All that was needed, in 1922, to make certain that the guns—or an improved version of them—would sound again was a new merger of German and Austrian claims; that is to say, the *Anschluss* that would give Germany a mission to recover the territory in central Europe and the Balkans lost by the Dual Monarchy in the war.

With the signing of the Protocol of 1922 by Austria, reinforcing Article 88 of the Treaty of St.-Germain, and the pledge of cooperation in its behalf by the great and lesser powers, the scheme of the League's experts for the rehabilitation of Austrian finances went forward swiftly. Though the details of the plan were complex, its main outline was simple. The first step was to stop the printing of bank notes; right of issue was transferred by the Austrian government to an independent bank, under statutes approved by the League. Austria was asked to undertake internal reforms to balance expenditures and receipts, and the League appointed a commissioner general to supervise this painful but necessary process. Commercial loans to meet current deficits for two years were arranged, with customs and tobacco receipts as security and the states that had signed the protocol as guarantors. Belgium, Sweden, Denmark, Holland, Switzerland, and Spain associated themselves with the guarantee. The loans, amounting to some one hundred thirty million dollars, were quickly raised in the financial capitals of the world.

Within two years, Austrian currency was transformed from the least stable to the steadiest in Europe. Instead of a flight from the crown there was a flow of foreign exchange to it, and the city of Vienna became an asset to the countryside. These years of deflation brought a rise in unemployment, but the general economic condition of the country was immeasurably improved. The success of the plan was due to its comprehensiveness, to the courage and endeavors of the Austrians themselves once they were freed from the sense of hopelessness, to the degree of international good will and support, and to the skill of the League's experts and the appropriateness and availability of the League's machinery. The general pattern of this Austrian experiment was to be repeated, also under League auspices, in Hungary and Bulgaria. The realization of its full benefits for the Danube area depended upon whether some such rescue operation could be extended to disordered German finances—and that, of course, depended upon whether a comparably sound political basis would be laid there.

V . END OF THE EXPERIMENT

1. Cold War on Reparations

The German and Austrian financial disorders were very different in scale; and embedded in the problem of German finances was the intractable factor of reparations. There was never a serious effort by the Allies to collect reparations from the Austrian remnant of empire and any idea of doing so yielded quickly to postwar actualities. But a claim against Germany for damages was, by contrast, decidedly in order. On the western front, the war began and ended with German troops on French and Belgian soil. The invasion of 1914 engulfed virtually all Belgium and the manufacturing area of northeastern France almost to the gates of Paris. Much of that district was devastated in the four years of swaying entrenchments, and the French industrial plant that was behind the German lines during these years was systematically dismantled, or demolished in the scorched-earth policy of the German retreats. When the German commanders asked for an armistice, the powerful industrial plant of the Reich was intact. The terms of the Armistice included an Allied demand for compensation for damage done to civilian property, including damage at sea and from the air. German plenipotentiaries signed to escape rout and invasion.

Confident of victory, the German government had financed the war primarily by the sale of bonds, with relatively low taxation, thus anticipating repayment of monetary costs of the war by the losers through a heavy indemnity. Economic and political control of Belgium, transfer to Germany of French colonies, and the annexation of the French Longwy-Brie ore basin were also expected as fruits of victory. Such assumptions were shared by almost all in Germany, particularly the middle class that bought war bonds. This was the class that was to come to political power after General Erich Ludendorff lost his final gamble in 1918 and the monarchy collapsed. Prospects of limitless aggrandizement in the east simultaneously disappeared, and instead of that dream there was Poland. The German internal debt was one hundred forty-four billion marks. Adjustment was going to take time.

Before the completion of the Versailles Treaty there was correspondence between Allied and German officials about the amount of reparation. A German offer was invited. The German reply remains a curiosity, though a significant one. It suggested a sum of one hundred million gold marks (roughly twenty-five billion dollars) to be paid in annual installments, without interest, over a period of fifty to sixty years. It was a bargaining offer which, if accepted and paid, would have brought the Allies much more than they ever received. But it was also disingenuous and, indeed, an abstraction, for, along with the implausibly long period for interest-free payment, it was made conditional upon retention of German "territorial integrity" as of the time of the Armistice—that is, without the return of Alsace and Lorraine to France, without an independent Poland in the east, and with no obstacle to another try— payment of a fine for speeding but no loss of the driver's license.

The response of the victors was the "war guilt" clause of the Treaty, Article 231, which opened the section on reparations: "The Allied and Associated Governments affirm and Germany accepts the responsibility of Germany and her allies for causing all the loss and damage to which the Allied and Associated Governments and their nationals have been subjected as a consequence of the war imposed upon them by the aggression of Germany and her allies." Though the phrase "war guilt" nowhere appeared, this was an attempt to gain contractual obligation for unlimited restitution. It, too, was written in hot blood, and like the German territorial proposal, had an effect opposite to the one intended.

Sums suggested for reparations reached excessive heights when "loss and damage" were interpreted to mean war "costs." Projected outlays for soldiers' separation and disability allowances and for pensions were, for example, included in the bill. This was done particularly at British request and Lloyd George put what he thought might be the immediate receipts in his next official budget. The French doubted the practicability of this extension of claims and Woodrow Wilson opposed it. He yielded at the urging of the high-principled and unpredictable General Smuts, who subsequently encouraged John Maynard Keynes to write his brilliantly malicious attack on Wilson and every aspect of the Treaty.*

As was pointed out by various knowledgeable men (John Foster Dulles, for instance, in memoranda less readable but more responsible than Keynes') great sums of cash could not be collected from any foreign country without some degree of consent and could not be assimilated without major economic rearrangements, notably in regard to tariffs, by creditors. Though the United States asked no reparation, it was an international creditor to the extent of about ten billion dollars, plus interest, because of the Allied war debts, but the American government acknowledged no connection between the payment of these debts and payments sought by the Al-

---

* The tragedy of Keynes' *The Economic Consequences of the Peace* is that he turned the needed analysis of problems of international finance into a literary shocker that dazzled and misled the generation of English and American intellectuals to whom it was addressed and urged on to self-destruction the large audience it summoned in Germany. He was unscrupulous in his method. For example, arguing that Germany must have all of Upper Silesia, he disposed of the Polish interest in these words: "Unless her great neighbors are prosperous and orderly, Poland is an economic impossibility with no industry but Jew-baiting"—truth and venom in equal proportions, with the acid making the desired impression. (New York edition, Harcourt, Brace and Howe, 1921, p. 291). Keynes was intolerant of political authority. R. F. Harrod's *The Life of John Maynard Keynes* (New York: Harcourt, Brace, 1951) gives a full portrait.

lies from Germany, though the two accounts were, in fact and theory, inseparable. The American assumption that the former account was purely "commercial" and the full responsibility of the Allies whereas the latter was impurely political and a responsibility for which the United States must be excused exacerbated transatlantic relations for years and made the satisfactory adjustment of either account impossible.* Only Britain seriously attempted to repay its share of the indebtedness, and did so not from a sense of obligation transcending her own contributions to what became the common cause but from the desperate necessity of maintaining the reputation of the pound as an international currency. (The celebrated loan to Finland, paid in full, was made after the war.)

France remembered that after the Franco-Prussian War Bismarck had demanded an indemnity of five billion francs, a sum so large for those days that he was confident it would keep Prussian occupation troops in France indefinitely, and that Frenchmen had produced it in less than three years to get rid of them. The French reasoned, correctly, that the degree of German self-interest in the payment of reparations to the Allies could be determined only by some comparably rough calculus. Clauses of the Versailles Treaty provided not only for occupation of the Rhineland for fifteen years but also for Allied occupation of the right bank of the Rhine—the great industrial area of the Ruhr—in the event of default on payment of reparations. Thus the bargaining positions of the two sides took shape. Germany would use accommodation or intransigence on reparation payments as a means of obtaining territorial concessions; the Allies would use the threat of occupation of the Ruhr to exert leverage for fulfillment of all terms of the Treaty.

---

* The war loans to the Allies, begun in the period of American neutrality, were immensely important political acts, but the pretense that they were impersonal commercial transactions was mutual. Franklin D. Roosevelt solved this problem on the next round with lend-lease, on the homely and persuasive analogy of the loan of the garden hose to the neighbor whose house was on fire.

Determination of a concrete figure for reparations was postponed at Versailles. A Reparation Commission was instructed to recommend a total in May 1921, Germany being asked to pay about five billion dollars in the interval, in cash and goods; part of this was to cover the costs of occupation forces in the Rhineland and of raw materials and food shipped into Germany to meet immediate needs, to be subtracted from the total bill.

The bargaining began in earnest in 1920 and was marked by a dozen or more conferences within the next few years, with continuous probing by both sides to discover the intentions of their adversaries—and in the process their own. At Spa in 1920 the Allies made concessions on the question of trials of "war criminals"—wisely, most commentators now believe, for though sentences were light in the few cases that came to trial, they were imposed by German courts for indubitable crimes. But the Allies stood firm on the Treaty limitations on German arms and schedules for delivery of coal to France and Belgium. Conversations showed the two sides so far apart on reparation totals that the question was sidetracked. The high point of the conference was a speech by the Ruhr industrialist Hugo Stinnes, a member of the Reichstag but inept at politics, who railed at the Allied statesmen seated around the table and threatened defiance on the required delivery of coal. The Allied answer was to summon Marshal Ferdinand Foch and the English commander, Sir Henry Wilson, to prepare an occupation of the Ruhr. The German Foreign Minister, Dr. Walter Simons, sought to repair the damage, but the tone of the conference remained heated and the Allied ultimatum stood. Stinnes returned to Germany a hero for his bad manners, but Dr. Simons gave warning in the Reichstag of the actualities of the situation: "Up to the last few months many of our nation nourished the false notion that the peace treaty was not to be taken seriously and would not be taken seriously by the other side." The warning was, of course, no less revelatory of the terrible predicament of responsible German statesmen. Germany continued the delivery of coal, but that same month

the German government blocked the shipment of munitions to Poland, then in its life-and-death struggle with the Red army.*

In January 1921 the Allies proposed a total of fifty billion dollars, payable over forty-two years. It was rejected. In March the
Allies occupied three ports on the right bank of the Rhine—Düs-
seldorf, Duisburg, and Ruhrort—and seized customs revenues. In
April the German government asked the United States to intervene
as mediator. All this was political warfare and the United States
refused the role, which would have signaled an official change in
sides by the Associated Power. In May came a unanimous report
by the members of the Reparation Commission. (The United States'
member was now only an "observer.") It named a sum of thirty-
three billion dollars—payable with interest over thirty years—of
which about two billion, in the Commission's estimate, had already been paid. Annual payments were to be approximately five
hundred million dollars.† ¹ The note conveying these terms to Germany was accompanied by a restatement of the earlier ultimatum:
occupation of the Ruhr in the event of German rejection. The
Reichstag accepted the Allied terms by a vote of two hundred
twenty to one hundred seventy-two, on the day the ultimatum expired.

Such a scaling down of the monetary obligation brought it within
range of the original German proposal and, indeed, more or less
equaled the figure of one hundred thirty-seven billion marks that
Keynes had suggested. The Reparation Commission, moreover, established three orders of priority for the distribution of monetary
payments, by the device of issuing A, B, and C reparations bonds.
The C bonds, amounting to twenty billion dollars, were to be kept
in the hands of the Commission until the payments they represented became less theoretical. This division of prospective receipts

* The SS *Wimbleton* case, brought before the Court in 1923. As noted
above, the Court decided against Germany, and Germany made reparation.

† The multiplicity of conditional clauses in all proposals and counteroffers,
and fluctuations in currencies, make the citation of specific sums in dollars
meaningful only as general illustrations.

into classes labeled, in effect, "Good," "Indifferent," and "Bad" suggested the nature of an ultimate Allied offer in the bargaining for a peace of consent: further concessions on reparations in return for German acceptance of the political core of the Treaty. It also foreshadowed a further test of wills, in which Germany would seek to exploit the divergence of British and French interests on the Continent. As in the contest over Upper Silesia, the League was to be brought in at the climax, and again, its usefulness in forwarding a settlement depended upon the relationship between France and Britain.

France wanted and certainly needed all the money it could get to defray the costs of rebuilding; with even greater intensity it sought to assure that a renewed German invasion would be discouraged, or repulsed, by significant military power ready for use. "It has always been easy for the West to forget how close Germany came to victory in 1914 and in the spring of 1918," Edward W. Bennett has written. "After the Armistice the Allies counted the dead and wondered if the war could have been won more easily; the Germans counted the kilometers and knew that they had barely been stopped." [2] But France did not forget that the German army had been stopped only because it was fighting on two fronts.

In February 1921, as soon as Poland had signed a treaty of peace with the Soviet Union and organized its domestic affairs, France concluded an alliance with the reborn state. The treaty provided for "concerted action in case of unprovoked aggression" and contained military conventions. These were the essentials of an alliance, in the traditional sense of that word as understood by Continental statesmen—a binding commitment embracing specific measures to wage a war. The contradictory phrase "unprovoked aggression" was also customary and well understood—a check rein that one party to an alliance intended to be strictly defensive thought wise to have available in the event that the partner was tempted to adventure by the grant of power. France, in this case, was discouraging any Polish thought of renewed involvement with Russia. French policy toward the Soviet state was epitomized by the famous phrase *cordon sanitaire,* in effect "containment" and well suited to the postwar circumstances, though not to the requirements of good public relations between France and the English-speaking nations.

The alliance with Poland—a "middle" power, in the terminology that has become current in our day—plus comparable, though varying, arrangements with Czechoslovakia, Rumania, and Yugoslavia, formed the basic French Continental design for security against a third German war. Nevertheless, this arrangement was no substitute for the power of the former Russian ally, without whose eastern offensive, ill-starred as it was, the French army and the British Expeditionary Force would have been overwhelmed in August 1914. In 1919 and thereafter, France sought the binding alliance with Britain, with explicit military conventions, that had eluded it in the years before the First World War.

The American-British pledge of military assistance to France, signed in Paris, dissolved when Wilson returned to the United States. Though the pact was never submitted to the Senate and formally discarded, the rejection of the Versailles Treaty and the conclusion by the United States government of a separate peace with Germany on August 25, 1921, ended any possibility of American participation in the alliance. Under the terms of the three-cornered agreement, the American failure to ratify freed Britain from its obligation. France accepted the finality of the American decision, though not without bitterness, for what it received instead of the promised military pledge was an invitation to a disarmament conference. But in December of the same year, the French Ambassador in London approached the British Foreign Secretary, Lord Curzon, with a request for the negotiation of a new pact of mutual assistance.

Though Lord Curzon tended to think of European problems as personal affronts by irritating foreigners, there was comprehension and sympathy for the French request among leaders in all the British political parties, Curzon's own Conservative Party especially. Negotiations were opened and went on for about a year, with desire on both sides for an understanding. Ambassador Auguste Saint Aulaire made plain at the outset that France would go to war if Germany attacked Poland. "A Polish Sadowa would be the best preparation for Germany for a new Sedan," he said[3]—Sadowa being the battle in which Prussia defeated Austria in 1866, thus securing its rear in preparation for the Franco-Prussian War. Saint Aulaire was prophetic. Nevertheless, though Britain offered a guarantee of assistance to France if Germany attacked France directly, it would not enter an arrangement which covered the indirect attack. Lloyd George, quicksilver as always, took the opportunity to ask concessions from France in regard to submarines (Britain hoped to "outlaw" them at the Washington Naval Conference) and in regard to certain Franco-British disputes in Tangiers and the Middle East. The first round of the negotiations was fruitless.

As part of the outline of a pact, Saint Aulaire had suggested that if Britain would not make a direct commitment covering a German attack in the east the League guarantee might be strengthened to achieve this objective. To protect Poland and Czechoslovakia without naming them, Aristide Briand, then Foreign Minister, now pressed this idea of a general security pact. Briand, a powerful orator, prided himself on his ability to find words that could dissolve all diplomatic stalemates. At an international conference at Cannes in January 1922, Lloyd George employed his own eloquence in behalf of a program of disarmament, trade, and peace, and in Point Six offered a formula for security that was general indeed: "All countries should join in an understanding to refrain from aggression against their neighbors." This, in effect, anticipated the Kellogg-Briand Pact of 1928—and, indeed, the later nonaggression pacts of the dictators, woven of words to disguise purpose.

At the same time, however, Britain offered France a draft of a treaty that included a definite commitment for aid if France were the victim of unprovoked aggression, for "concert" with France in the event of German violation of the Rhineland provision of Versailles, and for "consultation" if the disarmament clauses were violated. This was a great advance over the uncertainties of the

EUROPE AND
THE MIDDLE EAST,
1923

prewar Entente; yet it omitted what the French considered the requirements of a prudent arrangement in the new circumstances—a military convention that would assure planning for an attack in the east. Briand said, "It remained only to protect Eastern and Central Europe." That was precisely the point, and Briand's colleagues in the Cabinet doubted his resolution. Whether Briand, in 1922, was on the verge of accepting a formula that would have jettisoned Poland and Czechoslovakia no one knows, perhaps because he himself did not know. At any rate, there was a Cabinet crisis in Paris, touched off by the most ludicrous of incidents—publication of a photograph showing Briand taking a lesson in golf from Lloyd George at Cannes. Briand lost his post and Poincaré, who had been President of the Republic during the war, came to power.

Raymond Poincaré's style was as pointed as Aristide Briand's was expansive, and his meticulously prepared briefs included no effort to please. Since he was a mathematician by profession, his foreign opponents used the presumed heartlessness of logic as the symbol of his deficiencies, much the way Briand's domestic critics used golf. But Poincaré's argument was passionate and plain: Germany would destroy the Versailles settlement if possible but would accept it if necessary. Germany would never accept it, however, as long as British policy wavered. Poincaré asked strict enforcement of the terms of the Treaty.

This insistence presaged a showdown, and it came quickly, though it was precipitated not by Poincaré but by the Weimar Republic. German finances were in extreme disorder, partly as a result of "normal" postwar inflation—intensified in this instance by the monarchy's methods of financing the war—partly from the difficulty of finding exchange to pay reparations, and still further from deliberate depreciation of the mark to escape payment of reparations. Through inflation, the state was also toughly cutting its own internal debt at the expense of bondholders. There was virtually full employment in Germany, and industrial profits were high. German gold reserves were double the total currency then in circulation, despite inflation. When the German government declared its inability to meet the reparations payments due in January and February 1922, the Reparation Commission granted a temporary moratorium and substantially reduced the payments in cash and goods scheduled for the rest of the year. In agreeing to this suspension and reduction of payments, however, the Commission demanded budgetary and tax reforms. A committee of experts, which included Robert H. Brand of England, (later Lord Brand), Keynes, and the Swedish economist Gustav Cassel, pointed out in a report to the Commission that the resources of the Reich, if used, were sufficient to stabilize the currency. In the background lay the threat of Allied occupation of the Ruhr, the trump card in the battle of wills over reparations.

In April of that year Lloyd George tried one more conference. This one, to be held at Genoa, was a major effort, in which Russia was included, to bring Europe, in the broadest sense of the term, together in a program of reconstruction. On the agenda was a proposal that, in return for some payment on the debts of the Czarist government, Bolshevik Russia be given credits. There could be credits for Germany also, if it would accept the needed tax and currency reforms. All emphasis was to be on reconciliation and trade. In an attempt to downgrade hard political problems, Poland and Czechoslovakia were pointedly omitted from the list of nations to attend preliminary discussions. Poincaré, skeptical on every count, refused to go and sent a deputy.

On the day the conference assembled, the Weimar government rejected the demand of the Reparation Commission for tax and budgetary reforms and currency control. When the conference had been in session only a few days, the German and Russian delegations astounded the assembly with the announcement that, some hours earlier, a treaty between Germany and Russia had been signed, in secret, in the neighboring town of Rapallo. The terms of the pact sounded innocent: the two former enemies mutually renounced claims to reparations and indemnities, promised reciprocal most-favored-nation rights in trade, and accorded one another full diplomatic recognition, with exchange of ambassadors and consular staffs. The two governments insisted that the treaty had no secret military clauses. No one believed them, since the only common interest of bourgeois Weimar and Bolshevik Moscow could be the dislocation of the new order in Europe—including its instrument, the League—and that meant force and war.

In fact, discussions between Russian and German emissaries looking to a quasi alliance had been begun much earlier. General Hans von Seeckt, Chief of the Army Command, was the prime mover on the German side, with the approval of the Chancellor of the Weimar coalition government, Dr. Wirth of the Center Party. The Rapallo Treaty was signed with the knowledge that the military arrangement would presently be concluded. It was completed three months later, masked as a Society for the Encouragement of Commercial Enterprises, and even so, supersecret. Its precise terms were not discovered for several years. They provided for German technical and financial aid to the Soviet armament industry (from funds secretly dispensed by the German Chancellor) and the manufacture in Russia, for delivery to Germany, of planes and munitions. In effect, the Weimar government set up a German arms industry in the Soviet Union. As it happened, no planes were delivered, and such ammunition as was shipped, particularly gas shells and grenades, was of little or no importance. The Reichswehr profited, however, from the opportunity to experiment with and train its officers in the new methods of warfare, notably with tanks. The Soviet dictatorship, then savagely liquidating the Russian intelligentsia, received assistance from German technicians; and there was the satisfaction of throwing the capitalist countries off stride, with the promise of greater opportunities for mischief in the future.

The bargain was struck in a spirit of perfect cynicism on both sides. Lenin had said publicly that Germany "would naturally be forced to ally herself with Russia," and Leninist revolutionary doctrine supplied the strategy and the apparatus by which the Soviet Union could take advantage of the German need. The theoretical separation of the functions of Soviet state and Communist party permitted the state to have formally correct relations with capitalist states while the Communist International worked surreptitiously to destroy them. Lenin believed that the next great Marxist upheaval would come in Germany. Civilian and military leaders in the Reich were exceedingly well aware of Bolshevik efforts to promote it and of their own intention to crush them.

What the Germans needed was help in destroying the Versailles settlement—in the short run, by a political blow eastward that would dislocate the already strained common front of the Allies in the west; in the longer run, by the recovery of military power, lost under the disarmament clauses of the treaty. "Whenever our policy in the West has run aground it has always been wise to try something in the East," Chancellor Wirth observed.[4] That was classic doctrine for Prussia and Imperial Germany, and though Communism had introduced an untested factor in the equation between east and west, German politicians, and Foreign Office professionals such as Ulrich von Brockdorff-Rantzau and Adolf von Maltzan, were confident that they could outwit the Russians in the game of profiting from disorder. Von Seeckt had a simpler objective: "Poland must disappear." In the course of the prolonged intrigue leading to the Rapallo Treaty, Reichswehr generals negotiated with one of the principal agents of the Comintern, Karl Radek, in Berlin. Dr. Walter Rathenau, the organizer of German industry during the war, who had become Foreign Minister shortly before Rapallo (and later was assassinated by anti-Semitic terrorists), visited Radek in a Berlin prison.

In the long run, German officials proved mistaken in their estimate of the new forces; the turn toward the east meant desolation and captivity for Germany. The immediate result of Rapallo, however, was a triumph for the Weimar government in the political duel with the Allies. When Germany and Russia reached out to clasp hands, the shadow of a new partition fell upon Poland. The threat of German-Russian collaboration—and of eventual German-Russian conflict over the spoils—shattered what remained of a joint French-British policy toward Germany. The warning of Rapallo was heard by France and Britain alike, but it impelled the island power and the Continental power to seek safety in opposite directions. France moved forward while it was strong, whereas Britain moved back to its source of strength. Discussion of the terms of an alliance continued, but any possibility of a meeting of minds disappeared. To a British suggestion—handsome, if intended as a serious declaration of policy—that the pact of assistance in the event of German aggression westward be extended to cover a period of fifteen years, Poincaré predictably replied, "It is not on the Rhine that a German offensive, destined to ruin the edifice of peace set up at Versailles, will take place." [5] The greatest danger to France and to peace, he repeated in speech after speech, was the illusion of security.

The Russian Foreign Minister, Chicherin, completed his foray into Europe at Genoa by asking the routed enemies for credits. That ended the conference. With it went Lloyd George's Russian policy, and presently Lloyd George himself, his coalition Cabinet being displaced in September by a Conservative government under the ailing Scotsman Bonar Law. The long-deferred occupation of the Ruhr by the Allies came in January 1923—but the "Allies" did not include Great Britain, which declared itself neutral in the climactic test of wills. Italy stood with France and Belgium in the vote in the Reparation Commission holding Germany formally in default, but the troops that advanced across the Rhine were Belgian and French only.

France shouldered the responsibility for the occupation throughout the ensuing months of turmoil. Poincaré's demand was for "protective guarantees" of reparation payments—that is, supervision of the management of Ruhr coal mining and industry. At first he sent only a small number of troops, as escort for commissioners dispatched to the several headquarters of Ruhr industrial organizations. The commissioners, who found that all records had been removed, met with uncompromising refusal by industrialists to plan for joint control. The Weimar government declared that the French effort at collection would be met with passive resistance. This resistance was made active by an order to coal miners and governmental railroad personnel to disregard French instructions, and mine owners were ordered to refuse delivery of coal even for payment in gold by the French. At the same time, the German government promised to feed the population of the Ruhr during the total shutdown of industrial activity.

Poincaré responded with large contingents of troops, and the inevitable violence occurred. Several hundred Germans were arrested and tried on various charges; several thousand were deported from the Ruhr; riots in Essen brought shootings and casualties; and acts of sabotage by bombing brought death to French soldiers and officials and death sentences for perhaps a dozen Germans. This sort of war went on for about nine months. In September Germany capitulated; a new Chancellor, Gustav Stresemann, declared resistance ended. An organization of Ruhr industrialists accepted the controls and signed the contracts for delivery of coal that Poincaré had asked in the beginning.

Though the degree of repression was small and the loss of life smaller in relation to comparable later episodes in the wars of our time, the experience of the Ruhr occupation cut deep into the minds of all who participated and all who watched. In these tense summer months of 1923 the German people learned that the unimaginable was actual: they had, in fact, lost the First World War. The frenzy with which they responded to this belated awareness frightened everyone, in particular those who observed from a distance—that is to say, Englishmen and Americans. Symbol and substance of the frenzy was the destruction of the German currency. At the pitch of the battle, the Weimar government was spending forty million gold marks daily to relieve distress among the Ruhr population; it was simultaneously printing forty-six billion paper marks daily. The President of the *Reichsbank* congratulated himself on the efficiency with which the problem of getting this torrent of paper notes off the printing presses every twenty-four hours had been mastered.

Passive resistance was a policy bereft of reason, passionately supported by the German nation and, though condemned by some, condemned on the ground that it was insufficiently defiant. Germany appeared to be going to pieces, politically as well as economically. Separatist movements (to which the French gave encouragement) budded, though never flowered, in the Rhineland; there was a Communist insurrection in Hamburg; a Communist government was briefly installed in Saxony-Thuringia; and successive Black Army and Nationalist risings occurred in Bavaria, culminating in the Ludendorff-Hitler November *putsch* after resistance in the Ruhr was ended. Signficantly, however, the Reichswehr command crushed such uprisings—either by using its own troops or backing the police—when any of them reached a stage that could have fractured the unity of the Reich.

The distressing spectacle of German inflation and its increasingly disastrous effect upon the Western monetary system brought Britain and the United States out of their detachment from Continental problems. The press in both countries found release from emotion in unmeasured anger at Poincaré, the *Manchester Guardian* setting the tone by a demand for the "moral isolation" of France. The French were, indeed, terribly isolated, with the result that French determination was strengthened and the German sense of victimization intensified. When Lord Curzon engaged in public polemics with Poincaré, many in Germany were convinced that British intervention on the German side, including the use of force, was a possibility or even a likelihood. As at the flash point in the Upper Silesian quarrel, however, Britain turned abruptly to form a common front with France. Stanley Baldwin, coming to power upon Bonar Law's death, reversed Curzon's policy and, in a joint statement with the French Premier, declared that "on no question is there any difference of purpose or principle which could impair the cooperation of the two countries."

With this communiqué, sanity began to return to the German mind. Stresemann's proclamation of the end of resistance in the Ruhr—"to preserve the life of the nation and the state"—came within a week. In October, under the guidance of Dr. Hjalmar

Schacht, the Weimar government took steps to stabilize German currency on the basis of new *Rentenmarks,* secured by mortgages. Theoretically redeemable at a ratio of something like a trillion to one, the old marks were thus declared worthless. The savings of the German people were wiped out, but the new currency was eagerly accepted. Though the *Rentenbank* that issued it could be no more than provisional, German acceptance of responsibility for the establishment of a firm currency, coupled with resumption of shipments of coal and iron to France and Belgium, brought the cold war to a full stop.

France had won the test of wills, but victory was costly. Inflation in France had put the franc on the downhill road; it seemed as though prostrate Germany would drag France into bankruptcy. And there was no possibility of France's receiving reparation payments in cash unless the precarious German stabilization was reinforced by international aid and the likelihood of future crises diminished. The time was ripe for renewed negotiations.

Prompted by Britain, the United States proposed a fresh study of the tangled problem. With American governmental approval, the Chicago banker General Charles G. Dawes (later Vice President of the United States) was asked by the Reparation Commission to be chairman of a committee of experts to recommend a plan for an agreed settlement. Owen D. Young, a prominent American industrialist, was named vice chairman. British bankers and students of governmental finance were especially influential members of the international group.

The American intervention signaled a dramatic return to Europe by isolationist America. But the United States took isolationism along. The Secretary of State of the United States, Charles Evans Hughes, had earlier expressed the condition of American participation in any such an effort:

> If statesmen cannot agree, then there should be called to their aid those who can point the way to a solution. Why should they not invite men of the highest authority in finance in their respective countries—men of such prestige, experience and honor that their

agreement upon the amount to be paid and upon a financial plan for working out the payments, would be accepted throughout the world as the most authoritative expression obtainable.[6]

Put in such mellow but weighted words as the condition of American participation, the question carried its own answer. Statesmen—that is to say, politicians—must yield to experts, and the experts must be insulated from politics. German "capacity to pay" was to be treated simply as an economic and financial question. This meant that the problem of Continental security was excluded from consideration. Germany would be asked for no political concessions in return for the concessions proffered her by the Allies on reparations and for the promise of American loans. In particular, the United States could in no way be associated with the problem of the guarantee of boundaries in Eastern Europe. It also meant, and by no means incidentally, that the political question of Allied war debts to the United States was out of bounds for the experts, as was the question of tariffs.

That "politics should be taken out of politics" was an ideal of government in that American age of innocence and *laissez faire*. Not a few financial experts and their colleagues in American banks and on the Federal Reserve Board, struggling with unprecedented problems in international finance, were well aware that major economic questions required political answers.[7] General Dawes, who knew his way around in the corridors of political power and was often amused by what he encountered there, is reported to have remarked, at the first meeting of his committee, "If the French were not in the Ruhr we experts would not be here." And Roland W. Boyden, the hard-pressed and heroic American observer with the Reparation Commission from 1920 to 1923, who greeted the idea of an objective study of German economic capacity to pay with heartfelt relief, also noted that the success of the plan would depend upon the intangible of "good faith." He hoped that the political problem of security would be met by a voluntary German pledge of respect for the eastern boundaries.[8]

The restricted approach had the virtue of its defect, however.

The Dawes Report, when it came in 1924, was recognized as reasonably impartial and was accepted by the Allied and German governments, after argument and emendation at an international conference, as the best solution obtainable from their respective points of view.

In many respects the plan followed the lines of the scheme for Austrian rehabilitation devised by the League experts, providing for a new bank of issue in Germany, a new currency, and foreign—largely American—credits to Germany, with securities and certain revenues pledged as backing for the loans, and a supervisory organization. The feature of the plan for Germany, however, was an ingenious arrangement to meet the so-called transfer problem. Reparations were to be paid in Germany and in German marks. Germany was relieved of responsibility for converting its money into francs, pounds, lire, and dollars. This irritating and hitherto insoluble problem was the task of an Agent-General for Reparations—an American. If payments accumulated in amounts that endangered international financial stability, he had power to reduce, or suspend, German payments. During two five-year periods annual payments would be regulated by an index of the health of the German economy (based on railroad travel, foreign trade, population growth, consumption of certain commodities,—*e.g.,* wine, though the word could not be mentioned in the era of prohibition.) Beginning with a small amount the first year, payments would increase by one-half the percentage of increase in German prosperity. The purpose of this regulation of payments by a "prosperity index" was to restore hope and confidence to the German people, while assuring receipt of reparations by the Allies in proportion to German capacity to pay. In the words of the Report: "Under this system Germany will retain her incentive to develop, as it retains the major part of the advantage of any increase of prosperity, while the Allies obtain a reasonable share in this increase and avoid the risk of losing through a premature estimate of future capacity."

The Report did not attempt to set a figure for total payments. (The idea of the twenty billion dollars in C bonds was quietly dropped.) It was hoped that the annual payments would reach about six hundred million dollars in five years (as, in fact, they did) and that, through further negotiations, there would be a final determination of Germany's liability for reparations. The obligation would then be funded as a long-term German commercial debt.

It was a knowledgeable outline of a financial solution. What was lacking was the political foundation.

2. Climax of the League

For three fateful years after the contest of wills in the Ruhr ended in German collapse, the central question of international politics was whether a program of German reconstruction would be accompanied by an effective guarantee of the territorial provisions of Versailles. In the negotiations with France, Britain had offered a treaty of assistance to deter or repulse a German attack on the western frontier, but with pointed omission of concern for the new eastern boundaries. The United States, taking the leadership in the restoration of the economic base of German military strength, had emphasized its earlier rejection of responsibility for either eastern or western territorial settlements. As a last hope, France and its Continental allies turned to Geneva in their quest for protection against a potentially resurgent German Central Power. It was a hazardous move, since under the terms of the Covenant the path to collective security led through the bristling thickets of "disarmament." We know how the journey to Geneva ended; but the effort to link national reduction of arms and collective security remains the most significant episode of the League's story.

The Articles of the Covenant did not use the popular word disarmament. They spoke of limitation, reduction, control of national arms, and they spoke also of enforcement of the League's pledge of protection against war-makers. Article 8—the so-called disarmament article—linked the two objectives in Paragraph 1: "The Members of the League recognize that the maintenance of peace requires the reduction of national armaments to the lowest point consistent with national safety and the enforcement by common action of international obligations." Even so, there was a significant order of priorities there, and still more significant was the contrast between the hesitant suggestion for use of military force under the so-called sanction clauses of the Covenant (Article 16) and the confidence with which Article 8 outlined a program for control of national arms in paragraphs 2, 3, and 4:

> 2. The Council, taking account of the geographical situation and circumstances of each State, shall formulate plans for such reduction for the consideration and action of the several Governments.
> 3. Such plans shall be subject to reconsideration and revision at least every ten years.
> 4. After these plans shall have been adopted by the several Governments, the limits of armaments therein fixed shall not be exceeded without the concurrence of the Council.

Nothing in the Covenant conferred such governmental powers upon the League of Nations. The directive was, in part, the expression of the Wilsonian vision of a moral world, at peace because all governments had voluntarily put their means of waging war into the hands of a committee of the whole, the source of whose authority was, simply and magnificently, the consciousness of common interest. Even more simply, Article 8 was the expression of the popular equation—shared or reflected by most leaders of government—"disarmament equals peace." Now that Germany was disarmed, why should there not be disarmament all around, since the League of Nations would make sure that no new competition in armaments started?

So confident were the peacemakers at Versailles of the validity of the equation (or so powerful was the pressure of it upon the skeptics among them) that the actuality of a system of League control of arms was assumed in the arrangements for German disarmament. Paragraph 1 of Article 8 was incorporated in each of the Peace Treaties, and the Preamble to Part V of the Treaty of Versailles, dealing with the limit on German arms read: "In order to render possible the initiation of a general limitation of the armaments of all nations, Germany undertakes strictly to observe the military, naval and air clauses which follow."

The German delegation at Versailles asked clarification of this statement, and Clemenceau, replying for the Allies and the United States, said in a note handed to von Brockdorff-Rantzau on June 16, 1919:

> The Allied and Associated Powers wish to make it clear that their requirements in regard to German armaments were not made solely with the object of rendering it impossible for Germany to resume her policy of military aggression. They are also the first steps towards that general reduction and limitation of armaments which they seek to bring about as one of the most fruitful preventives of war, and which it will be one of the first duties of the League of Nations to promote.

The note emphasized that "Germany must consent unconditionally to disarm in advance of the Allied and Associated Powers." But it closed with a significant concession: "No deviation from the organization in armament [*la constitution de l'armament*] laid down in the present Treaty can be permitted *until Germany is admitted to the League of Nations, which may then agree to such modifications as may seem desirable.*" (Italics added.)

This was a way of telling Germany that the severe limitations on German arms were not intended to last forever. That had to be said. The blow to German self-respect and sense of security in a demand that this great nation accept a permanent military status inferior to all save a handful of the smallest countries of Europe, unlike the blow to pride in asking the German people to accustom themselves to the existence of an independent Poland, would be one that time could only exacerbate. But this way of introducing the idea of modification laid a time bomb under the League and the Treaty. Suppose there were no system of control of the instruments of offense and defense of the members of the League when the time came for Germany to join? Had the Allies made promises that would hold good in that event? Would they disarm while Germany armed?

For two years the Assembly of the League made disarmament its first order of business, appointing committees and conducting constant debate, but without accomplishment. There was actually an early plan to achieve reductions of arms by limiting each nation to a quota of "units" of troops—thirty thousand men to a unit, with six units for one country, four for another, one for a third—on the theory that if each nation cut its army in the same proportion, no country would thereby gain an advantage, none would lose, and there would be no arms race. Reduction by units of capital ships—battleships and aircraft carriers—had been applied with apparent success at the Washington Naval Conference, but the attempt to extend the mathematical approach to Continental air forces and armies was quickly abandoned. Disarmament by percentages of existing strength left decisive political, economic, and scientific variables out of account—as, indeed, they had been omitted at Washington.[9] The innocent (sometimes not so innocent) formula for reduction of arms by ratios of existing strength was to be brought forward more than once; but the Assembly reconstituted its committee on disarmament to include men competent to examine the political and economic problems of armaments as well as the technical aspects of weapons.

This committee, known by the odd name of Temporary Mixed Commission, brought the question down to earth with an incisive report. Reasoning that progress toward voluntary reduction of national armaments was hopeless without arrangements that would ensure prompt and effective aid to an endangered state, it reversed the order of priority of Articles 8 and 16. It recommended that the search for disarmament begin with a plan for enforcement and proposed a treaty of mutual guarantee supported by special defensive arrangements—"partial alliances." To many in the Assembly this was the old heresy of the arms race, and they condemned it with a new slogan: enforcement equals war. But there were those in the Assembly who perceived in such a planned use of international power the one instrument that could defuse the time bomb ticking under the peace of Europe. They were able and experienced men, and in the debate they carried the day. The Assembly accepted the committee's report, with some amendment and elaboration, in the famous Resolution XIV of the Third Assembly. Since that resolution has probably never been improved upon as a summary of principles and methods for achieving the twin objectives of reduction of national arms and collective security, it is worth quoting. The Assembly was of the opinion that

1. No scheme for the reduction of armaments, within the meaning of Article 8 of the Covenant, can be fully successful unless it is general.

2. In the present state of the world many Governments would be unable to accept the responsibility for a serious reduction of armaments unless they received in exchange a satisfactory guarantee of the safety of their country.

3. Such a guarantee can be found in a defensive agreement which should be open to all countries, binding them to provide immediate and effective assistance in accordance with a pre-arranged plan in the event of one of them being attacked, provided that the obligation to render assistance to a country attacked shall be limited in principle to those countries situated in the same part of the globe. In cases, however, where, for historical, geographical, or other reasons, a country is in special danger of attack, detailed arrangements should be made for its defense in accordance with the above-mentioned plan.

4. As a general reduction of armaments is the object of the three preceding statements, and the Treaty of Mutual Guarantee the means of achieving that object, previous consent to this reduction is therefore the first condition of the Treaty.

This reduction could be carried out either by means of a general treaty, which is the most desirable plan, or by means of partial treaties designed to be extended and open to all countries.

In the former case, the Treaty will carry with it a general reduction of armaments. In the latter case, the reduction should be proportionate to the guarantees afforded by the Treaty.

In brief: if a satisfactory general plan is not now within reach, start with a particular plan covering the area of greatest danger and heaviest armaments. It went without saying that that area was Europe.

The Assembly requested the Council of the League to submit the proposals of Resolution XIV to members for their observations and instructed the Commission to draft a treaty. The results of the inquiries to governments vindicated the good judgment of the Assembly in allowing for alternative approaches. Half the members of the League failed to answer the letter. No reply came from the Latin American nations and only one from the British Dominions. That was from Canada, and it was explicitly unfavorable. More ominously, the British Foreign Office found no time for a reply. If that was the accurate expression of the British interest in the League's initiative, both collective security and control of national arms were obviously doomed.

Within the Commission, however, British and French representatives were collaborating, as had happened before in crises. The French representative was Colonel Réquin of the French general staff; France was taking the League seriously and was eager to reduce the burden of its large standing army, if there were a grouping of forces under a guarantee that covered Eastern and Western Europe. The British representative was Lord Robert Cecil, not then a member of the British government and, indeed, present in Geneva only as a delegate from the Union of South Africa. But like Balfour in earlier instances—if without his authority in the Cabinet—Cecil was a leader. He knew that it was now or never for control of national arms and that French fears of a resurgent Germany were justified. He was determined to get a draft of a collective defense agreement that could be put before governments, his own especially, and was now ready to adapt to current necessities the

French specifications for effective enforcement action that he and Wilson had wholly rejected at Paris five years before.

Cecil and Réquin, working with renewed purpose in the summer of 1923 when the conflict in the Ruhr was drawing to its appointed end and new opportunities for an agreed political settlement were opening, prepared a draft of a Treaty of Mutual Assistance that was a compromise between British and French desires but was the plainest outline of an effective system to maintain the peace in Europe under League control that was put forward in the interwar years.

Its basic proposition was simple: that the collectivity of some fifty nations required a core of organized power. At Paris the French had proposed to meet the problem of enforcement by the creation of a military staff, appointed by the Council, authorized to organize and train an army of national contingents, and, in an emergency, to devise a stategy for a particular war. That grant of power, as we have noted, was too great for the theory of the general interest to bear. The Draft Treaty of Mutual Assistance, as put before the Assembly of the League in the autumn of 1923, made a bow to the theory and reduced it to particulars. The Treaty would be general, in the sense that it could be signed by any member of the League—or any nonmember—that wished to subscribe; but it underpinned the collectivity with a center of power in Europe based on an awareness of special interests. There could, indeed, be comparable centers of power in other parts of the world, if the signatories so desired. Taking the hint from the third paragraph of the Assembly's Resolution, the Commission inserted into this question of enforcement the idea of regional responsibilities and exemptions. No signatory to the general treaty was "in principle" required to cooperate in military, naval, or air operations carried on in a "continent" other than the one in which it was situated. This was a new version of collective action, but there was no element of counter-theory in it. The Commission was asking not for what it would most like to have but for the most the survey had indicated it could hope to get and for the minimum it must have if the peace was to be maintained—namely, Britain in Europe, without the Dominions if necessary.

Like Article 16, the Draft Treaty was constructed on the assumption that other articles of the Covenant had failed in their purpose and a war had begun. In more direct language than Article 16, though in a pledge of narrowed scope, the contracting parties undertook to furnish assistance "to any one of their number should the latter be the object of a war of aggression." The Council would name the aggressor—action implicit in Article 16 but here made explicit, with the additional stipulation that the Council act quickly, "within four days." Economic pressure against the offender would immediately be organized, again as under Article 16; but the Council would not "recommend" to all the members of the League what military forces they were to contribute. The Council would "invoke by name the signatories" of the Treaty whose assistance it "required." It would "determine" the forces these states would contribute. It would "prescribe" measures for necessary communications and transport, would prepare a plan for financial cooperation, and would "appoint" the Higher Command. These were the terms of an agreement to fight a war, based on recognition among the signatories of a vital self-interest.

The heart of the plan for mutual assistance was the provision that any group of signatories might conclude "complementary defensive agreements" in anticipation of a call from the Council of the League. Such agreements were to be submitted to the Council for consideration, revision, and approval. Given that approval, the signatories might put provisions of their defensive arrangements into effect even before the Council designated the enemy whose attack it was their obligation to repulse. This was the safeguard, lacking in Article 16, against being caught flat-footed by a prepared attack, and reinsurance if the Council could not make up its mind.

Arrangements for bringing the Treaty into force by regions showed that the Commission was aware that countries that did not consider themselves in danger of attack would be unlikely to sign it. Since political factors would determine their estimate of the risks involved, the drafters had to modify the convenient division of the world into "continents" in outlining these arrangements. They displayed considerable geographical originality. Six distinct areas were found: North America, Central America and the West Indies, South America, Asia, Africa and Oceania, and Europe. There was, however, no regional division within Europe; the Treaty would come into force "in Europe when it shall have been ratified by five States, of which three shall be permanently represented on the Council." Provisions for bringing the Treaty into force in other areas were along comparable lines, except for North America. Procedure in the North American area was stated succinctly: the Treaty would come into force in North America "when ratified by the United States of America."

Finally, as the leverage for disarmament, an over-all clause provided that only states agreeing to a planned reduction of national arms, under League control, would be entitled to the protection the Treaty offered. Arrangements for inspection were blurred; signatories were pledged to "cooperate" with the League in supplying information.

The Commission did not attempt to offer details of the plan for control of arms. It did, however, insert in the Preamble a short sentence of powerful appeal to League adherents throughout the world for whom disarmament and peace were synonymous. It sought to outlaw aggressive war: "The High Contracting Parties solemnly declare that aggressive war is a crime and severally undertake that no one of them will be guilty of its commission." The finality of the words "crime" and "guilty" went beyond anything in the Covenant. Were this assertion retained it would certainly have to be clarified.

As presented by the Commission, the Treaty was, of course, a draft only, inviting amendment. The Assembly debated it hotly, did not vote to approve or disapprove, and sent a copy to every government in the world for comment.

Two of the three great non-League states returned the expected negatives. The American letter coldly explained that the link to League and Covenant was reason enough for rejection. The Soviet government gave itself the dialectical pleasure of noting the inconsistency between "Cecil's and Réquin's" objectives, but indignantly —or with Bolshevik humor—termed the League plan "equivalent to an international dictatorship." As for disarmament, the letter said, no state was more eager for it than the USSR, but the way to disarm was for every state to go ahead and do it; there was no need for "measures of constraint." Leninist ideas on the subject came as no surprise, for Russia, like the United States, had staged its own disarmament conference. At that conference, held in Moscow in 1922, the USSR had proposed to its invited guests—the neighboring states of Eastern Europe—that all clasp hands in nonaggression pacts and reduced armed forces seventy-five per cent forthwith. Aware of the earlier Bolshevik proposal that Poland cut its army to the vanishing point and defend itself with a workers' militia, the visiting statesmen went home quickly.

The reply to the League's inquiry from the third great non-League state was, however, news. German comments on the League had hitherto been bitter. This communication, signed by Gustav Stresemann, who associated with his own the names of eight German legislators, jurists, and scholars, was, in effect, an application for membership in the League—though a League whose purpose would be limitless revision, not maintenance, of the Versailles settlement. The letter praised the clarity with which the Draft Treaty of Mutual Assistance defined its objective—security and disarmament—and declared that "its significance and value were beyond all manner of doubt." But the reply was obliged to "question seriously the method adopted" to achieve the objective. Not only were the complementary defensive agreements against the spirit of the Covenant, but the Treaty would not rectify the current inequality of arms or provide security, since the verdicts of the Council were not impartial but inescapably political. The identification of aggression required time, scientific research, and histori-

cal scholarship; and peace required the correction of injustice. The
letter proposed an ideal approach:

> Side by side with the Court of International Justice for purely
> legal disputes, create a court of arbitration for political conflicts
> and endow it with every guarantee for the political independence
> of its members. Decree compulsory adherence thereto as well as
> to the Permanent Court of International Justice. . . . See to it
> that the justified wishes of the population for an adjustment of
> frontiers be met by means of properly regulated legal procedure
> . . . and above all, make disarmament obligatory upon all na-
> tions.[10]

Stresemann, who had pounded his way to the top in German
politics like one of Admiral Hipper's battle cruisers coming up at
Jutland and was a representative of the class that had devised these
powerful machines, thus gave notice of the extent of his remarkable
talents. The letter, at once disingenuous and sincere, and adroit in
its appeal to the pacifist illusions of the time, was the signal of the
beginning of the political contest over conditions of German membership in the League and other things thereby determined.

Eighteen governments, including Italy and Japan, approved the
Treaty of Mutual Assistance "in principle," the League's report
said. In fact, only the Continental countries that feared an attack
from an easily identifiable source were clearly in favor of it. The
report summarized the "misgivings" to which it gave rise among
the other members in rounded phrases: the Treaty did not imply
reduction of armaments with "sufficient definiteness"; it made no
provision for development of the "moral elements" of the Covenant—"the extension of arbitration and international jurisdiction";
and the articles relating to partial treaties were considered by "several governments" to lead to "the establishment of groups of Powers animated by hostility toward other Powers."

The draft was too plain; the emphasis would have to be shifted.

When the reply from the British government was received in Geneva, over the signature of J. Ramsay MacDonald, who had taken

office as Prime Minister of a Labor government, there was no mistaking that the effort to underpin the general guarantee of the League with a special arrangement that could include Britain but exempt the Dominions had backfired. The British letter not only offered no suggestion for amendment but the severity of criticism of every aspect of the Treaty seemed a retreat from the Covenant itself. It was reported that the Foreign Office had composed the reply. *The Round Table,* the quarterly review of Commonwealth affairs,[11] speaking for the most influential sector of British opinion on foreign relations, said forthrightly in explanation that the Treaty "contained the elements of disruption of the British Empire." This was so not only because of the regional arrangements, which profered the intolerable suggestion that parts of the Empire could be at peace while other parts were at war, but also because the demand that Britain be a guarantor of "the whole territorial system in Central and Eastern Europe" would make Britain a "part of the European balance of power." Such a commitment would be "contrary to the whole tradition of British policy in Europe since that policy first took shape."

The Draft Treaty remained on the table in Geneva, but at the opening session of the Assembly in September 1924 MacDonald outdistanced the Foreign Office in his disesteem for the effort to link security and disarmament. The only security lay in disarmament, he said. Warning the small nationalities of the world against the "whited sepulchre of security through military pacts" with a fervor reminiscent of Lodge's appeal to wives, sisters, and sweethearts to rescue America from the menace of the League, the British Prime Minister praised a recent proposal of the Danish government to abolish its army and navy as one that "has really led the way for all sane countries all the world over," and outlined British policy toward the League in these words:

> Our interests for peace are far greater than our interests in creating a machinery of defense. A machinery of defense is easy to create, but beware lest in creating it you destroy the chances of

peace. What the League has to do is to advance the interests of peace.

The world has to be habituated to our existence, the world has to be habituated to our influence. We have to embody in the world confidence in the order and the rectitude of law, and then nations, with the League of Nations enjoying the authority, with the League of Nations looked up to not because its arm is great, but because its mind is calm and its nature just, can pursue their destinies in the feeling of perfect security, none daring to make them afraid.

That is the outlook, and that is the policy that the British Government stands by, and to which it invites the League of Nations to adhere.

He said that Germany must come into the League and that he intended to invite the nations of the world to a disarmament conference. But the strangest part about this strange speech was that his purpose turned out to be not so much to demolish the Draft Treaty as to suggest how it should be revised; and his indicated revision did not consist in severing the link between collective security and disarmament but in putting a new objective ahead of both. The words were rambling, but they led to a point: "An essential condition of security and peace is justice. Justice must be allowed to speak before passion. That is arbitration. . . . The test is, are you willing to arbitrate." [12] Refusal to submit to arbitration should be the criterion for aggression. The formula to which he asked the League to adhere was *arbitration, security, disarmament.*

The appeal of the trilogy was instantaneous. Everyone in the Assembly found in it what he wanted—from the neutrals, for whom compulsory arbitration was a favored panacea, to the French, for whom it promised a closing of the "gap" in the Covenant at which they feared they might find themselves standing alone against an aggressor who had availed himself of the opportunity to fight "legally." [13] The French were now represented not by Poincaré but by Edouard Herriot, a younger and more amiable man, who had come to office as head of a Radical-Socialist ministry. He and MacDonald had agreed upon the new approach in talks behind the scenes, and although Herriot did not expect the British presentation to take the form MacDonald's oratory had given it, he willingly accepted MacDonald's prescription for revision of the Draft Treaty. In his seconding speech, Herriot said:

> We admit that it is an extremely intricate and perplexing task to determine which state is the aggressor . . . We earnestly hope, therefore, that one of the acts of the Fifth Assembly will be to accept the principle of arbitration, which will once again settle our difficulties, since henceforth the aggressor will be the party which refuses arbitration.

This was sanguine indeed. With the change of ministries France had moved to the defensive. Since the possibility of reconciliation with Germany was thereby increased, the peril of an irrevocable misstep increased proportionately. The possibility of a closing of the French-British gap in postwar policies brought the Assembly to the height of enthusiasm and authority. Seventeen speakers took part in the opening debate, which brought an Assembly directive to the legal and political committees of the League for preparation of a new draft. As P. J. Noel Baker has written:

> Four of them were Prime Ministers in power, including the Prime Ministers of Great Britain and of France. Four of them were Ministers of Foreign Affairs in power. Two others were Cabinet Ministers of the highest rank. Two were ex-Prime Ministers, two others were ex-Ministers of Foreign Affairs—all four recently in power, likely to come to power again, and speaking by instructions and in the name of their governments at home.[14]

The work in the committees and subcommittees was done by ministers of Cabinet rank and delegates acting on behalf of governments. The product of their work was the Protocol for the Pacific Settlement of International Disputes—called a protocol because it was offered as a supplement to the Covenant rather than as an international treaty. It was presented to the same Assembly before its adjournment and accepted by unanimous vote of the delegates of the forty-eight governments represented, including the Dominions and British governments.

The popular appeal of this Protocol lay in the shift of emphasis from enforcement to peaceful settlement. The Preamble repeated in stronger words the condemnation of wars of aggression as an "international crime." The articles and clauses of the text, under which the signatories would pledge themselves to follow peaceful procedures in all disputes, followed the scheme of Article 15 of the Covenant. If a dispute referred to the Council could not be resolved by political methods, the Council would seek to persuade the parties to resort first to judicial settlement, then to arbitration. The role of the Permanent Court was enlarged by a requirement that all signatories to the Protocol subscribe to the optional clause of the Court's statute. This extension of the Court's authority was, however, limited to the same justiciable types of dispute as before, with the opportunity for prior national reservations. An "American plan," submitted to the League by a private group in New York, had sought to confer virtually total political power upon the Court by making a refusal to accept the jurisdiction of the Court and comply with its decision in *any* dispute the criterion for aggressive war. By way of sanctions, the American plan proposed that the aggressor state be denied the protection of international law, national law, or treaty, and that all property of the government or of citizens of such a state be seized by any signatory to the treaty that could lay hands on it. Concerning force to be used, each signatory would "consult its own interests and obligations." This draft was gallantly, if rather alarmingly, designed to achieve American support for the objectives of Article 16 of the Covenant without mentioning those unmentionable words.[15] It was hoped in Geneva that the American initiative heralded renewed popular interest in the League, and the effort to strengthen the hand of the Court was, in part, a response to this intervention.

Similarly in search of the absolute, the Protocol placed its bet upon compulsory arbitration. Traditionally, arbitration was an adjunct of diplomacy, useful, as we have noted, in minor disputes in which both parties desired a compromise and were able to agree in advance on the main lines of a settlement. The disputants themselves chose the arbitrators and defined their powers; the statement submitting the controversy to arbitration (called the *comprimis*) might prescribe the law to be applied if they agreed that there was any. The arbitrators, whose function was to complete and make easy of acceptance an understanding already virtually achieved by diplomatic exchanges, carefully avoided harsh judgments or anything savoring of judicial legislation.

The procedures by which the drafters of the Protocol elaborated this diplomatic device into what they hoped would be an ironclad legal prohibition of private war were exceedingly complex. They wound their way through some eighteen or twenty stages and variations of the problem. These ranged from failure of the Council to effect a settlement at the outset, through the machinery for selection of arbitrators (an adaptation of the method used by the Council to select judges of the Permanent court) and the procedure to be used by the Assembly if a disputant demanded resort to that body, to the return of the case to the Council for obligatory arbitration if the Assembly failed. If the disputants still could not agree on the composition of the Committee of Arbitrators, the Council was to choose the committee. The decision that named the aggressor would thus be a political decision, though disguised and long deferred. Formal amendment of Article 15 would be required to incorporate these changes in the Covenant, and there were provisions for interim application. The obligation to accept and abide by these procedures would, moreover, be extended to all disputants who were members of the League even if none wanted it and to cases in which one or both parties were outside the League. While all this was going on there was to be no warlike move by anyone. Any belligerent who refused to accept the terms of an armistice or violated a demilitarized zone would by definition be deemed an aggressor.

This was a large package. Even so, the *rapporteur* for the First Committee noted in his report that there were significant omissions.

The arbitral procedures would not be expected to apply "in disputes which aimed at revising treaties and international acts in force, or which seek to jeopardize the existing territorial integrity of signatory states." M. Politis explained that his committee had considered inserting such a provision in the document but that "both from the legal and political point of view, the impossibility of applying compulsory arbitration to such cases was so obvious that it was quite superfluous to make them the subject of a special provision. It was thought sufficient to mention them in this report."

But these were the very cases that Gustav Stresemann and his advisers wanted to put before a "court of arbitration." The search for the absolute was an exercise in illusion. Arnold J. Toynbee summed up the elaborate provisions for compulsory arbitration in an exact observation: "preliminary guarantees of security which were subjective and psychological." [16] The ambiguity was slurred over in the debate; the temptation to believe was too great. No one wanted the promise of peace severely analyzed. If Germany entered the League without reservation and signed the Protocol there would, in truth, be a peace of consent. Eduard Beneš, the chief among the draftsmen, a man of peace, was probably the most skillful diplomatist on the Continent, excluding the newcomer, Stresemann. He hoped that Germany would sign and was eager to make it as easy as possible for it to do so. Strength and weakness inseparable, he was never so confident as when his hand was upon a writing pad.

By contrast with these provisions for peaceful settlement, the articles dealing with enforcement were modest and straightforward. The artificial arrangements of the Draft Treaty of Mutual Assistance for continental divisions within a general treaty, which had so distressed the British Foreign Office because of its challenge to the unity of Empire and Commonwealth, were abandoned. The provocative terminology of the Draft Treaty, by which the Council "required," "determined," "prescribed," and "appointed" armed forces and commanders in case of aggression, was also deleted. In Article 10 the Protocol merely noted, in the words of the Covenant, that when the Council called upon signatory states to apply sanctions the obligations of Article 16 of the Covenant would become operative, and in unexceptionable language it interpreted them as obliging each of the signatory states "to co-operate loyally and effectively in support of the Covenant of the League of Nations, and in resistance to any act of aggression, in the degree which its geographical position and particular situation as regards armaments allow." In the context of the Protocol this last qualification was mere common sense. Bolivia (as it were) would not be expected to contribute warships, or Denmark an army. "Loyal and effective" support of the Covenant, however, inescapably meant support of the safety of all members of the League, Eastern as well as Western European countries.

Nor did the Protocol dodge the problem of the weakness of Article 16 of the Covenant. "In view of the contingent military, naval and air sanctions provided for by Article 16 of the Covenant, and by Article 11 of the present Protocol," Article 13 of the Protocol read, *"the Council shall be entitled to receive undertakings from States determining in advance* the military, naval and air forces which they would be able to bring into action immediately to ensure the fulfilment of their obligations in regard to sanctions. . . ." (Italics added.) Furthermore, in response to a call from the Council, the said states might "in accordance with any agreements which they may previously have concluded, bring to the assistance of a particular State, which is the victim of aggression, their military, naval and air forces." The League would issue no orders to its sovereign member states. Everything was *may,* not *must.* But the Covenant's prohibition of special arrangements between League members—in substance, if not in name, alliances—such as those over which Wilson and Clemenceau had quarreled at Paris, was lifted. This was the minimum that could be done to make effective the League's pledge of protection, and the quiet words said everything that needed to be said.

In event of an attack in Europe (for example), the loyal members of the League would be prepared, politically and militarily. The precise form their arrangements would take was up to them.

They would fight only by authorization of the Council and in the name of the League of Nations; but by readiness to do so, it might reasonably be supposed, they would discourage attack. There could be no uncertainty, as there had been within the Entente in prewar years, whether a commitment under the terms of the Protocol included military as well as diplomatic support in a crisis. The "undertakings" referred explicitly to the use of armed forces. Nor could there be any doubt that, soon after the Protocol was ratified, one of Paul Cambon's successors would make polite inquiry at Whitehall as to a mutually convenient date for renewed conversations.

If the result of such conversations were in substance an alliance, it would, at any rate, be a new-fashioned one—the first of the series that attempted, as we now know, to give validity to a code of international behavior to which large numbers of states are pleased to subscribe in principle, but upon whose principles few intend to insist. Not only would the "undertakings" be subordinate to Council and Assembly, but, following the directive of Resolution XIV, Article 13 of the Protocol emphasized that any agreement between signatory states "shall remain open to all States Members of the League which may desire to accede thereto." This, in theory, met the objection raised by several members of the League to the "competing alliances" possible under the regional arrangements of the Draft Treaty. Here, again, was the open door for Germany. Had it availed itself of the opportunity to enter, it would, we may fleetingly speculate, thereby effectively have ended any possibility of a British-French grouping directed against it—but by the pleasing act of rendering such a grouping unnecessary. The fact was that the Weimar government had a quite different arrangement with Britain and France in mind, to obviate any possibility that German, British, and French staff officers would sit down together for candid talk about the strength of their armed forces and existing arrangements such as the Rapallo Treaty.

The Geneva Protocol was completed by articles tying measures for enforcement tightly to control of national arms. The Protocol

UNITED KINGDOM
of GREAT BRITAIN
and
NORTHERN
IRELAND

N

THE HEBRIDES

SHETLAND IS.

NORWAY

Bergen

Oslo

SCOTLAND

Glasgow

Edinburgh

Belfast

Dublin

IRELAND

Manchester

North Sea

DENMARK

Copenhagen

EAST

Atlantic Ocean

Liverpool

Birmingham

WALES

London

Amsterdam

The Hague

Antw.

BELGIUM

Rotterdam

NETH.

Hamburg

East Berlin

Potsdam

GERMAN

English Channel

Lille

Le Havre

Brussels

Essen

Cologne

WEST

Leipzig

Bonn

Frankfurt

Prague

Bay of Biscay

Nantes

Loire

Seine

Paris

Marne

GERMANY

Stuttgart

Munich

Salzburg

AUSTI

Vie

Graz

Rhine

Zurich

Bern

LIECH.

SWITZERLAND

Geneva

Lausanne

Lyons

Bordeaux

Garonne

Toulouse

Rhône

Milan

Verona

Venice

Triest

Rieka

Od

Bilbao

Ebro

Oporto

Douro

ANDORRA

Nice

Genoa

Po

Ferrara

Florence

SAN MARINO

ITALY

Madrid

SPAIN

Barcelona

MONACO

Marseilles

CORSICA

Lisbon

Tagus

Toledo

Valencia

MAJORCA

MINORCA

SARDINIA

Rome

Nap

Córdoba

Guadalquivir

Málaga

Granada

BELEARIC IS.

Tyrrhenian Sea

Str. of Gibraltar

Tangier

GIBRALTAR

MOROCCO

SICILY

Rabat

Casablanca

Fez

Oran

Algiers

MALTA

Medi

MOROCCO

Marrakesh

ALGERIA

Bizerte

Tunis

TUNISIA

EUROPE AND
THE MIDDLE EAST,
1967
*Territorial changes after the Second World War
are provisional in absence of peace treaties.*

Tripoli

LIBYA

TRIPOLITANIA

would come into effect not after ratification by groups of states in various areas but as a general agreement ratified by a majority of the permanent members of the Council and ten other members of the League, and *after adoption of a plan for the reduction of armaments*. If the plan were not carried out, the Protocol would be declared null and void. An early date was set for a disarmament conference: June 15, 1925. But Beneš and his colleagues, who had been through a good deal of this kind of thing in recent years, hedged the bet on quick success in control of national arms; the disarmament conference itself would lay down the ground for a Council judgment of nonperformance. Presumably, modest initial progress would be enough. Given security, further reduction might be expected to follow in national self-interest.

The Protocol was immediately signed by seventeen governments, including France, and ratified by one more—Czechoslovakia. The British delegates were not authorized to sign, however; the MacDonald government was in trouble at home. Other governments waited to learn what Britain intended to do.

3. The Blue Sky of Locarno

In a few weeks the news came. The Labor government was defeated in the House of Commons on a secondary issue, and a general election in November 1924 brought Stanley Baldwin back to power with a heavy Conservative majority. That meant the end of the Protocol. The MacDonald government may or may not have been prepared to put money on the bet that every small war and any large one could be outlawed by compulsory arbitration under the League of Nations. But the Conservatives certainly would not back the immense gamble with their blue chip, the British navy, unsupported. Were the Protocol to be amended and the world-wide "psychological guarantee" jettisoned, what remained would, in substance, be the rejected Draft Treaty of Mutual Assistance, focused on the Continent and cutting across the Commonwealth. But if the Protocol were rejected in entirety, what then would be the British proposal to maintain stability in Europe? Sir Austen Chamberlain, Secretary of State for Foreign Affairs in the new Cabinet, could not go to Geneva without a foreign policy. Was the answer, after all, the still more explicit commitment of the French alliance? In the six years since the Paris Conference, the British search for a policy that would relate the Empire and Commonwealth to the Continent and the League had come full circle.

Stanley Baldwin had small interest in foreign affairs but a great concern for party unity. He had assembled a strong Cabinet. The sensational development was Winston Churchill's return to the Conservative Party to accept the offer of the Chancellorship of the Exchequer. Like his father, who had held the same office, Churchill was no friend of a program that might mean an increase in army estimates or a commitment to fight on the Continent. Leopold Amery, a lieutenant of Lord Milner in the lost cause of imperial federation and, like Churchill, a former First Lord of the Admiralty, was Secretary of State for the Colonies. Balfour was, of course, within the circle. Lord Robert Cecil was included. Baldwin's choice of a post for Austen Chamberlain—a son of Joseph Chamberlain, the Colonial Secretary who had split the Unionist (Tory) Party at the turn of the century with his campaign for an imperial tariff—was another surprise. Sir Austen had figured as an attractive compromise candidate in Conservative Party rivalries but had had little experience in the field in which he was now to be chief. He was reputedly in favor of a French alliance. The driving force within the Cabinet in such matters would, however, lie elsewhere.

The new government requested the Council of the League to postpone a scheduled consideration of the Protocol until March 1925 and referred the question of British adherence to a subcommittee of the Committee of Imperial Defence under Balfour's chairmanship. The Dominions were invited to attend an Imperial Conference to devise a common policy.

The Dominion governments were having second thoughts about the uncritical votes their delegates had cast for the Protocol in the Geneva Assembly. All continued to be pleased with the idea of disarmament, and all favored the principle of arbitration; enthusiasm for the added obligations of enforcement was rapidly diminishing. "We live in a fireproof house, far from inflammable materials," noted Senator Raoul Dandurand of Canada in a speech that, unfortunately for the speaker, became famous. (The Senator's fame is not his alone. A discreet British inquiry at Washington as to what the American response might be in the event of application of sanctions by the League brought from the State Department a chilly reminder of the principle of the rights of neutrals.[17]) Other Dominions—Australia especially—were troubled about the answer given in a clause of the Protocol to a question ever so innocently raised by Japan during the drafting sessions. The question was whether international disputes concerning national immigration laws would be subject to compulsory arbitration. The embarrassed answer was, "No, but. . . . Questions of immigration, Article 5 said, without using that dread word, were matters of domestic jurisdiction reserved to the sovereign members of the League—though, naturally, the Protocol did not repeal Article 11 of the Covenant, which gave to each member of the League the "friendly right" to bring to the attention of the Assembly or the Council "any circumstance" affecting international peace or good understanding between nations. Redrafting this clause of the Protocol would not be easy.

Notwithstanding such anxieties, the Dominions did not speak of rejection but of amendments. Yet among the Dominions New Zealand alone accepted the British invitation to the Imperial Conference for the purpose of forging a British Commonwealth policy. Canada, Newfoundland (then a self-governing Dominion), Australia, and the Union of South Africa regretted that impending elections or other pressing business would prevent their Prime Ministers from attending. The Irish Free State did not reply. Great Britain would have to make its own decisions.

Two forceful leading articles in the December 1924 issue of *The Round Table*[18] disclosed the elements of the reorientation of British policy toward the League and Europe that the British government had in mind. The Protocol was dismissed. The procedures of compulsory arbitration would involve the world in every trivial dispute and be futile in great ones: "The struggles which really convulse humanity do not take place over petty disputes, but over deep and seemingly unbridgeable differences in conviction and moral sense." A temporary committee of "five just men" could not legislate such vast forces out of existence. The enforcement of all the obligations of the Protocol would, moreover, impose limitless burdens upon the Empire, including the possibility of conflict with the United States and the adoption of the Protocol would end any possibility of American membership in the League. Wiser to move in the opposite direction: eliminate Article 10 of the Covenant—already, in effect, eliminated—and reduce rather than extend the obligations of Article 16. The League should be used only for discussion and conciliation. In serious disputes it could strive for delay. For the time being the most useful thing it could do was to relax. "If the League is ever to do its work it will be because it is a League of all nations, with both Germany and the United States inside. The first and greatest step towards world peace, therefore, is to make the League one which all nations can reasonably be expected to join, and then patiently wait until the logic of the League's case brings them in."

But what of the impatient Continent? "The real question underlying the Protocol is that of British policy towards Europe," *The Round Table* continued with its customary candor, "for the Protocol is frankly the product of purely European necessities and is primarily an attempt to stabilize, not the world, but Europe." Should Europe, then, be encouraged to try to solve its problems on the basis of a permanent British guarantee? The answer was a flat no. "Europe is a continent, and its nations have the characteristics, the interests and the traditions of Powers with only land frontiers between themselves and their neighbors. Great Britain is an island and the centre of a world-wide Commonwealth far larger than Europe in extent, containing within its boundaries more people than the whole of Europe, and having problems and interests and traditions entirely different from those of Europe." Europe must solve its internal problems for itself. The world-within-a-world of Empire and Commonwealth had task enough in managing its own affairs.

The journalists who wrote in this vein, like the men whose ideas and power they reflected, were "imperialists"—a word that for most of them had lost the traditional connotation. They did not envisage Britain as a ruler of vassal states and had, moreover,

abandoned as utterly impracticable the objective of imperial federation which Milner and his group had passionately advanced. For
most of the imperialists outside that group, indeed, the passion the
idea engendered and required made it unattractive. It was too thorough: un-English.* Balfour's epochal definition, or description, of
the relations of the Commonwealth in his Report—"autonomous
Communities within the British Empire, equal in status, in no way
subordinate one to another in any aspect of their domestic or external affairs, though united by a common allegiance to the Crown"—
was not to appear in print for a year or so, but it was already
unmistakable that the emphasis in Commonwealth relations was on
the negative side. Seldom absent from the consciousness of these
responsible British writers and statesmen, though usually suppressed, was the shadow thrown by the simple and terrible phrase,
"unity or dissolution."

The anxiety of *The Round Table* was disclosed in a peremptory
statement addressed obviously to the self-governing Dominions
which had shown such an undesired degree of interest in the Protocol: "As the Empire must be either at war or at peace as a whole, it
is clear that unless there is a unanimous decision of the self-
governing parts of the empire in favor of ratifying the Protocol, no
one part, whether it is Great Britain or a Dominion, can ratify it."

* Edward Crankshaw, writing cogently, and with passion, in *The Forsaken
Idea: A Study of Viscount Milner* (New York: Longman's Green, 1952)
about the total failure of the effort to achieve the organic unity of the Empire, asked himself the central question: Why did not Lord Milner, with his
tremendous gifts, dominate his time? His own answer epitomizes the story:
the greatest Prime Ministers have not only vision and ability but "an instinc-
tive sense of the way the nation does things." It is not an insular observation.
Some twenty-three schemes for a federated Empire were advanced at one
time or another, but none became a serious enough political possibility to be
put before the British electorate. England would no more subordinate the
House of Commons to an Imperial legislature than the Dominions would
subordinate their parliaments to the House; and India was unassimilable in
any scheme. For interesting examples of the proposed "constitutions" the curi-
ous reader may be referred to Seymour Ching-Yuan Cheng, *Schemes for the
Federation of the British Empire* (New York: Columbia University Press,
1931).

And with regard to the League demand that Britain and Dominions turn aside from their own great problem to soothe a worried Europe, the anxiety became downright annoyance. The talk about the necessity to " 'do something' " to prevent Europe sinking into political chaos was "rubbish." To suggest that France needed military guarantees for security was "sheer rubbish." Europe was now stabilized. Were a greater degree of stabilization desired, France could best contribute to it by reducing its preponderant armament. Thus *The Round Table* accurately revealed what were to become the main outlines of British policy toward the Continent and the League for the next fifteen years.

In the event, a note to the Dominions on March 3, 1925, advised them that the Cabinet could not accept the Geneva Protocol or recommend its acceptance to the other governments of the Empire, and since this note was entirely negative, all were happy to subscribe to the rejection, and each did so for itself, making it, in a way, a common policy.

What was to take the place of the Protocol soon appeared. Since it was, after all, necessary to "do something," the Baldwin government reverted to the solution for the maintenance of stability on the Continent that had been adopted after the Napoleonic Wars. Britain would fight on the Continent if, in its estimate, fighting were necessary to protect the Low Countries and the Channel ports. It would maintain the balance of power on the Continent—this time between France and Germany—from the outside. It would mediate between Germany and France, in case of trouble, on the general principle of the free hand. It would pledge itself to oppose Germany if Germany attacked France and to oppose France if France invaded Germany. Belgian neutrality was implicit. Implicit and sensationally plain was a disclaimer of interest and responsibility in the event of trouble on the eastern frontiers of central Europe. There Germany would have a free hand. This solution of the problem of implementing the new British policy toward Europe had been brought to the attention of the Foreign Office by Gustav

Stresemann, no longer Chancellor but now Foreign Minister of the Weimar Republic and more powerful than before.

The substance of the proposal, which was to take shape in the group of treaties signed at Locarno "guaranteeing" western but not eastern frontiers, had been put forward three times before by German governments: by Chancellor Wilhelm Cuno in a speech at Hamburg in December 1922, again in a note to the Allied governments and the United States in May 1923, and tentatively by Stresemann in September 1923. French governments had rejected it decisively. Stresemann revived it now on the advice of the British Ambassador in Berlin, Lord D'Abernon, who knew that the time for it was ripe. Unwisely, however, the German Foreign Minister embodied it in a secret letter to the British Foreign Office, which quickly and correctly replied that it should be communicated also to the French government. That was done, again with the request that, for the time being, it remain confidential. Herriot, distraught for lack of a program to recommend to his own divided government, listened with hope and trembling. If Britain would pledge firm support for the western frontiers, why perhaps half a loaf, in the hungry political present . . . and might not the promise of British aid for threatened French allies be smuggled in by resolute diplomacy?

But there was nothing resolute in Herriot's character and little in that of Briand, who became Foreign Minister when the mournful game of musical chairs was next played in Paris. Herriot's readiness to entertain the German-British proposal settled the matter.

When Chamberlain stopped in Paris on March 7, 1925, on the way to Geneva to deliver the postponed verdict on the Protocol, he found Herriot in a state of nerves. "I tell you I look forward with terror to her [Germany] making war upon us again in ten years," he cried.[19] The British Foreign Secretary was so alarmed by Herriot's reaction that he wrote to the Prime Minister for instruction. There was a stormy session of the Cabinet, with Churchill, Amery, and Lord Birkenhead apparently up in arms lest Chamberlain's

French sympathies were leading him to make undue concessions.* But Baldwin reassured his Foreign Secretary that the government was firmly behind him—at any rate, in the rejection of the Protocol and in his recommendation that Herriot look favorably upon the German proposal.[20]

Sir Austen delivered the death sentence at Geneva on March 12, 1925, in a speech less forthright than *The Round Table*'s closely reasoned preview but plain enough: "The fresh emphasis laid upon sanctions, the new occasions discovered for their employment, the elaboration of military procedure, insensibly suggest the idea that the vital business of the League is not so much to promote friendly co-operation and reasoned harmony in the management of international affairs as to preserve peace by organizing war. . . ." Collective security under the League was thus officially buried.

In the period of diplomatic jockeying that ensued, Stresemann was devious and brilliant. At home he had to persuade enemies such as von Seeckt, and his colleagues in the Weimar coalition, the extreme German Nationalists, that in pledging acceptance of the postwar western boundaries he was actually opening the door for limitless revision of the Versailles settlement; he had to persuade Briand of the opposite; and, most difficult of all, he had to quiet the intense suspicions of his Rapallo partner, the Soviet government, as to the import of the whole intricate maneuver.

Von Seeckt hated the idea of a pact of any kind with France, especially one that seemed intended to make the loss of Alsace-Lorraine irremediable, and he was no less hostile to the League of Nations, which he looked upon simply as a vicious instrument of Allied oppression. The Versailles Treaty provided that the Allied Military Control Commission would be withdrawn when it was sat-

---

* Exactly what went on in the episode is unclear. Amery and Churchill seem to have wanted less of a commitment than Landsdowne and Grey had made before the war. In their memoirs they describe themselves as strong supporters of the Locarno idea, Amery suggesting that it was he who first brought it forward. To the end of his life Churchill insisted that it was a master stroke and wanted to apply it to German-Russian problems after the Second World War.

isfied that German disarmament had been accomplished, but it also provided (Article 213) that thereafter the responsibility for investigation would devolve upon a Commission of the League. Stresemann's intention of gaining German membership in the League as part of a plan that promised the inviolability of French frontiers seemed to von Seeckt not only another disgraceful capitulation but a direct threat to his burgeoning plans for secret rearmament. The German Foreign Minister persuaded him to soften his opposition with the argument that "if one wanted to ruin an organization or club, it was always better to be a member," [21] but the unpolitical general did not perceive the sagacity of Stresemann's policy of revising the Treaty by "undermining" (*aushöhlen*) during the period of hidden rearmament until the fruits of the Locarno arrangements began to ripen several years later. Then von Seeckt yielded him his grudging admiration and the two dissimilar men became friends.

Briand, coming to the Foreign Ministry in April 1925 in a government headed by Paul Painlevé, was less recalcitrant. He twisted and turned in an effort to broaden the envisaged guarantees of frontiers, but with Britain as well as Germany adamant in refusing to entertain such an extension he was in a vise. The resourceful German Foreign Minister then found the formula which enabled Briand to rise above the problem: Germany would sign arbitration treaties with Poland and Czechoslovakia, which, though not "coordinated" with the western pacts as Briand asked, would nonetheless be "simultaneous." [22] That is to say, various pens would put ink upon the several pieces of paper the same day, but Britain and Italy—now drawn into the settlement—would be guarantors of the western boundaries only. The French plenipotentiaries could sign eastern arbitration agreements if it gave them pleasure—with the understanding that there were two separate sets of documents, one enforceable, the other not. It was an artistic solution and Briand, appreciating it, began to enjoy—and really believe in—his grand role as peacemaker. The two Ministers wound up their collaboration in a feast of friendship.

In his efforts to placate Alfred Hugenberg's Nationalists, Gustav

Stresemann revealed his own interpretation of the significance of the proposed pacts in letters and speeches at closed party meetings which might have wrecked his plans had they become known and believed at the time. A letter to Ambassador von Maltzan, then in Washington, explained that the Locarno Treaties would protect Germany from punitive action by France, would "split the Entente, and open new possibilities in the east." [23] In an unsigned letter to the Crown Prince, with whom he was on good terms, for circulation among the Nationalists, he argued that until Germany had recovered power, its policy must be to *finassieren* (a word difficult to translate, suggesting something between "maneuver" and the use of tricks). Among German aims he listed the recovery of lost colonies, *Anschluss* with Austria, and sweeping territorial revision in the east. In anonymous articles in German periodicals he reaffirmed such ideas and reasoned further that the pact with France would constitute a renunciation not of Alsace-Lorraine but only of the recovery of the provinces by force; procedures of "peaceful change" could be used to achieve that objective. Once Germany was in the League, an active German diplomacy could make things very uncomfortable for its opponents, both in the west and the east, he suggested.[24]

In an open document he named the concessions the Weimar Republic asked from the Allies and the League in return for German willingness to accept membership. The demands included the immediate evacuation of Allied forces from the Cologne zone in the Rhineland, evacuation of the remaining zones of occupation earlier than specified in the Versailles Treaty, a seat among the permanent members of the Council of the League, and exemption from obligations under Article 16. This last point—in effect, a demand for a special position of neutrality within the League—was vital for the success of Stresemann's plans, for the continuation of the Weimar Republic's collaboration with Russia depended upon it.

The Soviet government gave Stresemann a rougher time than either the French or the German Nationalists. In Communist eyes the League was "a consortium of bandits," the proposed Locarno arrangements a British plot to send Germany marching eastward. A Communist leader in the Reichstag replied to an exposition by the German Foreign Minister in these words:

> Herr Stresemann, you are not deceiving anyone. Everybody knows that you have offered German soil and German workers for a future war against Russia as the price of reconciliation with England and France. Your foreign policy is attempting to turn Germany into a village of timorous vassals who seek union with the great British robber baron in order to share in further spoils.[25]

This was a notable exaggeration, for the British were not plotting to start a war in Europe. Their serious thoughts about the future were several thousand miles away. In the Locarno scheme they merely hoped to make sure that if a war did come in Eastern Europe they would keep out of it, in the spirit of go it mother-in-law, go it bear. They wanted no more of Article 16 of the Covenant than did Stresemann or the Comintern, but it was difficult for the Russians to believe that the English would undermine the stability of Europe so casually.[26] Furthermore, Krestinsky, the Russian Ambassador to Berlin, asked whether the Weimar government, as a member of the League, expected to aid Poland or to permit France to send help across German territory in the event of Polish-Russian hostilities? Stresemann assured him that before Germany joined the League it would see that Article 16 was stripped of all dangerous implications.[27] But this assurance did not suffice. The Russians were not novices at such games. Their response was to initiate advances for a *rapprochement* with Poland. And what, in fact, *was* the German view of the Polish future? demanded the Soviet Foreign Minister, Chicherin, who turned up suddenly in Berlin. Gustav Stresemann gave a brief and comprehensive answer: "Naturally we refuse to see any justification for the continued existence of the present Polish state: we shall therefore never recognize the Polish borders of our own free will." [28]

Gustav Stresemann was not an "easterner," as many ranking officials of the German Foreign Office were, or as von Seeckt was;

he not only disliked and distrusted Communism as a political philosophy but also was alert to the danger of German ties with the Kremlin. But the Rapallo agreement was essential leverage for his power play against the West. First came economic strength, he constantly asserted, then military power, and when Germany was strong enough, it would have its own policy. That he intended deliberately to make war seems unlikely. He drew away in alarm from a Russian inquiry as to whether Germany was actually prepared to undertake military action with Russia to "push Poland back to her ethnic borders"—a suggestion apparently made by the German Foreign Office without his knowledge—and he rejected a Soviet request for a treaty strengthening the Rapallo understanding. He nonetheless gave Krestinsky a reason for his disinclination to sign such a treaty that the Russians understood and accepted under the rules of the game. He explained that he could not do it while the negotiations leading to Locarno were in progress: "If I am asked whether we have a secret treaty with Russia, I wish to be able to say no." [29] He promised that he would sign an agreement reaffirming the Rapallo Treaty after the Locarno Treaty was signed, and he kept his promise.

And so, in due course, the representatives of the Western powers met in the October sunshine of Locarno and, turning their backs to the distant clouds, rejoiced to see only clear skies. In a boat ride on the lovely Italian lake, Chamberlain, Briand, and Stresemann settled their final problem—the choice of words that would exempt Germany from responsibilities under Article 16. This, too, was a neat solution—the use of a phrase lifted from the shattered Protocol. It was decided that an annex to the Treaty would state that, though the signatories were aware that they were not in a position to speak in the name of the League, they had agreed that, in the case of Germany, the obligations of each state member of the League to cooperate loyally and effectively in support of the Covenant and in resistance to any act of aggression should be understood to mean "to an extent which is compatible with its military situation and takes its geographical position into account." This was the reservation intended to make continued League membership possible for Denmark, the weakest and most thoroughly pacifist country in Europe.

Thus Europe's Central Power, not disarmed and already rearming, was "neutralized," and Briand and Chamberlain, knowing that the League considered such a reservation for German benefit improper and ruinous, nonetheless pledged themselves to see it through. Such was the political foundation for the Dawes Plan and the rehabilitation of the German economy. Stresemann had taken every trick in the hand.

The group of pacts—usually called simply the Treaty of Locarno—was initialed on October 16, 1925, Sir Austen Chamberlain's birthday. Chief among the set of documents was the treaty guaranteeing Franco-German and German-Belgian boundaries. This was signed by Germany, Belgium, France, Great Britain, and Italy. There were also arbitration conventions between Germany and Belgium, between Germany and France, between Poland and Germany, and between Germany and Czechoslovakia. France took the opportunity to conclude treaties of mutual assistance with Poland and Czechoslovakia. All these were bilateral. France was linked with all; Britain with none. They built a house of paper.

The relation of the guarantees of the Treaty to the provisions of the Treaty of Versailles and of the Covenant was carefully worded. The relevant passages from the text merit close reading:

> *Article* 1. The High Contracting Parties collectively and severally guarantee . . . the maintenance of the territorial *status quo* resulting from the frontiers between Germany and Belguim and between Germany and France and the inviolability of the said frontiers as fixed in persuance of the treaty of peace signed at Versailles on June 28, 1919, and also the observance of the stipulations of Articles 42 and 43 of the said treaty concerning the demilitarized zone.
>
> *Article* 2. Germany and Belgium, and Germany and France mutually undertake that they will in no case attack or invade each other. This stipulation shall not, however, apply in case of:
>
> 1. The exercise of the rights of legitimate defense, that is to

say, resistance to a violation of the undertaking contained in the previous paragraph or to a flagrant breach of Articles 42 or 43 of the said Treaty of Versailles if said breach constitute an unprovoked act of aggression and by reason of the assembly of armed forces in the demilitarized zone some immediate action is necessary.

2. Action in pursuance of Article 16 of the Covenant of the League of Nations. . . .

Article 4. If one of the parties alleges that a violation of Article 2 or a breach of Articles 42 or 43 of the Treaty of Versailles has been committed it shall bring the question at once before the Council of the League of Nations. . . . *The Council will notify the signatories of its findings.*

In case of a flagrant violation . . . *each of the other Contracting Parties* hereby undertakes immediately to come to the help of the party against whom such a violation or breach has been directed [Italics added.]

What could sound more reassuring, if the absence of any reference to the frontiers between Germany and Poland and between Germany and Czechoslovakia remained unnoticed? Yet the loophole through which Hitler was to march to destroy the Continent, the League, and the British Empire, was evident even in the one wall of the foundation under the new structure of peace. In the view of the signatories to the Locarno Treaty, the Treaty was "not to be interpreted as restricting the duty of the League to take whatever action may be deemed wise and effective to safeguard the peace of the world," Article 7 insisted. But the upshot of the double negative was that the League was obliged merely to report. In the event that aggression was deemed "unprovoked" and "flagrant," only Italy and Great Britain undertook to act—that is to say, to go to war on the side of the victim. And the Dominions were, after all, constitutionally free to remain at peace if Britain decided to fight: "The present treaty shall impose no obligation upon any of the British Dominions, or upon India, unless the Government of such Dominion, or of India, signifies its acceptance thereof," Article 19 of the Locarno Treaty explained. No Dominion signed.

When the statesmen at Locarno emerged from the ceremony of initialing this masterpiece of doubletalk they were met by a crowd of people cheering in Italian, German, French, and English, and church bells were rung. "The wonderful week is over," said the British Foreign Secretary in a letter written that night, "so simple, so natural, so easy. . . . We did what we had to do because it was inevitable." Austen Chamberlain, Aristide Briand, and Gustav Stresemann received Nobel Prizes for their work. General Dawes got one too. Mussolini was not on the honors list, though Sir Austen had words of appreciation for him also: "the simplest and sincerest of men, when he is not posing as the Dictator." [30] This was the spirit of Locarno.

That the public should have thought the shadow play assuaged the feud between France and Germany and strengthened the League is perhaps not surprising, since almost without exception the statesmen of Europe thought best to proclaim that it did. Beneš noted that Locarno was devised to meet only one danger spot, yet, as was his way, he put a good face on his disappointment: the pacts were, he said, "an undoubted strengthening of the League of Nations." [31] The Polish Foreign Minister allegedly described the pact to the French Ambassador as "a dagger thrust in the back of the alliance between our two countries," but said publicly that he was pleased by it because "our friendship with France will be stronger." [32] Poincaré analyzed the Treaty unsparingly, but Briand drew cheers even in France when he declaimed on the day that Germany took her seat on the Security Council of the League, "Away with rifles, away with machine guns, away with cannons! Make room for reconciliation, for courts of arbitration, for peace." The Briand-Kellogg Pact, in which the round world renounced the use of force in international affairs, followed two years later. France began to pour concrete for the Maginot Line the same year, but the flank of the great forts on the Belgian boundary was left hanging in air as Belgium moved to neutrality.

With all limits lifted or marked for removal, Germany did not settle down but, quite naturally, blew up. By 1929 it had received some twenty-five billion gold marks in loans, paying about eight billion in reparations. Some four to five billion of the loans were short term. Money flowed into German savings accounts at the rate of more than a billion a year, attracted by high interest rates, but the savings accounts could not begin to finance the booming German economy. Industrial productivity rose to one hundred and twenty-two per cent, as compared with the production of the last year before the war. The American Agent-General for Reparations warned against the hazardous financial structure, protesting in particular the overspending by municipalities and the disregard of the unfavorable German trade balance, but he could not control the boom, or the American bond salesmen.

In a newly constituted German Economic General Staff the excitement was controlled, for German industry was being planned and rebuilt for another war. A survey had outlined the requirements of an army of sixty-three divisions. Contracts for material were placed in Austria, Switzerland, Sweden, Spain, Holland, and Italy. The Reichswehr budget rose from 490,000,000 marks in 1924 to 827,000,000 in 1928 and continued to mount. Tanks were in production in 1928, a year after the withdrawal of the Allied Control Commission. It is customary and convenient to charge these things to the wickedness of German soldiers, but that is neither just nor rational. Who were the deceived and who were the deceivers? The fact of German-Russian collaboration in arms production was by then public knowledge, having been revealed in the Reichstag itself by a Socialist deputy. It was thought best to disregard the information, as the final five-hundred-page report of the Arms Control Commission was disregarded. "It was no longer possible that a settlement should be delayed indefinitely by technical controversies between experts now that the statesmen were of one mind in feeling that the time for a settlement had come and were also in agreement over the broad lines of their political bargain," Arnold J. Toynbee explained to the readers of the *Survey of International Affairs, 1927*.[33]

At a conference at the Hague in 1929, the total withdrawal of

Allied occupation forces from the Rhineland was pledged for 1930, five years ahead of the date set in the Versailles Treaty. This concession was part of a bargain by which Germany was induced to accept a revised schedule of reparation payments and a funding of the external German debt under the ephemeral Young Plan. Gustav Stresemann died in October 1929. The withdrawal of Allied troops was completed in June 1930. That was the year that the Nazi Party won one hundred and seven seats in the Reichstag. The Locarno Treaty did not itself produce Hitler. It merely guaranteed the success of his strategy.

The Power of Illusion

Before the new German leader could strike, in the East, the blow that would bring down the West, one more concession was required of the one-time Allies and their Associated Power. Adolf Hitler had to secure their assent to the *open* rearmament of Germany during the period that would be necessary to transform the skeletal arrangements for economic and military mobilization into a full-fledged fighting machine. When he gained power, this evil political genius achieved the incredible with ease, using the "language of Geneva" (the phrase is Alan Bullock's) and then the League itself, as his instruments.[1] *Did not the world want peace? That is what he wanted too. Was not war useless and horrible? Be certain he thought so. But was not justice the basis of peace, as written in the Covenant? And did not even the Treaty of Versailles, that catalogue of injustices, provide that, through the League, Germany would be received by former enemies as a respected equal? Germany was now in the League, but where was the promised equality? What could be plainer than the meaning of that word, as defined by the victors themselves? It meant the reduction of their armaments to the German level. Was the war over or was it not? Did they or did they not want peace?*

They desperately wanted peace. Hitler's new tone was not the one he had taken in *Mein Kampf,* but what he was saying now was what everyone wanted to hear. He riveted the attention of his audience abroad by illustrating his disquisition on the horrors of war with remorseless acts of terror against his own countrymen—Social Democrats in general (he was aided in this by the Communist street-fighters who followed the book of Marx and Lenin) and Jews in particular. Foreign Offices that were not convinced that Hitler's approach pointed the way to peace were simply paralyzed, except in Japan and Mussolini's Italy, where plans for supplementary action began to mature.

The problem of the pacific powers was that in the era of every man for himself it was even more difficult to agree on how to disarm themselves than it had been in the dawn of the era of collective security. Since the death of the Protocol they had wrangled incessantly among themselves over disarmament in a series of preparatory conferences, some under League auspices, some not, but all leaving political relations worse than before.

A Three-Power Naval Conference—Japan, Great Britain, and the United States—ended in disagreement on every count, the sharpest words being exchanged by the English-speaking countries. At another Naval Conference, in London, three years later, Britain and America did drop the assumption that they were preparing to fight each other, though they had no policies for the use of their fleets. When Japan agreed to accept a slight reduction in its quota of ships and the United States agreed to an extension of the battleship-building "holiday," the naval problem was considered solved. But the Japanese army moved against the Chinese at Mukden eight months after the Treaty—signed also, resentfully, by Italy and France—went into effect. British and American statesmen, passionately urged on by press and pulpit, then came together in an effort to persuade France to reduce its army.

The General Disarmament Conference that had been scheduled for June 1925 in the rejected Protocol was held in Geneva in February 1932. It went on for two years. There were two high points. One was the intervention of the United States, in full diplomatic force, with a Presidential plan for a slash in land armaments; its main proposal was a one-third reduction of existing strengths and the abolition of "offensive" weapons, notably tanks—in sum, the nonpolitical approach abandoned by the League as hopeless in 1922. In practice, this plan would be a means of drastically reducing the forces of France and its allies, since Germany was assumed to be already disarmed and the Anglo-Saxon countries had drifted into a satisfactory degree of disarmament. France suffered severe international odium for its refusal to cooperate. The French government and military staff did, at any rate, refrain from the further offense of deliberately strengthening and modernizing the tank forces that they possessed, suggested by an obscure, though tall, young French officer.

The second high point was German withdrawal from the Conference and the League in October 1933, while these matters were being fruitlessly debated. Though Hitler's patience was nearing an end, he was still trying to be reasonable. He had welcomed every proposal for disarmament, from abolition of offensive weapons to the principle of total dissolution of all armed forces except the police (Maxim Litvinov's new version of the old workers' militia idea), but now, in "self-respect," as he said, he had to withdraw. He also issued orders to the German High Command for a secret alert in the event that the League took some action. It took none. In these years, in accordance with the role prescribed for it by the Treaty of Locarno, the Assembly was busy endeavoring to amend the Covenant to harmonize it with the nerveless Kellogg Pact—an impossible feat—and perfecting the machinery of peace by drawing up a dozen or more model treaties of arbitration and conciliation—all abstractions. The General Disarmament Conference angrily disbanded.

The end of the Locarno road was now in sight, and the pace quickened. Shocked to a degree of awareness, Britain issued a White Paper noting the "general feeling of insecurity" and began languidly to rearm. France instinctively doubled the period of service for conscripts. Hitler's response to these provocations was an announcement of the existence of a German Air Force, in open contravention of the Treaty of Versailles, and, in March 1935, a law ordering the conscription of recruits for an army of thirty-six divisions. France begged Geneva to take note of this repudiation of international obligations, and the League obliged with a satisfying vote of censure. It also appointed a committee to study the question of the kind of action that might be taken if anything of the sort were done again.

This time, however, Britain, with Baldwin again in power, did take decisive action. Within two months, without informing either France or Italy, it negotiated and then signed a separate arms accord with Hitler—the Anglo-German Naval Agreement of June 1935—whereby Hitler promised not to rebuild the German navy beyond thirty-five per cent of Britain's strength. British assent to the creation of the thirty-six divisions was implicit in the bargain. There followed the Alice-in-Wonderland episode of League sanctions against *Italy* for disregard of international obligations, in Africa, with the British representative on the rostrum at Geneva demanding enforcement of the Covenant.

Ethiopia had appealed to the League on the very day that Hitler promulgated the order for conscription, and the Fascist aggression was no less flagrant than Hitler's violations of treaties. But, as Mussolini understood perfectly, there was not the remotest possibility that France, in sanity, could or would turn her back upon the German army and go to war with Italy. Mussolini had withdrawn from the Corfu adventure twelve years earlier when Britain and France formed a common front against him, but the only common front in existence in Europe now was the German-British understanding.

It was all too clear that the Führer was planning war, but not against Italy. Nor, for that matter, did Britain intend to lead a war against Italy; the excited and bewildered League was asked for economic sanctions only, oil excepted from the embargo. The Council and the Assembly recommended the sanctions in October

1935, and a special Committee of the League began organizing them. Hitler gave the *coup de grâce* to the misjudged and hopeless project on March 7, 1936, when he denounced the Treaty of Locarno and occupied the Rhineland.

His pretext for the violation of both the Locarno and Versailles Treaties was a treaty of mutual assistance which France had signed with the Soviet Union and an appended treaty between Russia and Czechoslovakia whereby the USSR promised to aid the Czechs in the event of German attack, if France first intervened actively in their behalf—the empty agreement made famous at Munich. Hitler said that the pacts violated "the inner meaning" of Locarno and proclaimed the Locarno Treaty dissolved.

What happened thereafter is familiar and almost too painful even for summary. France protested vehemently in private, feebly in public. The violations of the Treaty of Locarno and the Treaty of Versailles were referred to the League *for report only,* the French being told by Sir Anthony Eden (now British Foreign Secretary) that if any military action were demanded at Geneva there would be no support from Great Britain. Ten years of paralysis do not yield to health in an afternoon: France remained where Hitler, truly an expert in pathology, had foreseen—behind the growing Maginot Line. The United States was entrenched behind its Neutrality Laws; and the League unrolled the red carpet for retreat. A period of delay while the League took the problem under advisement assured that there would be no rash resistance to the aggressor, and another formal condemnation made total surrender seemly. Poland wanted to fight and isolated itself dangerously by saying so; Hitler brought it to heel shortly after with a ten-year pact promising coexistence.

Even more deadly was the effect of the unopposed occupation of the Rhineland upon the only serious remaining source of opposition to the German dictator within the Reich—the German army. It too was brought to heel. The small, highly trained force of commissioned and noncommissioned officers had been fragmented for the purpose of training the new recruits. It could not have held the Rhineland or barred the road to Berlin against a determined thrust. The Reichswehr High Command was aghast at the rashness of Hitler's gamble and advised against it. Hitler gave orders for the immediate withdrawal of the occupying force if there were any opposition, but he assured his officers that there would be none. He was right, and they were wrong. That settled the fate of the officers corps.

Strategically secure now for his eastward adventure, Hitler was politeness itself toward his tremulous adversaries. He could not, unfortunately, agree to Eden's request that he promise not to fortify the Rhineland, but he did suggest that there might be a new demilitarized zone on both sides of the French-German boundary, and that Germany was ready to consider rejoining the League. The existence of the Maginot Line interfered with the creation of a demilitarized zone in France, but the League played its part for peace and reconciliation by acknowledging the sovereignty of Italy over Ethiopia and removing the name of that unfortunate country from the roster of League members. Since the Soviet Union was now in the League and the United States was taking part in its nonpolitical social and economic activities, the magic word universality was heard again in Geneva. Now that Article 16 of the Covenant was a dead letter, why could not everyone come in? Mussolini spoiled the dream by taking Italy out of the organization the following year. The dictators had a project of their own—the Berlin-Rome Axis. Mussolini was silent when Hitler seized Austria, and the threat of war was lifted when Czechoslovakia was prevailed upon at Munich to yield peacefully to Hitler's demands.

Peace can be ensured if the demands of a war-maker are always granted; but the pendulum of history swings, retreats come to an end, and dreamers awake. The power of illusion is doubly dangerous for the suddenness with which it can explode and for the fury of the disillusioned. The awakening came five months after peace was proclaimed at Munich. In March 1939 Great Britain gave the eastern guarantee that France and Poland had sought twenty years earlier in the form of a restricted alliance, and that the League had sought in terms of collective security under the Draft Treaty of Mutual Assistance and the Geneva Protocol in 1924 and 1925. The British pledge was unconditional: Britain would take up arms whenever Poland found it necessary to do so. The Dominions did not join in the guarantee, for they had not been told about it. The British Prime Minister, Sir Neville Chamberlain, explained that there had been no time to consult with them.

German tanks and planes crossed the Polish boundary September 1, 1939. The Poles resisted, and there was war. The French mobilized and manned their forts, but the Rhineland bristled with German fortifications, and the Soviet Union was now Hitler's ally. The British pledge was bravely redeemed in the most disadvantageous possible circumstances.

To have constructive meaning, collective security within such an organization as the League of Nations requires a core of organized power, whether by old-fashioned restricted alliance or by some new variation of an alliance such as was attempted under the League by the Draft Treaty of Mutual Assistance and the Geneva Protocol. Lacking that center of political and military strength, the power of the large, loose "world" grouping is the power of illusion. In questions of war and peace illusion is a great and deadly force. The high principles of the parliamentary organization are turned against those members who most respect them. Peace becomes the conqueror's most powerful weapon. The policy of appeasement—the sacrifice of a friend to placate an aggressor—began in the interwar years as early as 1925, at Locarno; there the League of Nations became an instrument of that policy. At the end, the League was dominated by the man who hated it most—Adolf Hitler.

If peace becomes the overruling objective of an international organization such as the League of Nations, the influence of that organization will be used to advance the objectives of the most war-

like power. That is the lesson of the years of lost opportunity of the League. Corollaries seem to be that disarmament and economic betterment may follow but cannot precede the establishment of political security. Efforts to avoid the hard political problem and to reverse the order of priorities undermined the League.

COVENANT OF
THE LEAGUE OF NATIONS

CHARTER OF
THE UNITED NATIONS

NOTES

INDEX

Covenant of the League of Nations

The High Contracting Parties,

In order to promote international cooperation and to achieve international peace and security by the acceptance of obligations not to resort to war, by the prescription of open, just and honourable relations between nations, by the firm establishment of the understandings of international law as the actual rule of conduct among Governments, and by the maintenance of justice and a scrupulous respect for all treaty obligations in the dealings of organised peoples with one another;

Agree to this Covenant of the League of Nations.

Article I

1. The original Members of the League shall be those of the Signatories which are named in the Annex to this Covenant[3] and also such of those other States named in the Annex as shall accede without reservation to this Covenant.[4] Such accession shall be effected by a Declaration deposited with the Secretariat within two months of the coming into force of the Covenant. Notice thereof shall be sent to all other Members of the League.

2. Any fully self-governing State, Dominion or Colony not named in the Annex may become a Member of the League if its admission is agreed to by two-thirds of the Assembly, provided that it shall give effective guarantees of its sincere intention to observe its international obligations and shall accept such regulations as may be prescribed by the League in regard to its military, naval and air forces and armaments.[6]

3. Any Member of the League may, after two years' notice of its intention so to do, withdraw from the League, provided that all its international obligations and all its obligations under this Covenant shall have been fulfilled at the time of its withdrawal.[7]

Article II

The action of the League under this Covenant shall be effected through the instrumentality of an Assembly and of a Council, with a permanent Secretariat.

Article III

1. The Assembly shall consist of Representatives of the Members of the League.
2. The Assembly shall meet at stated intervals and from time to time, as occasion may require, at the Seat of the League or at such other place as may be decided upon.
3. The Assembly may deal at its meeting with any matter within the sphere of action of the League or affecting the peace of the world.
4. At meetings of the Assembly, each Member of the League shall have one vote and may have not more than three Representatives.

Article IV

1. The Council shall consist of Representatives of the Principal Allied and Associated Powers[8] together with Representatives of four other Members of the League. These four Members of the League shall be selected by the Assembly from time to time in its discretion. Until the appointment of the Representatives of the four Members of the League first selected by the Assembly, Representatives of Belgium, Brazil, Greece and Spain shall be Members of the Council.
2. With the approval of the majority of the Assembly, the Council may name additional Members of the League whose Representatives shall always be Members of the Council, the Council with like approval may increase the number of Members of the League to be selected by the Assembly for representation on the Council.
2b. The Assembly shall fix by a two-thirds majority the rules dealing with the election of the non-permanent members of the Council, and particularly such regulations as relate to their term of office and the conditions of re-eligibility.
3. The Council shall meet from time to time as occasion may require,

and at least once a year, at the Seat of the League or at such other place as may be decided upon.

4. The Council may deal at its meetings with any matter within the sphere of action of the League or affecting the peace of the world.

5. Any Member of the League not represented on the Council shall be invited to send a Representative to sit as a member at any meeting of the Council during the consideration of matters specially affecting the interests of that Member of the League.

6. At meetings of the Council, each Member of the League represented on the Council shall have one vote and may have not more than one Representative.

Article V

1. Except where otherwise expressly provided in this Covenant, or by the terms of the present Treaty, decisions at any meeting of the Assembly or of the Council shall require the agreement of all the Members of the League represented at the meeting.

2. All matters of procedure at meetings of the Assembly or of the Council, including the appointment of Committees to investigate particular matters, shall be regulated by the Assembly or by the Council and may be decided by a majority of the Members of the League represented at the meeting.

3. The first meeting of the Assembly and the first meeting of the Council shall be summoned by the President of the United States of America.

Article VI

1. The permanent Secretariat shall be established at the Seat of the League. The Secretariat shall comprise a Secretary-General and such secretaries and staff as may be required.

2. The first Secretary-General shall be the person named in the Annex; there-after the Secretary-General shall be appointed by the Council with the approval of the majority of the Assembly.

3. The secretaries and staff of the Secretariat shall be appointed by the Secretary-General with the approval of the Council.

4. The Secretary-General shall act in that capacity at all meetings of the Assembly and of the Council.

5. The expenses of the League shall be borne by the Members of the League in the proportion decided by the Assembly.

Article VII

1. The Seat of the League is established at Geneva.
2. The Council may at any time decide that the Seat of the League shall be established elsewhere.
3. All positions under or in connection with the League, including the Secretariat, shall be open equally to men and women.
4. Representatives of the Members of the League and officials of the League when engaged on the business of the League shall enjoy diplomatic privileges and immunities.
5. The buildings and other property occupied by the League or its officials or by Representatives attending its meetings shall be inviolable.

Article VIII

1. The Members of the League recognise that the maintenance of peace requires the reduction of national armaments to the lowest point consistent with national safety and the enforcement by common action of international obligations.
2. The Council, taking account of the geographical situation and circumstances of each State, shall formulate plans for such reduction for the consideration and action of the several Governments.
3. Such plans shall be subject to reconsideration and revision at least every ten years.
4. After these plans shall have been adopted by the several Governments, the limits of armaments therein fixed shall not be exceeded without the concurrence of the Council.
5. The Members of the League agree that the manufacture by private enterprise of munitions and implements of war is open to grave objections. The Council shall advise how the evil effects attendant upon such manufacture can be prevented, due regard being had to the necessities of those Members of the League which are not able to manufacture the munitions and implements of war necessary for their safety.
6. The Members of the League undertake to interchange full and frank information as to the scale of their armaments, their military, naval and air programmes, and the condition of such of their industries as are adaptable to warlike purposes.

Article IX

A permanent Commission shall be constituted to advise the Council on the execution of the provisions of Articles I and VIII, and on military, naval and air questions generally.

Article X

The Members of the League undertake to respect and preserve as against external aggression the territorial integrity and existing political independence of all Members of the League. In case of any aggression, or in case of any threat or danger of such aggression, the Council shall advise upon the means by which this obligation shall be fulfilled.

Article XI

1. Any war or threat of war, whether immediately affecting any of the Members of the League or not, is hereby declared a matter of concern to the whole League, and the League shall take any action that may be deemed wise and effectual to safeguard the peace of nations. In case any such emergency should arise, the Secretary-General shall on the request of any Member of the League forthwith summon a meeting of the Council.
2. It is also declared to be the friendly right of each Member of the League to bring to the attention of the Assembly or of the Council any circumstance whatever affecting international relations which threatens to disturb international peace or the good understanding between nations upon which peace depends.

Article XII

1. The Members of the League agree that, if there should arise between them any dispute likely to lead to a rupture, they will submit the matter either to arbitration or judicial settlement or to inquiry by the Council, and they agree in no case to resort to war until three months after the award by the arbitrators or the judicial decision, or the report by the Council.
2. In any case under this Article the award of the arbitrators or the judicial decision shall be made within a reasonable time, and the report of the Council shall be made within six months after the submission of the dispute.

Article XIII

1. The Members of the League agree that whenever any dispute shall arise between them which they recognise to be suitable for submission to arbitration or judicial settlement, and which cannot be satisfactorily

settled by diplomacy, they will submit the whole subject-matter to arbitration or judicial settlement.

2. Disputes as to the interpretation of a treaty, as to any question of international law, as to the existence of any fact which, if established, would constitute a breach of any international obligation, or as to the extent and nature of the reparation to be made for any such breach, are declared, to be among those which are generally suitable for submission to arbitration or judicial settlement.

3. For the consideration of any such dispute, the court to which the case is referred shall be the Permanent Court of International Justice, established in accordance with Article XIV, or any tribunal agreed on by the parties to the dispute or stipulated in any convention existing between them.

4. The Members of the League agree that they will carry out in full good faith any award or decision that may be rendered, and that they will not resort to war against a Member of the League which complies therewith. In the event of any failure to carry out such an award or decision the Council shall propose what steps should be taken to give effect thereto.

Article XIV

The Council shall formulate and submit to the Members of the League for adoption plans for the establishment of a Permanent Court of International Justice. The Court shall be competent to hear and determine any dispute of an international character which the parties thereto submit to it. The Court may also give an advisory opinion upon any dispute or question referred to it by the Council or by the Assembly.

Article XV

1. If there should arise between Members of the League any dispute likely to lead to a rupture which is not submitted to arbitration or judicial settlement in accordance with Article XIII, the Members of the League agree that they will submit the matter to the Council. Any party to the dispute may effect such submission by giving notice of the existence of the dispute to the Secretary-General, who will make all necessary arrangements for a full investigation and consideration thereof.

2. For this purpose the parties to the dispute will communicate to the Secretary-General, as promptly as possible, statements of their case with all the relevant facts and papers, and the Council may forthwith direct the publication thereof.

3. The Council shall endeavour to effect a settlement of the dispute, and, if such efforts are successful, a statement shall be made public giving such facts and explanations regarding the dispute and the terms of settlement thereof as the Council may deem appropriate.

4. If the dispute is not thus settled, the Council, either unanimously or by a majority vote, shall make and publish a report containing a statement of the facts of the dispute and the recommendations which are deemed just and proper in regard thereto.

5. Any Member of the League represented on the Council may make public a statement of the facts of the dispute and of its conclusions regarding the same.

6. If a report by the Council is unanimously agreed to by the Members thereof, other than the Representatives of one or more of the parties to the dispute, the Members of the League agree that they will not go to war with any party to the dispute which complies with the recommendations of the report.

7. If the Council fails to reach a report which is unanimously agreed to by the Members thereof other than the Representatives of one or more of the parties to the dispute, the Members of the League reserve to themselves the right to take such action as they shall consider necessary for the maintenance of right and justice.

8. If the dispute between the parties is claimed by one of them, and is found by the Council to arise out of a matter which by international law is solely within the domestic jurisdiction of that party, the Council shall so report and shall make no recommendation as to its settlement.

9. The Council may in any case under this Article refer the dispute to the Assembly. The dispute shall be so referred at the request of either party to the dispute, provided that such request be made within fourteen days after the submission of the dispute to the Council.

10. In any case referred to the Assembly, all the provisions of this Article and of Article XII relating to the action and powers of the Council shall apply to the action and powers of the Assembly, provided that a report made by the Assembly, if concurred in by the Representatives of those Members of the League represented on the Council and of a majority of the other Members of the League, exclusive in each case of the Representatives of the parties to the dispute, shall have the same force as a report by the Council concurred in by all the Members thereof, other than the Representatives of one or more of the parties to the dispute.

Article XVI

1. Should any Member of the League resort to war, in disregard of its covenants under Articles XII, XIII, or XV, it shall *ipso facto* be

deemed to have committed an act of war against all other Members of the League, which hereby undertake immediately to submit it to the severance of all trade or financial relations, the prohibition of all intercourse between their nationals and the nationals of the Covenant-breaking State, and the prevention of all financial, commercial or personal intercourse between the nationals of the Covenant-breaking State and the nationals of any other State, whether a Member of the League or not.

2. It shall be the duty of the Council in such case to recommend to the several Governments concerned what effective military, naval or air force the Members of the League shall severally contribute to the armed forces to be used to protect the Covenants of the League.

3. The Members of the League agree, further that they will mutually support one another in the financial and economic measures which are taken under this Article, in order to minimise the loss and inconveniences resulting from the above measures, and that they will mutually support one another in resisting any special measures aimed at one of their number by the Covenant-breaking State, and that they will take the necessary steps to afford passage through their territory to the forces of any of the Members of the League which are co-operating to protect the Covenants of the League.

4. Any Member of the League which has violated any Covenant of the League may be declared to be no longer a Member of the League by a vote of the Council concurred in by the Representatives of all the other Members of the League represented thereon.

Article XVII

1. In the event of a dispute between a Member of the League and a State which is not a Member of the League, or between States not Members of the League, the State or States not Members of the League shall be invited to accept the obligations of membership in the League for the purposes of such dispute, upon such conditions as the Council may deem just. If such invitation is accepted, the provisions of Articles XII to XVI inclusive shall be applied with such modifications as may be deemed necessary by the Council.

2. Upon such invitation being given, the Council shall immediately institute an inquiry into the circumstances of the dispute and recommend such action as may seem best and most effectual in the circumstances.

3. If a State so invited shall refuse to accept the obligations of membership in the League for the purposes of such dispute and shall resort to war against a Member of the League, the provisions of Article XVI shall be applicable as against the State taking such action.

4. If both parties to the dispute, when so invited, refuse to accept the obligations of membership in the League for the purposes of such dispute, the Council may take such measures and make such recommendations as will prevent hostilities and will result in the settlement of the dispute.

Article XVIII

Every treaty or international engagement entered into hereafter by any Member of the League shall be forthwith registered with the Secretariat and shall as soon as possible be published by it. No such treaty or international engagement shall be binding until so registered.

Article XIX

The Assembly may from time to time advise the reconsideration by Members of the League of treaties which have become inapplicable and the consideration of international conditions whose continuance might endanger the peace of the world.

Article XX

1. The Members of the League severally agree that this Covenant is accepted as abrogating all obligations or understandings *inter se* which are inconsistent with the terms thereof, and solemnly undertake that they will not hereafter enter into any engagements inconsistent with the terms thereof.

2. In case any Member of the League shall, before becoming a Member of the League, have undertaken any obligations inconsistent with the terms of this Covenant, it shall be the duty of such Member to take immediate steps to procure its release from such obligations.

Article XXI

Nothing in this Covenant shall be deemed to affect the validity of international engagements, such as treaties of arbitration or regional understandings like the Monroe Doctrine, for securing the maintenance of peace.

Article XXII

1. To those colonies and territories which as a consequence of the late war have ceased to be under the sovereignty of the States which formerly governed them, and which are inhabited by peoples not yet able to stand by themselves under the strenuous conditions of the modern world, there should be applied the principle that the well-being and development of such peoples form a sacred trust of civilisation and that securities for the performance of this trust should be embodied in this Covenant.

2. The best method of giving practical effect to this principle is that the tutelage of such peoples should be entrusted to advanced nations which, by reason of their resources, their experience or their geographical position, can best undertake this responsibility and which are willing to accept it, and that this tutelage should be exercised by them as Mandatories on behalf of the League.

3. The character of the mandate must differ according to the stage of the development of the people, the geographical situation of the territory, its economic conditions and other similar circumstances.

4. Certain communities formerly belonging to the Turkish Empire have reached a stage of development where their existence as independent nations can be provisionally recognised, subject to the rendering of administrative advice and assistance by a Mandatory until such time as they are able to stand alone. The wishes of these communities must be a principal consideration in the selection of the Mandatory.

5. Other peoples, especially those of Central Africa, are at such a stage that the Mandatory must be responsible for the administration of the territory under conditions which will guarantee freedom of conscience or religion, subject only to the maintenance of public order and morals, the prohibition of abuses, such as the slave trade, the arms traffic and the liquor traffic, and the prevention of the establishment of fortifications or military and naval bases and of military training of the natives for other than police purposes and the defence of territory, and will also secure equal opportunities for the trade and commerce of other Members of the League.

6. There are territories, such as South-West Africa and certain of the South Pacific Islands, which, owing to the sparseness of their population, or their small size, or their remoteness from the centres of civilisation, or their geographical contiguity to the territory of the Mandatory, or other circumstances, can be best administered under the laws of the Mandatory as integral portions of its territory, subject to the safeguards above mentioned in the interests of the indigenous population.

7. In every case of mandate, the Mandatory shall render to the

Council an annual report in reference to the territory committed to its charge.

8. The degree of authority, control or administration to be exercised by the Mandatory shall, if not previously agreed upon by the League, be explicitly defined in each case by the Council.

9. A permanent Commission shall be constituted to receive and examine the annual reports of the Mandatories and to advise the Council on all matters relating to the observance of the mandates.

Article XXIII

Subject to and in accordance with the provisions of international conventions existing or hereafter to be agreed upon, the Members of the League

a) Will endeavour to secure and maintain fair and humane conditions of labour for men, women and children, both in their own countries and in all countries to which their commercial and industrial relations extend, and for that purpose will establish and maintain the necessary international organisations;

b) Undertake to secure just treatment of the native inhabitants of territories under their control;

c) Will entrust the League with the general supervision over the execution of agreements with regard to the traffic in women and children and the traffic in opium and other dangerous drugs;

d) Will entrust the League with the general supervision of the trade in arms and ammunition with the countries in which the control of this traffic is necessary in the common interest;

e) Will make provision to secure and maintain freedom of communications and of transit and equitable treatment for the commerce of all Members of the League. In this connection, the special necessities of the regions devastated during the war of 1914–1918 shall be borne in mind;

f) Will endeavour to take steps in matters of international concern for the prevention and control of disease.

Article XXIV

1. There shall be placed under the direction of the League all international bureaus already established by general treaties if the parties to such treaties consent. All such international bureaus and all commissions for the regulation of matters of international interest hereafter constituted shall be placed under the direction of the League.

2. In all matters of international interest which are regulated by general conventions but which are not placed under the control of international bureaus or commissions, the Secretariat of the League shall, subject to the consent of the Council and if desired by the parties, collect and distribute all relevant information and shall render any other assistance which may be necessary or desirable.

3. The Council may include as part of the expenses of the Secretariat the expenses of any bureau or commission which is placed under the direction of the League.

Article XXV

The Members of the League agree to encourage and promote the establishment and co-operation of duly authorised voluntary national Red Cross organisations having as purposes the improvement of health, the prevention of disease and the mitigation of suffering throughout the world.

Article XXVI

1. Amendments to this Covenant will take effect when ratified by the Members of the League whose Representatives compose the Council and by a majority of the Members of the League whose Representatives compose the Assembly.

2. No such amendment shall bind any Member of the League which signifies its dissent therefrom, but in that case it shall cease to be a Member of the League.

Charter of the United Nations

We the peoples of the United Nations, determined to save succeeding generations from the scourge of war, which twice in our lifetime has brought untold sorrow to mankind, and to reaffirm faith in fundamental human rights, in the dignity and worth of the human person, in the equal rights of men and women and of nations large and small, and to establish conditions under which justice and respect for the obligations arising from treaties and other sources of international law can be maintained, and to promote social progress and better standards of life in larger freedom, and for these ends to practice tolerance and live together in peace with one another as good neighbors, and to unite our strength to maintain international peace and security, and to ensure, by the acceptance of principles and the institution of methods, that armed force shall not be used, save in the common interest, and to employ international machinery for the promotion of the economic and social advancement of all peoples, have resolved to combine our efforts to accomplish these aims.

Accordingly, our respective Governments, through representatives assembled in the city of San Francisco, who have exhibited their full powers found to be in good and due form, have agreed to the present Charter of the United Nations and do hereby establish an international organization to be known as the United Nations.

Chapter I: PURPOSES AND PRINCIPLES

Article 1. The purposes of the United Nations are [1] To maintain international peace and security, and to that end: to take effective collective measures for the prevention and removal of threats to the peace, and for the suppression of acts of aggression or other breaches of the peace, and to bring about by peaceful means, and in conformity with the principles of justice and international law, adjustment or settlement of international disputes or situations which might lead to a breach of the peace;

[2] To develop friendly relations among nations based on respect for the principle of equal rights and self-determination of peoples, and to take other appropriate measures to strengthen universal peace;

[3] To achieve international cooperation in solving international problems of an economic, social, cultural, or humanitarian character, and in promoting and encouraging respect for human rights and for fundamental freedoms for all without distinction as to race, sex, language, or religion; and

[4] To be a center for harmonizing the actions of nations in the attainment of these common ends.

Article 2. The Organization and its Members, in pursuit of the Purposes stated in Article 1, shall act in accordance with the following Principles.

[1] The Organization is based on the principle of the sovereign equality of all its Members.

[2] All Members, in order to ensure to all of them the rights and benefits resulting from membership, shall fulfil in good faith the obligations assumed by them in accordance with the present Charter.

[3] All Members shall settle their international disputes by peaceful means in such a manner that international peace and security, and justice, are not endangered.

[4] All Members shall refrain in their international relations from the threat or use of force against the territorial integrity or political independence of any state, or in any other manner inconsistent with the Purposes of the United Nations.

[5] All Members shall give the United Nations every assistance in any action it takes in accordance with the present Charter, and shall refrain from giving assistance to any state against which the United Nations is taking preventive or enforcement action.

[6] The Organization shall ensure that states which are not Members of the United Nations act in accordance with these Principles so far as may be necessary for the maintenance of international peace and security.

[7] Nothing contained in the present Charter shall authorize the United Nations to intervene in matters which are essentially within the domestic jurisdiction of any state or shall require the Members to submit such matters to settlement under the present Charter; but this principle shall not prejudice the application of enforcement measures under Chapter VII.

Chapter II: MEMBERSHIP

Article 3. The original members of the United Nations shall be the states which, having participated in the United Nations Conference on International Organization at San Francisco, or having previously signed the Declaration by United Nations of January 1, 1942, sign the present Charter and ratify it in accordance with Article 110.

Article 4. [1] Membership in the United Nations is open to all other peace-loving states which accept the obligations contained in the present Charter and, in the judgment of the Organization, are able and willing to carry out these obligations.

[2] The admission of any such state to membership in the United Nations will be effected by a decision of the General Assembly upon the recommendation of the Security Council.

Article 5. A Member of the United Nations against which preventive or enforcement action has been taken by the Security Council may be suspended from the exercise of the rights and privileges of membership by the General Assembly upon the recommendation of the Security Council. The exercise of these rights and privileges may be restored by the Security Council.

Article 6. A Member of the United Nations which has persistently violated the Principles contained in the present Charter may be expelled from the Organization by the General Assembly upon the recommendation of the Security Council.

Chapter III: ORGANS

Article 7. [1] There are established as the principal organs of the United Nations: a General Assembly, a Security Council, an Economic and Social Council, a Trusteeship Council, an International Court of Justice, and a Secretariat.

[2] Such subsidiary organs as may be found necessary may be established in accordance with the present Charter.

Article 8. The United Nations shall place no restrictions on the eligibility of men and women to participate in any capacity and under conditions of equality in its principal and subsidiary organs.

Chapter IV: THE GENERAL ASSEMBLY

COMPOSITION

Article 9. [1] The General Assembly shall consist of all the Members of the United Nations.

[2] Each Member shall have not more than five representatives in the General Assembly.

FUNCTIONS AND POWERS

Article 10. The General Assembly may discuss any questions or any matters within the scope of the present Charter or relating to the powers and functions of any organs provided for in the present Charter, and, except as provided in Article 12, may make recommendations to the Members of the United Nations or to the Security Council or to both on any such questions or matters.

Article 11. [1] The General Assembly may consider the general principles of cooperation in the maintenance of international peace and security, including the principles governing disarmament and the regulation of armaments, and may make recommendations with regard to such principles to the Members or to the Security Council or to both.

[2] The General Assembly may discuss any questions relating to the maintenance of international peace and security brought before it by any Member of the United Nations, or by the Security Council, or by a state which is not a Member of the United Nations in accordance with Article 35, paragraph 2, and, except as provided in Article 12, may make recommendations with regard to any such questions to the state or states concerned or to the Security Council or to both. Any such question on which action is necessary shall be referred to the Security Council by the General Assembly either before or after discussion.

[3] The General Assembly may call the attention of the Security Council to situations which are likely to endanger international peace and security.

[4] The powers of the General Assembly set forth in this Article shall not limit the general scope of Article 10.

Article 12 [1] While the Security Council is exercising in respect of any dispute or situation the functions assigned to it in the present Charter, the General Assembly shall not make any recommendation with regard to that dispute or situation unless the Security Council so requests.

[2] The Secretary-General, with the consent of the Security Council, shall notify the General Assembly at each session of any matters rela-

tive to the maintenance of international peace and security which are being dealt with by the Security Council and shall similarly notify the General Assembly, or the Members of the United Nations if the General Assembly is not in session, immediately the Security Council ceases to deal with such matters.

Article 13. [1] The General Assembly shall initiate studies and make recommendations for the purpose of: (a) promoting international cooperation in the political field and encouraging the progressive development of international law and its codification; (b) promoting international cooperation in the economic, social, cultural, educational, and health fields, and assisting in the realization of human rights and fundamental freedoms for all without distinction as to race, sex, language, or religion.

[2] The further responsibilities, functions, and powers of the General Assembly with respect to matters mentioned in paragraph 1 (b) above are set forth in Chapters IX and X.

Article 14. Subject to the provisions of Article 12, the General Assembly may recommend measures for the peaceful adjustment of any situation, regardless of origin, which it deems likely to impair the general welfare or friendly relations among nations, including situations resulting from a violation of the provisions of the present Charter setting forth the Purposes and Principles of the United Nations.

Article 15. [1] The General Assembly shall receive and consider annual and special reports from the Security Council; these reports shall include an account of the measures that the Security Council has decided upon or taken to maintain international peace and security.

[2] The General Assembly shall receive and consider reports from the other organs of the United Nations.

Article 16. The General Assembly shall perform such functions with respect to the international trusteeship system as are assigned to it under Chapters XII and XIII, including the approval of the trusteeship agreements for areas not designated as strategic.

Article 17 [1] The General Assembly shall consider and approve the budget of the Organization.

[2] The expenses of the Organization shall be borne by the Members as apportioned by the General Assembly.

[3] The General Assembly shall consider and approve any financial and budgetary arrangements with specialized agencies referred to in Article 57 and shall examine the administrative budgets of such specialized agencies with a view to making recommendations to the agencies concerned.

VOTING

Article 18. [1] Each member of the General Assembly shall have one vote.

[2] Decisions of the General Assembly on important questions shall be made by a two-thirds majority of the members present and voting. These questions shall include: recommendations with respect to the maintenance of international peace and security, the election of the non-permanent members of the Security Council, the election of the members of the Economic and Social Council, the election of members of the Trusteeship Council in accordance with paragraph 1 (c) of Article 86, the admission of new Members to the United Nations, the suspension of the rights and privileges of membership, the expulsion of Members, questions relating to the operation of the trusteeship system, and budgetary questions.

[3] Decisions on other questions, including the determination of additional categories of questions to be decided by a two-thirds majority, shall be made by a majority of the members present and voting.

Article 19. A Member of the United Nations which is in arrears in the payment of its financial contributions to the Organization shall have no vote in the General Assembly if the amount of its arrears equals or exceeds the amount of the contributions due from it for the preceding two full years. The General Assembly may, nevertheless, permit such a Member to vote if it is satisfied that the failure to pay is due to conditions beyond the control of the Member.

PROCEDURE

Article 20. The General Assembly shall meet in regular annual sessions and in such special sessions as occasion may require. Special sessions shall be convoked by the Secretary-General at the request of the Security Council or of a majority of the Members of the United Nations.

Article 21. The General Assembly shall adopt its own rules of procedure. It shall elect its President for each session.

Article 22. The General Assembly may establish such subsidiary organs as it deems necessary for the performance of its functions.

Chapter V: SECURITY COUNCIL

COMPOSITION

Article 23. The Security Council shall consist of eleven Members of the United Nations. The Republic of China, France, the Union of Soviet Socialist Republics, the United Kingdom of Great Britain and Northern Ireland, and the United States of America shall be permanent members of the Security Council. The General Assembly shall elect six other Members of the United Nations to be non-permanent members of the Security Council, due regard being specially paid, in the first instance to the contribution of Members of the United Nations to the maintenance of international peace and security and to the other purposes of the Organization, and also to equitable geographical distribution.

[2] The non-permanent members of the Security Council shall be elected for a term of two years. In the first election of the non-permanent members, however, three shall be chosen for a term of one year. A retiring member shall not be eligible for immediate re-election.

[3] Each member of the Security Council shall have one representative.

FUNCTIONS AND POWERS

Article 24. [1] In order to ensure prompt and effective action by the United Nations, its Members confer on the Security Council primary responsibility for the maintenance of international peace and security, and agree that in carrying out its duties under this responsibility the Security Council acts on their behalf.

[2] In discharging these duties the Security Council shall act in accordance with the Purposes and Principles of the United Nations. The specific powers granted to the Security Council for the discharge of these duties are laid down in Chapters VI, VII, VIII, and XII.

[3] The Security Council shall submit annual and, when necessary, special reports to the General Assembly for its consideration.

Article 25. The Members of the United Nations agree to accept and carry out the decisions of the Security Council in accordance with the present Charter.

Article 26. In order to promote the establishment and maintenance of international peace and security with the least diversion for armaments of the world's human and economic resources, the Security Council shall be responsible for formulating, with the assistance of the Military Staff Committee referred to in Article 47, plans to be submitted to the

Members of the United Nations for the establishment of a system for the regulation of armaments.

VOTING

Article 27. [1] Each member of the Security Council shall have one vote.

[2] Decisions of the Security Council on procedural matters shall be made by an affirmative vote of seven members.

[3] Decisions of the Security Council on all other matters shall be made by an affirmative vote of seven members including the concurring votes of the permanent members; provided that, in decisions under Chapter VI, and under paragraph 3 of Article 52, a party to a dispute shall abstain from voting.

PROCEDURE

Article 28. [1] The Security Council shall be so organized as to be able to function continuously. Each member of the Security Council shall for this purpose be represented at all times at the seat of the Organization.

[2] The Security Council shall hold periodic meetings at which each of its members may, if it so desires, be represented by a member of the government or by some other specially designated representative.

[3] The Security Council may hold meetings at such places other than the seat of the Organization as in its judgment will best facilitate its work.

Article 29. The Security Council may establish such subsidiary organs as it deems necessary for the performance of its functions.

Article 30. The Security Council shall adopt its own rules of procedure, including the method of selecting its President.

Article 31. Any Member of the United Nations which is not a member of the Security Council may participate, without vote, in the discussion of any question brought before the Security Council whenever the latter considers that the interests of that Member are specially affected.

Article 32. Any Member of the United Nations which is not a member of the Security Council or any state which is not a Member of the United Nations, if it is a party to a dispute under consideration by the Security Council, shall be invited to participate, without vote, in the discussion relating to the dispute. The Security Council shall lay down such conditions as it deems just for the participation of a state which is not a Member of the United Nations.

Chapter VI: PACIFIC SETTLEMENT OF DISPUTES

Article 33. [1] The parties to any dispute, the continuance of which is likely to endanger the maintenance of international peace and security, shall, first of all, seek a solution by negotiation, enquiry, mediation, conciliation, arbitration, judicial settlement, resort to regional agencies or arrangements, or other peaceful means of their own choice.

[2] The Security Council shall, when it deems necessary, call upon the parties to settle their dispute by such means.

Article 34. The Security Council may investigate any dispute, or any situation which might lead to international friction or give rise to a dispute, in order to determine whether the continuance of the dispute or situation is likely to endanger the maintenance of international peace and security.

Article 35. [1] Any Member of the United Nations may bring any dispute, or any situation of the nature referred to in Article 34, to the attention of the Security Council or of the General Assembly.

[2] A state which is not a Member of the United Nations may bring to the attention of the Security Council or of the General Assembly any dispute to which it is a party if it accepts in advance, for the purposes of the dispute, the obligations of pacific settlement provided in the present Charter.

[3] The proceedings of the General Assembly in respect of matters brought to its attention under this Article will be subject to the provisions of Articles 11 and 12.

Article 36. [1] The Security Council may, at any stage of a dispute of the nature referred to in Article 33 or of a situation of like nature, recommend appropriate procedures or methods of adjustment.

[2] The Security Council should take into consideration any procedures for the settlement of the dispute which have already been adopted by the parties.

[3] In making recommendations under this Article the Security Council should also take into consideration that legal disputes should as a general rule be referred by the parties to the International Court of Justice in accordance with the provisions of the Statute of the Court.

Article 37. [1] Should the parties to a dispute of the nature referred to in Article 33 fail to settle it by the means indicated in that Article, they shall refer it to the Security Council.

[2] If the Security Council deems that the continuance of the dispute is in fact likely to endanger the maintenance of international peace and security, it shall decide whether to take action under Article 36 or to recommend such terms of settlement as it may consider appropriate.

Article 38. Without prejudice to the provisions of Articles 33 to 37, the Security Council may, if all the parties to any dispute so request, make recommendations to the parties with a view to a pacific settlement of the dispute.

Chapter VII: ACTION WITH RESPECT TO THREATS TO THE PEACE, BREACHES OF THE PEACE, AND ACTS OF AGGRESSION

Article 39. The Security Council shall determine the existence of any threat to the peace, breach of the peace, or act of aggression and shall make recommendations, or decide what measures shall be taken in accordance with Articles 41 and 42, to maintain or restore international peace and security.

Article 40. In order to prevent an aggravation of the situation, the Security Council may, before making the recommendations or deciding upon the measures provided for in Article 39, call upon the parties concerned to comply with such provisional measures as it deems necessary or desirable. Such provisional measures shall be without prejudice to the rights, claims, or position of the parties concerned. The Security Council shall duly take account of failure to comply with such provisional measures.

Article 41. The Security Council may decide what measures not involving the use of armed force are to be employed to give effect to its decisions, and it may call upon the Members of the United Nations to apply such measures. These may include complete or partial interruption of economic relations and of rail, sea, air, postal, telegraphic, radio, and other means of communication, and the severance of diplomatic relations.

Article 42. Should the Security Council consider that measures provided for in Article 41 would be inadequate or have proved to be inadequate, it may take such action by air, sea, or land forces as may be necessary to maintain or restore international peace and security. Such action may include demonstrations, blockade, and other operations by air, sea, or land forces of Members of the United Nations.

Article 43. [1] All Members of the United Nations, in order to contribute to the maintenance of international peace and security, undertake to make available to the Security Council, on its call and in accordance with a special agreement or agreements, armed forces, assistance, and facilities, including rights of passage, necessary for the purpose of maintaining international peace and security.

　　[2] Such agreement or agreements shall govern the numbers and

types of forces, their degree of readiness and general location, and the nature of the facilities and assistance to be provided.

[3] The agreement or agreements shall be negotiated as soon as possible on the initiative of the Security Council. They shall be concluded between the Security Council and Members or between the Security Council and groups of Members and shall be subject to ratification by the signatory states in accordance with their respective constitutional processes.

Article 44. When the Security Council has decided to use force it shall, before calling upon a Member not represented on it to provide armed forces in fulfillment of the obligations assumed under Article 43, invite that Member, if the Member so desires, to participate in the decisions of the Security Council concerning the employment of contingents of that Member's armed forces.

Article 45. In order to enable the United Nations to take urgent military measures, Members shall hold immediately available national airforce contingents for combined international enforcement action. The strength and degree of readiness of these contingents and plans for their combined action shall be determined, within the limits laid down in the special agreement or agreements referred to in Article 43, by the Security Council with the assistance of the Military Staff Committee.

Article 46. Plans for the application of armed force shall be made by the Security Council with the assistance of the Military Staff Committee.

Article 47. [1] There shall be established a Military Staff Committee to advise and assist the Security Council on all questions relating to the Security Council's military requirements for the maintenance of international peace and security, the employment and command of forces placed at its disposal, the regulation of armaments, and possible disarmament.

[2] The Military Staff Committee shall consist of the Chiefs of Staff of the permanent members of the Security Council or their representatives. Any Member of the United Nations not permanently represented on the Committee shall be invited by the Committee to be associated with it when the efficient discharge of the Committee's responsibilities requires the participation of that Member in its work.

[3] The Military Staff Committee shall be responsible under the Security Council for the strategic direction of any armed forces placed at the disposal of the Security Council. Questions relating to the command of such forces shall be worked out subsequently.

[4] The Military Staff Committee, with the authorization of the Security Council and after consultation with appropriate regional agencies, may establish regional subcommittees.

Article 48. [1] The action required to carry out the decisions of the Security Council for the maintenance of international peace and security shall be taken by all the Members of the United Nations or by some of them, as the Security Council may determine.

[2] Such decisions shall be carried out by the Members of the United Nations directly and through their action in the appropriate international agencies of which they are members.

Article 49. The Members of the United Nations shall join in affording mutual assistance in carrying out the measures decided upon by the Security Council.

Article 50. If preventive or enforcement measures against any state are taken by the Security Council, any other state, whether a Member of the United Nations or not, which finds itself confronted with special economic problems arising from the carrying out of those measures shall have the right to consult the Security Council with regard to a solution of those problems.

Article 51. Nothing in the present Charter shall impair the inherent right of individual or collective self-defense if an armed attack occurs against a Member of the United Nations, until the Security Council has taken the measures necessary to maintain international peace and security. Measures taken by Members in the exercise of this right of self-defense shall be immediately reported to the Security Council and shall not in any way affect the authority and responsibility of the Security Council under the present Charter to take at any time such action as it deems necessary in order to maintain or restore international peace and security.

Chapter VIII: REGIONAL ARRANGEMENTS

Article 52. [1] Nothing in the present Charter precludes the existence of regional arrangements or agencies for dealing with such matters relating to the maintenance of international peace and security as are appropriate for regional action, provided that such arrangements or agencies and their activities are consistent with the Purposes and Principles of the United Nations.

[2] The Members of the United Nations entering into such arrangements or constituting such agencies shall make every effort to achieve pacific settlement of local disputes through such regional arrangements or by such regional agencies before referring them to the Security Council.

[3] The Security Council shall encourage the development of pacific settlement of local disputes through such regional arrangements or

by such regional agencies either on the initiative of the states concerned or by reference from the Security Council.

[4] This Article in no way impairs the application of Articles 34 and 35.

Article 53. [1] The Security Council shall, where appropriate, utilize such regional arrangements or agencies for enforcement action under its authority. But no enforcement action shall be taken under regional arrangements or by regional agencies without the authorization of the Security Council, with the exception of measures against any enemy state, as defined in paragraph 2 of this Article, provided for pursuant to Article 107 or in regional arrangements directed against renewal of aggressive policy on the part of any such state, until such time as the Organization may, on request of the Governments concerned, be charged with the responsibility for preventing further aggression by such state.

[2] The term enemy state as used in paragraph 1 of this Article applies to any state which during the Second World War has been an enemy of any signatory of the present Charter.

Article 54. The Security Council shall at all times be kept fully informed of activities undertaken or in contemplation under regional arrangements or by regional agencies for the maintenance of international peace and security.

Chapter IX: INTERNATIONAL ECONOMIC AND SOCIAL COOPERATION

Article 55. With a view to the creation of conditions of stability and well-being which are necessary for peaceful and friendly relations among nations based on respect for the principle of equal rights and self-determination of peoples, the United Nations shall promote: (a) higher standards of living, full employment, and conditions of economic and social progress and development; (b) solutions of international economic, social, health, and related problems; and international cultural and educational cooperation; and (c) universal respect for, and observance of, human rights and fundamental freedoms for all without distinction as to race, sex, language, or religion.

Article 56. All Members pledge themselves to take joint and separate action in cooperation with the Organization for the achievement of the purposes set forth in Article 55.

Article 57 [1] The various specialized agencies established by intergovernmental agreement and having wide international responsibilities, as defined in their basic instruments, in economic, social, cultural, educational, health, and related fields, shall be brought into relationship with the United Nations in accordance with the provisions of Article 63.

[2] Such agencies thus brought into relationship with the United Nations are hereinafter referred to as specialized agencies.

Article 58. The Organization shall make recommendations for the coordination of the policies and activities of the specialized agencies.

Article 59. The Organization shall, where appropriate, initiate negotiations among the states concerned for the creation of any new specialized agencies required for the accomplishment of the purposes set forth in Article 55.

Article 60. Responsibility for the discharge of the functions of the Organization set forth in this Chapter shall be vested in the General Assembly and, under the authority of the General Assembly, in the Economic and Social Council, which shall have for this purpose the powers set forth in Chapter X.

Chapter X: THE ECONOMIC AND SOCIAL COUNCIL

COMPOSITION

Article 61. [1] The Economic and Social Council shall consist of eighteen Members of the United Nations elected by the General Assembly.

[2] Subject to the provisions of paragraph 3, six members of the Economic and Social Council shall be elected each year for a term of three years. A retiring member shall be eligible for immediate re-election.

[3] At the first election, eighteen members of the Economic and Social Council shall be chosen. The term of office of six members so chosen shall expire at the end of one year, and of six other members at the end of two years, in accordance with arrangements made by the General Assembly.

[4] Each member of the Economic and Social Council shall have one representative.

FUNCTIONS AND POWERS

Article 62. [1] The Economic and Social Council may make or initiate studies and reports with respect to international economic, social, cultural, educational, health, and related matters and may make recommendations with respect to any such matters to the General Assembly, to the Members of the United Nations, and to the specialized agencies concerned.

[2] It may make recommendations for the purpose of promoting respect for, and observance of, human rights and fundamental freedoms for all.

[3] It may prepare draft conventions for submissions to the General Assembly, with respect to matters falling within its competence.

[4] It may call, in accordance with the rules prescribed by the United Nations, international conferences on matters falling within its competence.

Article 63. [1] The Economic and Social Council may enter into agreements with any of the agencies referred to in Article 57, defining the terms on which the agency concerned shall be brought into relationship with the United Nations. Such agreements shall be subject to approval by the General Assembly.

[2] It may coordinate the activities of the specialized agencies through consultation with and recommendations to such agencies and through recommendations to the General Assembly and to the Members of the United Nations.

Article 64. [1] The Economic and Social Council may take appropriate steps to obtain regular reports from the specialized agencies. It may make arrangements with the Members of the United Nations and with the specialized agencies to obtain reports on the steps taken to give effect to its own recommendations and to recommendations on matters falling within its competence made by the General Assembly.

[2] It may communicate its observations on these reports to the General Assembly.

Article 65. The Economic and Social Council may furnish information to the Security Council and shall assist the Security Council upon its request.

Article 66. [1] The Economic and Social Council shall perform such functions as fall within its competence in connection with the carrying out of the recommendations of the General Assembly.

[2] It may, with the approval of the General Assembly, perform services at the request of Members of the United Nations and at the request of specialized agencies.

[3] It shall perform such other functions as are specified elsewhere in the present Charter or as may be assigned to it by the General Assembly.

VOTING

Article 67. [1] Each member of the Economic and Social Council shall have one vote.

[2] Decisions of the Economic and Social Council shall be made by a majority of the members present and voting.

PROCEDURE

Article 68. The Economic and Social Council shall set up commissions in economic and social fields and for the promotion of human rights, and such other commissions as may be required for the performance of its functions.

Artice 69. The Economic and Social Council shall invite any Member of the United Nations to participate, without vote, in its deliberations on any matter of particular concern to that Member.

Article 70. The Economic and Social Council may make arrangements for representatives of the specialized agencies to participate, without vote, in its deliberations and in those of the commissions established by it, and for its representatives to participate in the deliberations of the specialized agencies.

Article 71. The Economic and Social Council may make suitable arrangements for consultation with non-governmental organizations which are concerned with matters within its competence. Such arrangements may be made with international organizations and, where appropriate with national organizations after consultation with the Member of the United Nations concerned.

Article 72. [1] The Economic and Social Council shall adopt its own rules of procedure, including the method of selecting its President.

[2] The Economic and Social Council shall meet as required in accordance with its rules, which shall include provision for the convening of meetings on the request of a majority of its members.

Chapter XI: DECLARATION REGARDING NON-SELF-GOVERNING TERRITORIES

Article 73. Members of the United Nations which have or assume responsibilities for the administration of territories whose peoples have not yet attained a full measure of self-government recognize the principle that the interests of the inhabitants of these territories are paramount, and accept as a sacred trust the obligation to promote to the utmost, within the system of international peace and security established by the present Charter, the well-being of the inhabitants of these territories, and, to this end: (a) to ensure, with due respect for the culture of the peoples concerned, their political, economic, social, and educational advancement, their just treatment, and their protection against abuses; (b) to develop self-government, to take due account of the political aspirations of the peoples, and to assist them in the progressive development of their free political institutions, according to the particular circumstances of each territory and its peoples and their varying stages of advancement; (c) to further international peace and security; (d) to promote constructive measures of development, to encourage research, and to cooperate with one another and, when and where appropriate, with specialized international bodies with a view to the practical achievement of the social, economic and scientific purposes set forth in this Article; and (e) to transmit regularly to the Secretary-General for information purposes, subject to such limitation as security and constitutional considerations may require, statistical and other information of a technical nature relating to economic, social, and educational conditions in the territories for which they are respectively responsible other than those territories to which Chapters XII and XIII apply.

Article 74. Members of the United Nations also agree that their policy in respect of the territories to which this Chapter applies, no less than in respect of their metropolitan areas, must be based on the general principle of good-neighborliness, due account being taken of the interests and well-being of the rest of the world, in social, economic, and commercial matters.

Chapter XII: INTERNATIONAL TRUSTEESHIP SYSTEM

Article 75. The United Nations shall establish under its authority an international trusteeship system for the administration and supervision of such territories as may be placed thereunder by subsequent individual agreements. These territories are hereinafter referred to as trust territories.

Article 76. The basic objectives of the trusteeship system, in accordance with the Purposes of the United Nations laid down in Article 1 of the present Charter, shall be: (a) to further international peace and security; (b) to promote the political, economic, social, and educational advancement of the inhabitants of the trust territories, and their progressive development towards self-government or independence as may be appropriate to the particular circumstances of each territory and its peoples and the freely expressed wishes of the peoples concerned, and as may be provided by the terms of each trusteeship agreement; (c) to encourage respect for human rights and for fundamental freedoms for all without distinction as to race, sex, language, or religion, and to encourage recognition of the interdependence of the peoples of the world; and (d) to ensure equal treatment in social, economic, and commercial matters for all Members of the United Nations and their nationals, and also equal treatment for the latter in the administration of justice, without prejudice to the attainment of the foregoing objectives and subject to the provisions of Article 80.

Article 77. [1] The trusteeship system shall apply to such territories in the following categories as may be placed thereunder by means of trusteeship agreements: (a) territories now held under mandate; (b) territories which may be detached from enemy states as a result of the Second World War; and (c) territories voluntarily placed under the system by states responsible for their administration.

[2] It will be a matter for subsequent agreement as to which territories in the foregoing categories will be brought under the trusteeship system and upon what terms.

Article 78. The trusteeship system shall not apply to territories which have become Members of the United Nations, relationship among which shall be based on respect for the principle of sovereign equality.

Article 79. The terms of trusteeship for each territory to be placed under the trusteeship system, including any alteration or amendment, shall be agreed upon by the states directly concerned, including the mandatory power in the case of territories held under mandate by a Member of the United Nations, and shall be approved as provided for in Articles 83 and 85.

Article 80. [1] Except as may be agreed upon in individual trusteeship agreements, made under Articles 77, 79, and 81, placing each territory under the trusteeship system, and until such agreements have been concluded, nothing in this Chapter shall be construed in or of itself to alter in any manner the rights whatsoever of any states or any peoples or the terms of existing international instruments to which Members of the United Nations may respectively be parties.

[2] Paragraph 1 of this Article shall not be interpreted as giving grounds for delay or postponement of the negotiation and conclusion of agreements for placing mandated and other territories under the trusteeship system as provided for in Article 77.

Article 81. The trusteeship agreement shall in each case include the terms under which the trust territory will be administered and designate the authority which will exercise the administration of the trust territory. Such authority, hereinafter called the administering authority, may be one or more states of the Organization itself.

Article 82. There may be designated, in any trusteeship agreement, a strategic area or areas which may include part or all of the trust territory to which the agreement applies, without prejudice to any special agreement or agreements made under Article 43.

Article 83. [1] All functions of the United Nations relating to strategic areas, including the approval of the terms of the trusteeship agreements and of their alteration or amendment, shall be exercised by the Security Council.

[2] The basic objectives set forth in Article 76 shall be applicable to the people of each strategic area.

[3] The Security Council shall, subject to the provisions of the trusteeship agreements and without prejudice to security considerations, avail itself of the assistance of the Trusteeship Council to perform those functions of the United Nations under the trusteeship system relating to political, economic, social, and educational matters in the strategic areas.

Article 84. It shall be the duty of the administering authority to ensure that the trust territory shall play its part in the maintenance of international peace and security. To this end the administering authority may make use of volunteer forces, facilities, and assistance from the trust territory in carrying out the obligations towards the Security Council undertaken in this regard by the administering authority, as well as for local defense and the maintenance of law and order within the trust territory.

Article 85. [1] The functions of the United Nations with regard to trusteeship agreements for all areas not designated as strategic, including the approval of the terms of the trusteeship agreements and of their alteration or amendment, shall be exercised by the General Assembly.

[2] The Trusteeship Council, operating under the authority of the General Assembly, shall assist the General Assembly in carrying out these functions.

Chapter XIII: THE TRUSTEESHIP COUNCIL

COMPOSITION

Article 86. [1] The Trusteeship Council shall consist of the following Members of the United Nations: (a) those Members administering trust territories; (b) such of those Members mentioned by name in Article 23 as are not administering trust territories; and (c) as many other Members elected for three-year terms by the General Assembly as may be necessary to ensure that the total number of members of the Trusteeship Council is equally divided between those Members of the United Nations which administer trust territories and those which do not.

[2] Each member of the Trusteeship Council shall designate one specially qualified person to represent it therein.

FUNCTIONS AND POWERS

Article 87. The General Assembly and, under its authority, the Trusteeship Council, in carrying out their functions, may: (a) consider reports submitted by the administering authority; (b) accept petitions and examine them in consultation with the administering authority; (c) provide for periodic visits to the respective trust territories at times agreed upon with the administering authority, and (d) take these and other actions in conformity with the terms of the trusteeship agreements.

Article 88. The Trusteeship Council shall formulate a questionnaire on the political, economic, social, and educational advancement of the inhabitants of each trust territory, and the administering authority for each trust territory within the competence of the General Assembly shall make an annual report to the General Assembly upon the basis of such questionnaire.

VOTING

Article 89. [1] Each member of the Trusteeship Council shall have one vote.

[2] Decisions of the Trusteeship Council shall be made by a majority of the members present and voting.

PROCEDURE

Article 90 [1] The Trusteeship Council shall adopt its own rules of procedure, including the method of selecting its President.

[2] The Trusteeship Council shall meet as required in accordance with its rules, which shall include provision for the convening of meetings on the request of a majority of its members.

Article 91. The Trusteeship Council shall, when appropriate, avail itself of the assistance of the Economic and Social Council and of the specialized agencies in regard to matters with which they are respectively concerned.

Chapter XIV: THE INTERNATIONAL COURT OF JUSTICE

Article 92. The International Court of Justice shall be the principal judicial organ of the United Nations. It shall function in accordance with the annexed Statute, which is based upon the Statute of the Permanent Court of International Justice and forms an integral part of the present Charter.

Article 93. [1] All Members of the United Nations are *ipso facto* parties to the Statute of the International Court of Justice.

[2] A state which is not a Member of the United Nations may become a party to the Statute of the International Court of Justice on conditions to be determined in each case by the General Assembly upon the recommendation of the Security Council.

Article 94. [1] Each Member of the United Nations undertakes to comply with the decision of the International Court of Justice in any case to which it is a party.

[2] If any party to a case fails to perform the obligations incumbent upon it under a judgment rendered by the Court, the other party may have recourse to the Security Council, which may, if it deems necessary, make recommendations or decide upon measures to be taken to give effect to the judgment.

Article 95. Nothing in the present Charter shall prevent Members of the United Nations from entrusting the solution of their differences to other tribunals by virtue of agreements already in existence or which may be concluded in the future.

Article 96. [1] The General Assembly or the Security Council may request the International Court of Justice to give an advisory opinion on any legal question.

[2] Other organs of the United Nations and specialized agencies, which may at any time be so authorized by the General Assembly, may also request advisory opinions of the Court on legal questions arising within the scope of their activities.

Chapter XV: SECRETARIAT

Article 97. The Secretariat shall comprise a Secretary-General and such staff as the Organization may require. The Secretary-General shall be appointed by the General Assembly upon the recommendation of the Security Council. He shall be the chief administrative officer of the Organization.

Article 98. The Secretary-General shall act in that capacity in all meetings of the General Assembly, of the Security Council, of the Economic and Social Council, and of the Trusteeship Council, and shall perform such other functions as are entrusted to him by these organs. The Secretary-General shall make an annual report to the General Assembly on the work of the Organization.

Article 99. The Secretary-General may bring to the attention of the Security Council any matter which in his opinion may threaten the maintenance of international peace and security.

Article 100. [1] In the performance of their duties the Secretary-General and the staff shall not seek or receive instructions from any government or from any other authority external to the Organization. They shall refrain from any action which might reflect on their position as international officials responsible only to the Organization.

[2] Each Member of the United Nations undertakes to respect the exclusively international character of the responsibilities of the Secretary-General and the staff and not to seek to influence them in the discharge of their responsibilities.

Article 101 [1] The staff shall be appointed by the Secretary-General under regulations established by the General Assembly.

[2] Appropriate staffs shall be permanently assigned to the Economic and Social Council, the Trusteeship Council, and, as required, to other organs of the United Nations. These staffs shall form a part of the Secretariat.

[3] The paramount consideration in the employment of the staff and in the determination of the conditions of service shall be the necessity of securing the highest standards of efficiency, competence, and integrity. Due regard shall be paid to the importance of recruiting the staff on as wide a geographical basis as possible.

Chapter XVI: MISCELLANEOUS PROVISIONS

Article 102. [1] Every treaty and every international agreement entered into by any Member of the United Nations after the present Charter comes into force shall as soon as possible be registered with the Secretariat and published by it.

[2] No party to any such treaty or international agreement which has not been registered in accordance with the provisions of paragraph 1 of this Article may invoke that treaty or agreement before any organ of the United Nations.

Article 103. In the event of a conflict between the obligations of the Members of the United Nations under the present Charter and their obligations under any other international agreement, their obligations under the present Charter shall prevail.

Article 104. The Organization shall enjoy in the territory of each of its Members such legal capacity as may be necessary for the exercise of its functions and the fulfillment of its purposes.

Article 105. [1] The Organization shall enjoy in the territory of each of its Members such privileges and immunities as are necessary for the fulfillment of its purposes.

[2] Representatives of the Members of the United Nations and offi-

cials of the Organization shall similarly enjoy such privileges and immunities as are necessary for the independent exercise of their functions in connection with the Organization.

[3] The General Assembly may make recommendations with a view to determining the details of the application of paragraphs 1 and 2 of this Article or may propose conventions to the Members of the United Nations for this purpose.

Chapter XVII: TRANSITIONAL SECURITY ARRANGEMENTS

Article 106. Pending the coming into force of such special agreements referred to in Article 43 as in the opinion of the Security Council enable it to begin the exercise of its responsibilites under Article 42, the parties to the Four-Nation Declaration, signed at Moscow, October 30, 1943, and France, shall, in accordance with the provisions of paragraph 5 of that Declaration, consult with one another and as occasion requires with other Members of the United Nations with a view to such joint action on behalf of the Organization as may be necessary for the purpose of maintaining international peace nd security.

Article 107. Nothing in the present Charter shall invalidate or preclude action, in relation to any state which during the Second World War has been an enemy of any signatory to the present Charter, taken or authorized as a result of that war by the Governments having responsibility for such action.

Chapter XVIII: AMENDMENTS

Article 108. Amendments to the present Charter shall come into force for all Members of the United Nations when they have been adopted by a vote of two thirds of the members of the General Assembly and ratified in accordance with their respective constitutional processes by two thirds of the Members of the United Nations, including all the permanent members of the Security Council.

Article 109. [1] A General Conference of the Members of the United Nations for the purpose of reviewing the present Charter may be held at a date and place to be fixed by a two-thirds vote of the members of the General Assembly and by a vote of any seven members of the Security Council. Each Member of the United Nations shall have one vote in the conference.

[2] Any alteration of the present Charter recommended by a two-thirds vote of the conference shall take effect when ratified in accordance with their respective constitutional processes by two thirds of the

Members of the United Nations including all the permanent members of the Security Council.

[3] If such a conference has not been held before the tenth annual session of the General Assembly following the coming into force of the present Charter, the proposal to call such a conference shall be placed on the agenda of that session of the General Assembly, and the conference shall be held if so decided by a majority vote of the members of the General Assembly and by a vote of any seven members of the Security Council.

Chapter XIX: RATIFICATION AND SIGNATURE

Article 110. [1] The present Charter shall be ratified by the signatory states in accordance with their respective constitutional processes.

[2] The ratifications shall be deposited with the Government of the United States of America, which shall notify all the signatory states of each deposit as well as the Secretary-General of the Organization when he has been appointed.

[3] The present Charter shall come into force upon the deposit of ratifications by the Republic of China, France, the Union of Soviet Socialist Republics, the United Kingdom of Great Britain and Northern Ireland, and the United States of America, and by a majority of the other signatory states. A protocol of the ratifications deposited shall thereupon be drawn up by the Government of the United States of America which shall communicate copies thereof to all signatory states.

[4] The states signatory to the present Charter which ratify it after it has come into force will become original Members of the United Nations on the date of the deposit of their respective ratifications.

Article 111. The present Charter, of which the Chinese, French, Russian, English, and Spanish texts are equally authentic, shall remain deposited in the archives of the Government of the United States of America. Duly certified copies thereof shall be transmitted by that Government to the Governments of the other signatory states.

In witness whereof the representatives of the Governments of the United Nations have signed the present Charter. Done at the city of San Francisco the twenty-sixth day of June, one thousand nine hundred and forty-five.

Notes

INTRODUCTION

1. Philip E. Mosely, "The Soviet Union and the United Nations," *The United Nations: Accomplishments and Prospects in International Organization,* Summer 1965.
2. Clyde Eagleton, "Excesses of Self-Determination," *Foreign Affairs,* July 1953.

I: THE LOGIC OF THE LEAGUE

1. H. A. L. Fisher, *A History of Europe* (Boston: Houghton Mifflin, 1939), p. 1126.
2. Viscount Grey of Fallodon, *Twenty-Five Years* (New York: Stokes, 1925), I, 259–60. By permission of the owner of the copyright.
3. R. W. Seton-Watson, *Britain in Europe* (London: Cambridge University Press, 1937), p. 566.
4. George Macaulay Trevelyan, *Grey of Fallodon* (Boston: Houghton Mifflin, 1937), p. 126.
5. André Geraud (Pertinax), "Diplomacy, Old and New," *Foreign Affairs* (January 1945).
6. Grey, *op. cit.,* I, 87.
7. *Ibid,* I, 74.
8. Halford J. Mackinder, *Democratic Ideals and Reality* (New York: Holt, 1942), p. 2. By permission of Constable Company Limited, London.
9. Quoted by Charles Kruszewski in "The Pivot of History," *Foreign Affairs* (April 1954).
10. Mackinder, *op. cit.,* p. 30.
11. *Ibid.,* p. 1.

12. *Ibid.,* p. 130.
13. *Ibid.,* p. 55.
14. *Iibd.,* p. 58.
15. *Ibid.,* p. 150.
16. *Ibid.,* p. 170.
17. *Ibid.,* p. 69.
18. Kruszewski, *op. cit.*
19. Halford J. Mackinder, "The Round World and the Winning of the Peace," *Foreign Affairs* (July 1943).

II: THE PROSPECTS FOR COLLECTIVE SECURITY

1. Readers seeking details can most readily find them in F. P. Walters, *A History of the League of Nations* (London: Oxford University Press). References here are to the one-volume edition, 1960. This is the definitive record of the League, to which students will always be indebted.
2. J. L. Brierly, *The Outlook for International Law* (Oxford: Clarendon Press, 1944), p. 62.
3. Felix Morley, "The Society of Nations," quoted by Egon Ranshofen-Wertheimer in "Geneva and the Evolution of a New Diplomacy," *World Organization* (Washington, D.C.: American Council on Public Affairs, 1942), p. 19.
4. Walters, *op. cit.,* p. 44.
5. Lord Robert Cecil, *The Great Experiment* (London: Oxford University Press, 1941), p. 90.
6. E. H. Carr, *International Relations Between the Two World Wars* (London: Macmillan, 1959), p. 16.
7. Robert Lansing, *The Peace Negotiations* (Boston: Houghton Mifflin, 1921), p. 10.
8. Robert Lansing, *War Memoirs of Robert Lansing* (New York: Bobbs, Merrill, 1935), p. 97.
9. Quoted by Hugh McKinnon Wood in "The World Court," *World Organization,* p. 280.
10. Robert Lansing, *The Peace Negotiations,* p. 68.
11. *Ibid.,* p. 85.
12. Sir Alfred Zimmern, *The American Road to Peace* (New York: Dutton, 1953), p. 90.
13. Quoted by Philip C. Jessup in *Elihu Root* (New York: Dodd Mead, 1938), Vol. II, p. 373.
14. *Ibid.,* Vol. II, p. 40.
15. Edwin S. Corwin, *The President, Office and Powers* (New York: New York University Press, 1957), p. 185.
16. Letter to Colonel House. Quoted by Henry Aaron Yeomans in *Abbott Lawrence Lowell* (Cambridge, Mass.: Harvard University Press, 1948), p. 454.

III: WITH BENEFIT OF HINDSIGHT

1. The regular budgets of the United Nations in 1965 (estimated), including the budget for the specialized agencies, amounted to $218,596,000. The United States contributed about thirty per cent of that total. Voluntary contributions for special programs came to $246,120,000, the shares of the United States ranging from twenty per cent to seventy per cent. Assessments for peace-keeping were about $29,000,000, the United States paying about thirty-six per cent. United States House of Representatives, *United States Contributions to International Organizations*, 13th report by the Secretary of State, H. Doc. No. 229, 89th Cong., 1st sess. [Washington: GPO, 1965].

Between January 1, 1957, and September 30, 1965, the United Nations spent $193,900,000 more than it received in income, mainly as the result of the failure of members to pay the costs of peace-keeping operations. As of September 30, 1965, long-term indebtedness of the United Nations included $156,000,000 outstanding on the repayment of United Nations bonds. (United Nations Document A/AC124/1. January 24, 1966.)

2. Anthony Eden, Earl of Avon, *The Memoirs of Anthony Eden, Earl of Avon: Facing the Dictators* (Boston: Houghton Mifflin, 1962), p. 8.

3. Isaiah Bowman, "The Strategy of Territorial Decisions," *Foreign Affairs,* January 1946.

4. Terms of peace with Hungary, Austria, and Bulgaria were spelled out in the treaties of Trianon, Saint Germain, and Neuilly. E. H. Carr's *International Relations Between the World Wars* (London: Macmillan, 1959) provides an authoritative summary. C. A. Macartney and A. W. Palmer's *Independent Eastern Europe* (New York: St. Martin's Press, Macmillan and Co. Ltd., 1962) is a detailed study, an over-all view which includes the contrast of "then" and "now" is to be found in Hugh Seton-Watson's *The East European Revolution* (New York: Praeger, 1956).

5. The figures are taken from a German source, *Statistisches Jahrbuch für das Deutsche Reich 1924-1925,* quoted by Étienne Mantoux in *The Carthaginian Peace, or the Economic Consequences of Mr. Keynes* (New York: Scribner's, 1952). Linguistic statistics can seldom be more than approximations. Mantoux used this source to show the German ethnic case at its strongest.

6. For the full terms of the proposal and the varying responses to it, see Piotr S. Wandycz, *France and Her Eastern Allies, 1919-1925* (Minneapolis: University of Minnesota Press, 1962), pp. 170, 171. This scholarly book provides new and important material for an understanding of the relations among the powers in this period.

7. Macartney and Palmer, *op, cit.,* pp. 71, 72.

8. See an interesting chapter, "Danubian Union or Little Entente?" in Wandycz, *op. cit.,* pp. 186 ff.

9. Quoted in Harry Elmer Barnes, *The League of Nations* (Boston: Atlantic Monthly Press, 1919), p. 171.

10. Brierly, *op. cit.,* p. 130.

IV: THE YEARS OF OPPORTUNITY

1. Judge Manley O. Hudson, *The World Court, 1921-1938* (World Peace Foundation, 1938), This handbook is the authoritative summary in English of the Court's cases.

2. Wood, *op. cit.*, p. 299.

3. Oliver J. Lissitzyn, *The International Court of Justice* (New York: Carnegie Endowment for International Peace, 1951), which includes a study of the experiences of the "old" and "new" World Courts, is especially valuable for its readable and discerning comments on the relation between law and power. Shabtai Rosenne's *The World Court: What It Is and How It Works* (New York: Oceana Publications, 1962) summarizes the work of the old Court and analyzes that of the new Court in more detail. Ambassador Rosenne's general conclusion is that the atmosphere today "is not propitious for any extended use of international judicial techniques."

4. Walters, *op. cit.*, p. 146. Readers interested in this significant Upper Silesian episode will find additional details, offered with varying emphases in G. P. Gooch, *Germany* (New York: Scribners, 1926), Erich Eyck, *A History of the Weimar Republic*, Vol. I (Cambridge, Mass.: Harvard University Press, 1962), and Piotr S. Wandycz, *France and Her Eastern Allies, 1919-1925,* cited.

5. Ernst Jäckh, *The Rising Crescent* (New York: Farrar and Rinehart, 1944), p. 159.

6. Ismet Inönü, "Negotiations and the National Interest," *Perspectives on Peace, 1910-1960* (New York: Praeger, for the Carnegie Endowment for International Peace, 1960), p. 137.

7. Harold Nicolson's *Curzon: The Last Phase* (London: Constable, 1934) presents the British view of Sèvres and Lausanne, with a sympathetic portrait of this complex, obtuse, yet brilliant viceroy and foreign secretary. Curzon's knowledge of the Near East was as ample as his understanding of Europe was slender. Though, like everyone else, he failed to estimate Kemal correctly, he had early sought to dissuade Lloyd Gorge and other colleagues from the plan for partition of Anatolia, especially from encouragement of the Greek attempt to re-establish an empire in Asia Minor two thousand years out of date.

8. William Linn Westermann, "Kurdish Independence and Russian Expansion," *Foreign Affairs,* July 1946.

9. Harold Jefferson Coolidge and Robert Howard Lord, *Archibald Cary Coolidge* (Boston: Houghton Mifflin, 1932), p. 256.

10. Walters, *op. cit.*, p. 314.

11. Hamilton Fish Armstrong, "The New Balkans," *Foreign Affairs,* December 1924.

12. Sir Arthur Salter, "The Reconstruction of Austria," *Foreign Affairs,* June 1924.

13. *Ibid.*

14. Erich Eyck, *A History of the Weimar Republic,* trans. Harlan P. Hanson and Robert G. L. Waite (Cambridge, Mass.: Harvard University Press, 1962, 1963), II, 306.

15. Bismarck, *op. cit.*, Vol. II, p. 278.

16. *Ibid.,* p. 277.
17. Barbara Tuchman, *The Guns of August* (New York: Macmillan, 1962), p. 18.

V: END OF THE EXPERIMENT

1. Volume I of Erich Eyck's *A History of the Weimar Republic* (Cambridge, Mass.: Harvard University Press, 1962) gives a thorough and objective account of the complicated story.
2. Edward W. Bennett, *Germany and the Diplomacy of the Financial Crisis, 1931* (Cambridge, Mass.: Harvard University Press, 1962), p. 1.
3. Wandycz, *op. cit.,* p. 254.
4. Eyck, *op. cit.,* Vol. I, p. 205.
5. Wandycz *op. cit.,* p. 261.
6. Charles Evans Hughes, speech at New Haven, December 29, 1922.
7. Letters of Benjamin Strong, Governor of the Federal Reserve Bank of New York (published in Lester V. Chandler, *Benjamin Strong: Central Banker* [Washington: Brookings Institution, 1958]) are interesting in this connection.
8. Roland W. Boyden, "The Dawes Report," *Foreign Affairs,* June 15, 1924. The article is an authoritative summary of the features and philosophy of the Plan.
9. An analysis of the problems created by that conference, in present perspective, can be found in Thaddeus V. Tuleja, *Statesman and Admirals* (New York: Norton, 1963).
10. "Arbitration, Security and Reduction of Armaments." General Report of the First Committee (M. Politis, Greece, *Rapporteur*) and the Third Committee (M. Beneš, Czechoslovakia, *Rapporteur*). League of Nations, Geneva, 1924.
11. *The Round Table* was founded in 1910 by a group of Lord Milner's young men in South Africa devoted to the ideal of imperial federation. The quotations here are from "Should We Guarantee a European Settlement?", June 1924.
12. League of Nations document cited. *See also* H. Hessell Tiltman, *J. Ramsay MacDonald* (New York: Stokes, 1929).
13. Paragraph 7 of Article 15 of the Covenant reserved to members the right "to take such action as they shall consider necessary for the maintenance of right and justice"—*i.e.* go to war—if resort to political settlement by the council, judicial settlement, or arbitration all failed. *See* p. 56 above
14. P. J. Noel Baker, *The Geneva Protocol* (London: King, 1925), p. 25.
15. The text is in the annex to the 1924 League reports on Security and Disarmament. *See also* James T. Shotwell and Marina Salvin, *Lessons in Security and Disarmament from the History of the League of Nations* (New York: King's Crown Press, for the Carnegie Endowment for International Peace, 1929) and James T. Shotwell, "Reflections on War and Peace," *Perspectives on Peace 1910-1960* (New York: Praeger, for the Carnegie Endowment for International Peace, 1960).
16. Arnold J. Toynbee, *Survey of International Affairs, 1924* (London: Oxford University Press; Humphrey Milford, 1926), p. 49.

17. Walters, *op. cit.*, p. 284.
18. "The Geneva Protocol: An Analysis" and "The British Commonwealth, The Protocol and the League," *The Round Table,* December 1924.
19. Sir Charles Petrie, *Life and Letters of the Right Honorable Sir Austen Chamberlain* (London: Cassell, 1940), Vol. II, p. 263.
20. For Sir Winston's effort to apply the Locarno idea in 1953, *see* Byron Dexter, "Locarno Again," *Foreign Affairs,* October 1953.
21. Hans W. Gatzke, *Stresemann and the Rearmament of Germany* (Baltimore: Johns Hopkins University Press, 1954), p. 38. This monograph has new material on Stresemann, gathered from his unpublished papers, which became available to scholars, through the courtesy of the German Documents Branch of the United States Department of State, after the Second World War.
22. Wandycz, *op. cit.,* p. 349.
23. Stresemann papers, quoted by Gatzke, *op. cit.,* p. 35.
24. Henry Ashby Turner, Jr., *Stresemann and the Politics of the Weimar Republic* (Princeton: Princeton University Press, 1963), pp. 189, 210 ff. This book is another valuable source of new information about the period.
25. Eyck, *op. cit.,* II, 13. There is also a wealth of new information relating to the Locarno episode in Volume II of this great history.
26. As recently as May 24, 1953, *Pravda* termed the word Locarno "notorious," since it gave Germany freedom of action in the East, "thus directing German aggression toward the USSR."
27. Eyck, *op. cit.,* II, 14.
28. Stresemann papers, quoted by Eyck, *op. cit.,* II, 25.
29. Eyck, *op. cit.,* II, 24.
30. Letter to Sir William Tyrell, Petrie, *op. cit.,* II, 290.
31. Eduard Beneš, "After Locarno: The Security Problem Today," *Foreign Affairs,* January 1926.
32. Wandycz, *op. cit.,* pp. 364, 365.
33. *Survey of International Affairs, 1927* (London: Oxford University Press, for the Royal Institute of International Affairs; Humphrey Milford, 1929), p. 96.

EPILOGUE: THE POWER OF ILLUSION

1. The story of Hitler's rise to power is definitively told by Alan Bullock, *Hitler* (New York: Harper and Row, rev. ed., 1962).

Index

Abdul Hamid, Sultan of Turkey, 126
Adams, Charles Francis, 60
Adriatic Sea, 44, 83, 117, 124
Afghanistan, 70
Africa, 70, 173, 208
Åland Islands, 96–98
Albania, 5, 6, 101*n.*, 117–21, 127
Alexandretta (Hatay), 128
Algeciras Conference (1906), 15
Alsace-Lorraine, 15, 82, 144, 194, 196
Ambassadors, Conference of, 107, 118, 119, 121, 122, 123, 124; *see also* Versailles, Treaty of
American Journal of International Law, The, 51
Amery, Leopold S., 22, 188, 193, 256
Anatolia, 95, 125–26, 128, 131; *see also* Sèvres, Treaty of; Turkey
Ankara, 128
Anschluss, *see* Austro-German Customs Union
Arabs, xx, xxi, 50, 126, 129
Arbitration, 54–59, 177–81, 199
Armenia, 118, 127
Armstrong, Hamilton Fish, 136, 254
Asia, 22, 23, 27, 69, 70, 173
Australia, 21, 22, 49, 70, 189
Austria, 67, 85, 118, 136–43
Austria-Hungary: empire of, 83, 85, 136; Empress Maria Theresa and, 108; and Bismarck, 14, 140, 141; annexation of Bosnia and Herzegovina by (1908), 16; and threat of war (1912), 16; ultimatum of (1914), 12; and Albania, 5; at London Conference, 5, 6, 7; in Triple Alliance, 3
Austro-German Customs Union, 102–103, 139, 141, 196, 208
Avon, Lord, *see* Eden, Sir Anthony
Azerbaijan, 118

Baghdad, 131
Baker, P. S. Noel, 178, 255
Baldwin, Stanley, 160, 187, 192–94, 208
Balfour, A. J., 138, 170, 188, 191

Balkan states, 4, 5, 85, 123; Russian intrigues in, 11; and Treaty of Versailles, 84–85, 89–92; influence of Republic of Turkey on, 125; "war" in (1925), 133–36; *see also* Corfu
Baltic Sea, 83, 86, 96
Barcelona Conference (1921), 79
Barnes, Harry Elmer, 253
Bavaria, 160
Belgium, 13, 69, 123, 143, 144; and occupation of Ruhr, 158; and Treaty of Locarno, 71, 199, 201, 202; neutrality of, 192, 201
Benckendorff, Count Alexander, 6
Beneš, Eduard, 90, 122–123, 137, 138, 181, 186, 201, 255, 256
Bennett, Edward W., 149, 255
Bering Strait, 29
Berlin, xiii, xvii, xxii
Berlin-Rome Axis, 210
Bessarabia, 88
Bethmann-Hollweg, Montz von, 12
Birkenhead, Lord, 193
Bismarck, Otto von, xv, 8, 11, 14, 110, 140–41, 146, 254, 255
Black Sea Straits, 126–28
Boer War, 48
Bohemia, 83
Bolivia, 74
Borah, Sen. William E., 59
Bosnia, 16
Bothnia, Gulf of, 96
Bourgeois, Léon, 38, 115
Bowman, Isaiah, 82, 253
Boyden, Roland W., 255
Brand, Robert H., 155
Branting, Karl, 98
Brazil, 67
Brenner Pass, 85
Brest-Litovsk, Treaty of, 88
Briand, Aristide, 115, 135, 136, 151, 154, 193, 194, 195, 198, 199, 201
Brierly, J. L., 33, 92, 252
Britain: in Entente Cordiale, 3, 9, 11–13, 15; strength of in 1914, 12, 13; view of alliances on Continent, 16, 17, 69; at Paris